CHRISTIANIZATION AND COMMUNICATION IN LATE ANTIQUITY

How did ordinary people and church authorities communicate with each other in Late Antiquity and how did this interaction affect the processes of Christianization in the Roman Empire? By studying the relationship between the preacher and his congregation within the context of classical, urban traditions of public speaking, this book explains some of the reasons for the popularity of Christian sermons during the period. Its focus on John Chrysostom's sermons allows us to see how an educated church leader responded to and was influenced by a congregation of ordinary Christians. As a preacher in Antioch, Chrysostom took great care to convey his lessons to his congregation, which included a broad cross-section of society. Because of this, his sermons provide a fascinating view into the variety of beliefs held by the laity, demonstrating that many people could be actively engaged in their religion while disagreeing with their preacher.

JACLYN MAXWELL is Assistant Professor in the Departments of History and Classics and World Religions at Ohio University. She studied at Princeton University and in 2002/3 held an Andrew J. Mellon Research Fellowship for Junior Faculty from the American Council of Learned Societies.

CHRISTIANIZATION AND COMMUNICATION IN LATE ANTIQUITY

John Chrysostom and his congregation in Antioch

JACLYN L. MAXWELL

Ohio University

CAMBRIDGE
UNIVERSITY PRESS

CAMBRIDGE UNIVERSITY PRESS
Cambridge, New York, Melbourne, Madrid, Cape Town, Singapore, São Paulo
Cambridge University Press
The Edinburgh Building, Cambridge CB2 2RU, UK

Published in the United States of America by Cambridge University Press, New York

www.cambridge.org
Information on this title: www.cambridge.org/9780521860406

© Jaclyn L. Maxwell 2006

First published 2006

Printed in the United Kingdom at the University Press, Cambridge

A catalogue record for this publication is available from the British Library

Library of Congress Cataloging-in-Publication Data
Maxwell, Jaclyn LaRae, 1973–
Christianization and communication in late antiquity : John Chrysostom and his congregation in
Antioch / Jaclyn L. Maxwell.
p.   cm.
Includes bibliographical references and index.
ISBN-13: 978-0-521-86040-6 (hardback)
ISBN-10: 0-521-86040-7 (hardback)
1. John Chrysostom, Saint, d. 407.   2. Preaching – History – Early church, ca. 30–600.
3. Communication – Religious aspects – Christianity.   4. Church history – Primitive and early
church, ca. 30–600.   I. Title.

BR1720.C5M39   2006
270.2092 – dc22

For my mother, Nancy Carol Gaddy Sorrels

Contents

Acknowledgments   *page* viii
List of abbreviations   x

Introduction   1

1 Philosophical preaching in the Roman world   11

2 Rhetoric and society: Contexts of public speaking in
   late antique Antioch   42

3 John Chrysostom's congregation in Antioch   65

4 Teaching to the converted: John Chrysostom's pedagogy   88

5 Practical knowledge and religious life   118

6 Habits and the Christianization of daily life   144

Conclusions   169

Bibliography   176
Index   194

Acknowledgments

I would like to thank a number of people and several institutions for their support while I worked on this project. First of all, I owe much to my undergraduate university and professors. I attended Tulane University, thanks to their generous Dean's Honor Scholarship program. I did not fully appreciate the extra time my advisers, Kenneth Harl and Jane Carter, spent with me translating Greek, discussing research papers, and helping me prepare for graduate school until I became a professor myself.

At Princeton University, I benefited from the collegial environments of the Department of History, the Program in the Ancient World, and the Group for the Study of Late Antiquity. A seminar on Greek rhetoric with Josiah Ober and a seminar on recently discovered sermons by Augustine with Peter Brown showed me the potential of public speeches as sources for social and intellectual history. Peter was a wonderful dissertation advisor, and I am thankful to both him and Betsy for making graduate school a friendly place. William Jordan's comments on early drafts of my dissertation improved the clarity of my writing and helped me learn to take criticism with good humor. Many friends in Princeton read drafts and shared ideas during the early stages of research and writing, including Lisa Bailey, Kirsti Copeland, Adam Davis, Michael Gaddis, Jennifer Hevelone-Harper, Christopher MacEvitt, Leonora Neville, Jarbel Rodriguez, Kevin Uhalde, and Joel Walker. Several scholars read all or part of the manuscript at various stages, offering valuable advice and criticism: Tia Kolbaba, Derek Krueger, Richard Lim, Wendy Mayer, Theresa Urbainczyk, Ruth Webb, and the anonymous reader for Cambridge University Press. At Ohio University, Lynne Lancaster answered numerous questions while I prepared the final manuscript. I would also like to thank Michael Sharp for his help and encouragement during the review process.

Several institutions provided financial support and scholarly communities that helped me immensely while I wrote my dissertation and revised it into a book. The Center for the Study of Religion at Princeton University in 1999–2000 provided a venue for discussion with a broader range of religion scholars while I finished the dissertation. A summer fellowship at Dumbarton Oaks in 2002 gave me the chance to do the research for the first chapter and exchange ideas with a group of Byzantinists and landscape architects. An Andrew J. Mellon Research Fellowship for Junior Faculty from the American Council of Learned Societies in 2003 allowed me to take time off from teaching for additional research and writing. Also, a course reduction in the Spring of 2005 from Ohio University helped me out during the final stages of editing.

Although the book benefited greatly from the input of the above-mentioned people, any shortcomings that remain are entirely my own. I should mention that some of the material in chapters 5 and 6 also appears in "Lay Piety and the Christianization of Habits in the Sermons of John Chrysostom" in *Byzantine Christianity*, ed. D. Krueger, *A People's History of Christianity* 3 (Minneapolis: Fortress, 2006).

Thanks also go to my folks, Nancy, Meredith, Ron, Casey, Alex, Jack, Rennie, Ray, Ruth, René, Amanda, and Yvette for their support and understanding while I spent so much time during the last few years working on this book. I owe even more thanks to Kevin Uhalde who has been a fellow graduate student, my best friend, a colleague and my husband. Finally, I have dedicated this book to my mom because she has always loved books.

Abbreviations

Journal abbreviations follow the conventions of *L'Année Philologique*.

Adv. Jud.	*Adversus Judaeos*
Adv. oppug.	*Adversus oppugnatores vitae monasticae*
Amm. Marc.	Ammianus Marcellinus
CAH	*Cambridge Ancient History*
Cateches.	*Catecheses*
CCSG	Corpus Christianorum. Series Graeca
CCSL	Corpus Christianorum. Series Latina
Chrysostom	John Chrysostom
Const. apost.	*Constitutiones apostolorum*
De Anna	*Sermones de Anna*
De eleem.	*De eleemosyna*
De inan.	*De inani gloria*
De incomp.	*De incomprehensibili Dei natura*
De Laz.	*De Lazaro*
De liberis educ.	*De liberis educandis*
De poen.	*Homilia de poenitentia*
De recta aud.	*De recta ratione audiendi*
De sac.	*De sacerdotio*
De stat.	*Homiliae de statuis*
Dia.	*Dialexis*
Dial.	*Dialogus de vita Johannis Chrysostomi*
Dio	Dio Chrysostom
Ep.	*Epistola*
FOTC	Fathers of the Church
G. Naz.	Gregory of Nazianzus
G. Nys.	Gregory of Nyssa
HE	*Historia ecclesiastica*
Hom.	*Homiliae*

HR	*Historia religiosa*
In Kalend.	*In Kalendas*
Or.	*Orationes*
PG	Patrologia Graeca
PL	Patrologia Latina
SC	Sources chrétiennes
VP	*Vitae philosophorum*
VS	*Vitae sophistarum*

Introduction

Sermons were popular in Late Antiquity – a number of priests and bishops became famous for their rhetorical skill and charisma as speakers. The importance of rhetoric in ancient higher education meant that many of the men who took on leadership roles in the clergy, especially after the conversion of Constantine, were trained for public speaking. On the same note, frequent rhetorical displays in cities taught the crowds to be listeners, and these people made up the urban Christian congregations. Communication across social and economic boundaries and the widespread appeal of rhetorical eloquence had long been an important part of urban life, and this played a part in the spread of Christianity and the formation of orthodoxy in Late Antiquity. By integrating this broader cultural context into the study of early sermons, we can better understand the relationship between the authors and the audiences of these important – and abundant – texts. In many cases, the needs and concerns of ordinary Christians shaped the style of sermons, as well as the questions they returned to again and again. Because of this element of interaction, it is possible to observe aspects of the world-views and daily lives of the preachers' congregations reflected in the subjects and presentation of their sermons. Therefore, sermons can provide information about the process of Christianization, the variety of religious beliefs and practices coexisting at one time, and about the ways in which laypeople interacted with church authorities.[1]

The ability and inclination of preachers and congregations to communicate with each other, however, is not always obvious. Church leaders in Late Antiquity often claimed to be proud of the simplicity of their faith and

---

[1] Several recent studies use late antique and medieval sermons to study interaction between church authorities and laity. See W. Klingshirn, *Caesarius of Arles: The Making of a Christian Community in Late Antique Gaul* (Cambridge, 1994); *Preacher and Audience: Studies in Early Christian and Byzantine Homiletics*, M. B. Cunningham and P. Allen, eds. (Leiden, 1998); C. Polecritti, *Preaching Peace in Renaissance Italy: Bernardino of Siena and His Audience* (Washington, DC, 2000); K. Jansen, *The Making of the Magdalen: Preaching and Popular Devotion in the Later Middle Ages* (Princeton, 2000).

its followers but at other times made elitist comments at the expense of the uneducated. Theological problems became more complex while the status and privileges of the clergy steadily rose, presumably creating more and more distance between preachers and their congregations. But Christian leaders in Late Antiquity could not afford to be indifferent to their followers. While competition with other sects was always a factor, a sincere belief in the necessity to instruct people inspired many priests and bishops. In addition to concerns about salvation, the prestige and popularity of public speaking helped to bridge the gap between the concerns and experiences of the church authorities and ordinary laypeople by equipping both sides with the tools and the incentives to understand each other.

John Chrysostom, perhaps more so than any other figure of the period, epitomizes the popularity of sermons and the ability of church leaders to capture the public's attention. Trained in rhetoric by the pagan rhetorician Libanius, this preacher became famous for his talent as a speaker, which inspired later admirers to add "Chrysostom" – Greek for "Goldenmouth" – to his name. He preached during the time when Christian emperors gradually outlawed pagan worship, closed ancient temples, and boosted the authority of Christian leaders. Both the quality and quantity of Christian sermons surged in this period, which became known as the Golden Age for this genre. This burst of activity was fostered by rivalry with other religious groups, including different sects of Christians, and also by a generation of particularly productive and skilled churchmen, whose sermons would form the handbooks for future generations of preachers in both the Latin and Greek traditions.[2]

JOHN CHRYSOSTOM IN ANTIOCH

Chrysostom's success as a preacher in Antioch (386–98) attracted the attention of other Christian leaders, who chose him to become the bishop of Constantinople in 398, where he continued to preach with enthusiasm. The mid-fifth-century church historian Sozomen commented on his popularity there: "He won over the masses, especially by refuting sinners in public frequently, even in the churches, and he freely expressed his anger at the wrongdoers as if he himself had been injured. This, naturally, was agreeable to the

[2] On the Golden Age, see J. Quaesten, *Patrology*, vol. III (Utrecht, 1963). For explanations of the subsequent decline of homiletic literature, see P. Rousseau, *The Early Christian Centuries* (New York, 2002) 299–300. On the popularity of sermons from this period, see M. B. Cunningham, "Preaching and Community" in *Church and People in Byzantium*, R. Morris, ed. (Birmingham, 1986) 29–46, at 29.

masses, but it was distressing to the wealthy and powerful, who committed most of the sins."[3] According to this account, the crowds tended to press close to Chrysostom in order to ask questions and listen to his responses, forcing him to stand on a platform above them. Even the pagan historian Zosimus noted this preacher's effect on his congregation and remarked dryly: "That man was clever at gaining the support of the irrational crowd."[4] Famous events of his career support these impressions of Chrysostom's widespread popularity. When he was chosen as bishop of Constantinople, he was taken away from Antioch secretly, so as not to upset the citizens of Antioch. In the capital, his sermons solidified his relationship with the laity, so that they did not abandon him when his enemies spread rumors that questioned his orthodoxy. Later, when he was sent into exile from Constantinople after a falling out with the imperial family, riots ensued.[5]

Although he is best known for events related to his career in Constantinople, several factors concerning the nature and quantity of the sources make Chrysostom's sermons in Antioch particularly fitting for this study. Chrysostom spent the major part of his career and preached most of his sermons in Antioch.[6] During roughly the same period in this city, Libanius wrote numerous orations and letters, which provide another perspective on the contemporary world outside Chrysostom's church. Most important, perhaps, is the preacher's congregation in Antioch. Since the intention of this study is to learn about the Christianization of late antique society, the congregation at Antioch, a thoroughly Hellenistic city, offers a more appropriate case-study than Constantinople, the newly built Christian capital dominated by the imperial court.[7]

---

[3] Sozomen, *HE* 8.2.11; cf. Socrates, *HE* 6.3–4. For the ancient biography of Chrysostom, see Palladius, *Dialogue on the Life of St. John Chrysostom* (SC 341 and 342). For the classic study, see C. Baur, *John Chrysostom and His Time*, M. Gonzaga, trans. (London, 1959). Most recently, see J. N. D. Kelly, *Golden Mouth: The Story of John Chrysostom – Ascetic, Preacher, Bishop* (Ithaca, NY, 1995); P. Allen and W. Mayer, *John Chrysostom* (London, 2000); and C. Tiersch, *Johannes Chrysostomus in Konstantinopel (398–404)* (Tübingen, 2002).

[4] Zosimus, *Historia Nova* 5.23.4.

[5] Sozomen, *HE* 8.18; Socrates, *HE* 6.16. A. Momigliano cites this as an instance of "mob theology": "Popular Religious Beliefs and the Late Roman Historians" in *Popular Belief and Practice*, G. Cuming and D. Baker, eds. (Cambridge, 1972) 1–18, at 18.

[6] See W. Mayer, "The Provenance of the Homilies of St. John Chrysostom: towards a New Assessment of Where He Preached What," Ph.D. dissertation, University of Queensland (Brisbane, 1996).

[7] On Antioch as a city that exemplified the changes of the times, see Rousseau, *Early Christian Centuries*, 191–2. On Greek culture in Antioch, see J.-P. Rey-Coquais, "La culture en Syrie à l'époque romaine" in *Donum Amicitiae: Studies in Ancient History*, E. Dabrowa, ed. (Krakow, 1997) 139–60. On various aspects of Antioch in Late Antiquity, see *Antioch: The Lost Ancient City*, C. Kondoleon, ed. (Princeton, 2000) and *Culture and Society in Later Roman Antioch*, I. Sandwell and J. Huskinson, eds. (Oxford, 2004).

In this period, Antioch was one of the most important cities of the Roman Empire: an occasional imperial residence, a city of merchants, administrators, and scholars, and the place where Christians were first called Christians. Vibrant Jewish and pagan communities lived alongside Chrysostom's followers – orthodox Christianity was far from being without rivals.[8] While Libanius carried on ancient cultural traditions with a school full of rhetoric students, Christian holy men began to retreat to the mountains surrounding the city. The tensions of contemporary urban life influenced the content of Chrysostom's sermons, leading him to concentrate on the problems of poverty and wealth in particular. At the same time, the diversity of the population in Antioch intensified the danger, from the preacher's point of view, of blurring the lines between Christian and non-Christian, or, perhaps worse, between orthodoxy and heresy. Every social interaction, every conversation in the marketplace could lead people astray. So Chrysostom made it his mission to explain carefully exactly what was and was not proper Christian belief and behavior, and attempted to persuade or intimidate his congregation into agreeing with him.

In such an environment, the urban preacher was faced with the job of explaining to his fellow Christians why they were not allowed to attend horse races with the pagans or celebrate Passover with the Jews. No orthodox "common sense" yet existed to guide people's actions, and so Chrysostom attempted to provide these basic guidelines. Discussions of such issues in the sermons illustrate how church authorities and lay Christians interacted: their points of confusion and conflict as well as instances of successful communication and compromise. Understanding this relationship more fully is particularly important for this crucial period in Christianity's development, when orthodoxy was being defined against the various alternatives. By examining the interaction of church authorities with their congregations, we can see the influence of ordinary people in this process.

SERMONS AS HISTORICAL SOURCES

Although it is difficult to tell the extent to which the congregation accepted or rejected advice from sermons, the preacher's instructions can give us an idea of basic elements of lay piety. These texts should not always be taken at face value because of their rhetorical and prescriptive nature: much of

---

[8] See R. Wilken, *John Chrysostom and the Jews: Rhetoric and Reality in the Late 4th Century* (Berkeley, 1983); A. J. Festugière, *Antioche païenne et chrétienne: Libanius, Chrysostome et les moines de Syrie* (Paris, 1959).

the behavior that was condemned or promoted served as stock subjects in Christian texts as well as pagan moral treatises. Moreover, sermons reflect first and foremost the preacher's point of view, which may or may not have corresponded to contemporary standards of lay Christians. But awareness of this last point allows us to look for indications of divergence and conflict between the preacher's views and those of his listeners. Although biblical and classical tropes make sermons challenging to read as historical texts, rhetorical technique did not overshadow the impact of the world that Chrysostom lived in. The purpose of the sermons was to provide spiritual guidance for laypeople living in a world with many alternatives to orthodox Christianity. This required the preacher to speak with the needs of his audience in mind. Indeed, dialogues emerge from the sermons in many instances, which allow us to examine beliefs and behaviors that people refused to accept, the condemned traditions that many Christians continued to observe, and the elements of orthodox Christian piety that people cherished.[9]

The importance of sermons in the liturgy and the care with which they were recorded contribute to our understanding of their social context and impact. In late antique Syrian churches, for instance, the centrality of preaching is reflected in the design of the buildings. Sermons were preached in the middle of the service, after the reading from the Scriptures and before communion.[10] Unbaptized Christians as well as outsiders were allowed to listen to sermons, but were required to leave the church before the communion ceremony. Sermons were given on Sundays and holidays throughout most of the year and more frequently during Lent.[11] Explicit references occasionally indicate at what point in the liturgical year a particular

---

[9] Klingshirn observes that sermons would not have had any rhetorical effect if they did not represent the views of the community: *Caesarius of Arles*, 14. R. Van Dam views late antique sermons as dialogues between preachers and audiences: *Becoming Christian: The Conversion of Roman Cappadocia* (Philadelphia, 2003) 101–50. Cf. Averil Cameron, *Christianity and the Rhetoric of Empire: The Development of Christian Discourse* (Berkeley, 1991) 79 and Philip Rousseau, *Basil of Caesarea* (Berkeley, 1994) 46.

[10] J. Lassus, *Sanctuaires chrétiens de Syrie: essai sur la genèse, la forme et l'usage liturgique des édifices du culte chrétien, en Syrie, du IIIe siècle à la conquête musulmane* (Paris, 1947) 214. The preacher's ambo was at the focus of the ceremony until the catechumens left and attention turned to the altar, see ibid., 216. Lassus describes the physical situation and order of the liturgy in a step-by-step recreation, 212–15. On the sermons' place in the liturgy, see F. van de Paverd, *Zur Geschichte der Messliturgie in Antiocheia und Konstantinopel gegen Ende des vierten Jahrhunderts: Analyse der Quellen bei Johannes Chrysostomos* (Rome, 1970), and Cunningham, "Preaching and Community," 30.

[11] On the origins and standardization of Lent, see P. Bradshaw, *The Search for the Origins of Christian Worship: Sources and Methods for the Study of Early Liturgy*, 2nd edn. (Oxford, 2002) 183–5 and 223–4. On liturgical services during Lent and their frequency, see F. van de Paverd, *St. John Chrysostom, the Homilies on the Statues: An Introduction* (Rome, 1991) 161–201.

sermon was delivered. In other instances, the subject matter may provide the same information. The dating and chronology of individual sermons by Chrysostom, however, is often uncertain. Scholars are now giving careful attention to systematic dating, organization into series, and the identification of the city in which each sermon was preached.[12] Because of these issues, as well as the likelihood that his congregation did not always consist of the same groups of people, this study will focus on sermons attributed to Antioch in order to examine the interaction between the preacher and laity in general, but cannot claim to study the developments of a particular group of people over time.

The exact relationship between the surviving texts and the original sermons preached in Antioch is impossible to know for certain, but the connection between oral and literate culture of the time, as well as the structure of the sermons themselves, points toward a close correlation between the spoken and the written versions. To begin with, verbatim records of public orations were widely used in antiquity. Court transcriptions, including some of Christian martyr trials, demonstrate the skills of stenographers.[13] In Antioch, Libanius complained that stenography had become such a popular profession that it threatened the prestige and livelihood of his rhetoric students.[14] Churches used the same methods. The church historian Socrates appears to have had access to Chrysostom's sermons, some of which had been published by the preacher, while others had been taken down in shorthand in church during their delivery.[15] In another revealing anecdote, Socrates reports that Atticus, Chrysostom's successor in Constantinople, did not receive applause, nor did anyone write down his sermons, regardless of whether he memorized them or spoke extempore.[16]

Chrysostom's sermons may have been polished after they were written down, but the structure, language, and tone of the texts indicate that they were presented, and probably even composed, orally. The texts contain

[12] See Mayer, "The Provenance of the Homilies of St. John Chrysostom" and "John Chrysostom and His Audiences: Distinguishing Different Congregations at Antioch and Constantinople," *Studia Patristica* 31 (1997) 70–5; P. Allen, "The Homilist and the Congregation: A Case Study of Chrysostom's Homilies on Hebrews," *Augustinianum* 36 (1996) 397–421 and "John Chrysostom's Homilies on I and II Thessalonians: The Preacher and His Audience," *Studia Patristica* 31 (1997) 3–21.

[13] On court stenographers, see J. Harries, *Law and Empire in Late Antiquity* (Cambridge, 1999) 108–10, 129–30.

[14] For Libanius' complaints about the growing popularity of shorthand secretaries (*hypographeis*), see *Or.* 2.43–6, 62.8, 31.33. Eunapius also remarks on shorthand specialists recording speeches during rhetorical contests, *VP* 489.

[15] Socrates, *HE* 6.4; Sozomen, *HE* 8.27. On the transcription of sermons, see Klingshirn, *Caesarius*, 9–10 and 14; Cunningham, "Preaching and Community," 44.

[16] *HE* 7.2.

all of the marks of impromptu speeches: repetitions, tangents, incomplete thoughts, and references to the audience's applause or evident boredom. They could end abruptly. Occasionally, Chrysostom observed that he had been talking for a long time and then wrapped up his sermon. The frequent references to interlocutors, who disagreed with him and refused to obey him, or else applauded and paid close attention, suggest exchanges between the preacher and audience.[17] In other words, we can perceive that these sermons were tailor-made for their audiences. Indications of this will appear throughout this study.

THE EFFECTS OF SERMONS

The motivations, sincerity, and awareness behind individual conversions to Christianity in Late Antiquity are difficult to guess at and impossible to know. Although we know of a few individuals, such as Augustine, who were convinced by texts, arguments, and philosophical introspection to convert to Christianity, miracles, exorcisms, and worldly benefits undoubtedly influenced many people.[18] Whatever the initial inspiration that led converts into the church, in Chrysostom's time most people who stood in preachers' audiences in the Greek East were already converted, often from families that had long been Christian.[19] The primary purpose of these sermons, therefore, was to deepen the laity's grasp of Christian doctrine and behavior.

In Late Antiquity, the chasm that separated Christians and non-Christians and the dramatic changes that came with conversion existed above all in the minds of churchmen such as Chrysostom and Augustine. Although they claimed that many of the beliefs and practices of ordinary people were inconsistent with Christianity, these same customs had been

---

[17] See A. Olivar, *La predicación cristiana antigua* (Barcelona, 1991). On oral style within written texts, see R. Wilken, *John Chrysostom and the Jews: Rhetoric and Reality in the Late 4th Century* (Berkeley, 1983) 109. On Chrysostom's rhetorical style, see K. Berger, "Antike Rhetorik und christliche Homiletik" in *Spätantike und Christentum: Beiträge zur Religions und Geistesgeschichte der griechisch-römischen Kultur und Zivilisation der Kaiserzeit,* C. Colpe, L. Honnefelder, and M. Lutz-Bachmann, eds. (Berlin, 1992) 173–87, at 176; M. B. Cunningham, "Andreas of Crete's Homilies on Lazarus and Palm Sunday: The Preacher and His Audience," *Studia Patristica* 31 (1997) 22–41, at 24; A. Hartney, *John Chrysostom and the Transformation of the City* (London, 2004) 53–65.

[18] R. MacMullen, *Christianizing the Roman Empire, AD 100–400* (New Haven, 1984) and "What Difference Did Christianity Make?" *Historia* 35 (1986) 322–43.

[19] P. Brown argues that the idea of new converts was a way for preachers to further their "hyper-Christianization" programs: "Christianization and Religious Conflict" in *Cambridge Ancient History,* vol. XIII (1998) 655; *The Cult of the Saints: Its Rise and Function in Latin Christianity* (Chicago, 1981) 29. On the Antiochene Christian communities, see S. Ashbrook-Harvey, "Antioch and Christianity" in *Antioch: The Lost Ancient City,* C. Kondoleon, ed. (Princeton, 2000) 39–49.

carried on by Christians for generations and were deemed acceptable by their practitioners. This was precisely the problem fourth- and fifth-century preachers faced as they spent many hours addressing laypeople, trying to explain why and how they needed to transform their lives. In reaction to their congregations, preachers were compelled to formulate strong statements and clear definitions to counter those who disagreed. But the fact that preachers considered this necessary does not mean that their congregations consisted of lukewarm Christians, or even crypto-pagans, who were attracted into the church solely by the social and economic aspects of the institution. Rather, their disagreements point to multiple views in the Christian community about acceptable beliefs and behaviors.

By focusing on sermons as points of contact between elites and masses, this study will examine aspects of cultural change and social communication brought about by the rise of Christianity.[20] The two parties (in this case, a famous, educated preacher and assemblies of otherwise obscure Antiochene Christians) did not encounter each other with the same views about correct beliefs and behaviors. The preacher's education and orthodox views did not make him entirely dominant; his listeners were neither meek nor indifferent Christians. Such a premise is quite different from the traditional approach of reading patristic literature disembodied from its social context, of assuming that the value of these works would have been lost on ordinary, uneducated listeners, whose very ignorance makes their religious sincerity suspect. Instead, my underlying assumption is that a lack of formal literary training does not preclude intelligence, spirituality, or an interest in listening to speeches.

ORGANIZATION OF THIS STUDY

The particular value of sermons as sources of information about the general population hinges on the fact that they were presented aloud to congregations. Much of their audience and their inspiration, if not the rhetorical skill with which they were presented, originated outside the circles of literate men. This point is often neglected because of the close identification of rhetorical skill with upper-class leisure and privilege. But the tradition of learned men using their positions and rhetorical skill to communicate with

[20] I use the terms "elites" and "masses" in a general sense, meaning the educated, influential upper classes for the former and the vast majority of people for the latter. The "gray area" of prosperous and/or literate workers falls into the latter category. The focus here is on elite Church Fathers in contrast to ordinary Christians from a range of social and economic levels who made up the majority of their congregations.

common people had its roots in a long past. The first chapter looks at this issue, focusing on Second Sophistic authors from the first to fourth centuries who either commented on or exemplified the figure of the philosopher who presented moralizing speeches to the crowds. Remarks by both pagan and Christian authors demonstrate that preachers had precedents among the philosophers, and that urban people would have had experience with such speakers and their topics. The second chapter examines occasions of public speaking more broadly, such as panegyrics, theatrical performances, and forensic speeches, but with a closer focus on Antioch in Late Antiquity. I argue that the frequency of public speaking contributed to the speakers' awareness of less educated listeners while providing opportunities for the general population to become familiar with listening to rhetoric. An awareness of the importance and accessibility of public speaking in Roman cities is vital to understanding the relationship between authorities and the general public, including the interaction between preachers and lay Christians that underlies the texts of sermons. The urban culture of the time affected the way preachers and their listeners responded to each other. The interactions between eloquent speakers and crowds of listeners indicate that this type of communication was not new, but, like many other elements of Christian culture, it was a transformation of an existing form rather than invented *ex nihilo*.

Subsequent chapters rely much more on Chrysostom's sermons, concentrating first on the composition of his congregation. The presence of workers as well as the wealthy, and women as well as men is examined through the direct addresses to various groups in the congregation and the preacher's care for their particular concerns. But does the presence of less educated people in the congregation necessarily mean that they were the target audience of Chrysostom's discourse? Although some have doubted that uneducated people would have been able to understand rhetorical speaking such as Chrysostom's, it is clear from the sermons themselves and accounts by contemporary observers that the preacher consciously attempted to communicate with different types of people. Moreover, his listeners responded to him and at times even adjusted their behavior according to his instructions. In this context, the fourth chapter examines the preacher's pedagogical strategies for a diverse audience and also provides a more general look at the related issues of literacy and memory.

After establishing the composition of the preacher's audience and his ability to communicate with diverse listeners, it is possible to discern dialogues in the sermons between his instructions and his congregation's views. Distinctive elements of lay piety emerge, differing in some ways from the preacher's lessons but still clearly Christian, which challenge the general depiction of lay Christians of this period as unenthusiastic and uninformed. Chapter 5 looks at disagreements over the definition of sins and virtues and the different levels of value placed upon various religious practices. Surprisingly, perhaps, the laypeople took a stricter stance in some matters. The last chapter is devoted to the religious transformation of life outside the church: what the preacher wanted the laity to change in their daily lives, how they reacted to this, and what types of Christian practices they developed on their own. In the discussion of daily habits, it becomes clear that the preacher and the laity had different ideas about which activities could be actively Christianized and which could be left alone as traditional or simply necessary parts of life.

Because texts providing direct evidence about the lives of ordinary people are scarce, we must try to detect their influence on the sources that do survive. Ultimately, this book illustrates the activity of a learned man speaking to ordinary people, addressing their concerns, questions, arguments, and behavior, and shaping both the style and the content of his sermons in response to them. From this, much can be learned about the people who listened to what Chrysostom said. At the same time, we find out that the preacher, too, heard his audience, revealing that the process of Christianization was gradual, interactive, and communicative.

CHAPTER I

Philosophical preaching in the Roman world

In Late Antiquity, Christian preachers attempted to shape entire communities according to moral ideals traditionally associated with philosophers and their circles.[1] They hoped to persuade the laity to reject worldly pleasures and honors in order to embrace the spiritual life prescribed by their sacred texts. Many of their ethical precepts were not new, but through frequent sermons Christians developed a systematic approach to instructing the laity in proper thinking and living. People listened: the widespread acclaim of many Christian leaders as popular speakers demonstrates that their sermons were well received. The rapid rise of Christians in this role requires an explanation, part of which can be found in the preexisting social framework for this type of contact between educated speakers and mass audiences.

The impact of pagan thought on the development of Christian theology is well known. Vocabulary and fundamental concepts of Greek thinkers, especially Platonists, helped many Christian apologists and exegetes interpret their Scriptures. Scholars have also observed the resemblance between sophists, rhetors, and Christian writers, focusing primarily on the connections of *paideia* and class.[2] Their approach to the public, though, was another element of their common ground. Christian leaders, largely from aristocratic backgrounds, expressed concern for ordinary laypeople and self-consciously promoted the use of a "low style" to communicate with them. They drew on traditions of "popular philosophy" in the Roman Empire, which had played a role in

---

[1] An attitude of moderation, or even asceticism, was traditional among educated, philosophical circles. See J. A. Francis, *Subversive Virtue: Asceticism and Authority in the Second-Century Pagan World* (University Park, PA, 1995); F. G. Downing, *Cynics and Christian Origins* (Edinburgh, 1992). The Christian concern for almsgiving was a notable exception. See P. Brown, *Poverty and Leadership in the Late Roman Empire* (Hannover, NH, 2002).

[2] On the education and theories of education of Christian leaders, see W. Jaeger, *Early Christianity and Greek Paideia* (Cambridge, MA, 1961); D. B. Saddington, "The Function of Education according to Christian Writers of the Latter Part of the Fourth Century," *Acta Classica* 8 (1965) 86–101; R. Kaster, *Guardians of Language: The Grammarian and Society in Late Antiquity* (Berkeley, 1988).

shaping both pagan and Christian audiences' expectations of public preachers.[3]

During the revival of Greek literature and culture known as the Second Sophistic, which lasted through the first four centuries CE, a range of rhetors and philosophers made their voices heard in the arenas of imperial and local politics, public entertainment, and education. One of the defining characteristics of this movement was its double focus on philosophical content and rhetorical form.[4] This combination led philosophers to larger audiences and sophists to more serious content, making it difficult – for both contemporary commentators and modern scholars – to draw a definitive line between the two groups. Additionally, the influence of Cynic philosophers directed more attention to ethics and public image and less to logic and metaphysics, making some philosophical discussions more accessible to lay audiences.[5] In order to examine the influence of Second Sophistic practices and attitudes on Christian preachers and their listeners, this chapter will concentrate first on several pagan figures and their relationship to the broader society: their debates over the role of the philosopher in society, their discussions of language and style fit for public speeches, and examples of pagan intellectuals appealing to popular audiences.[6] The focus will then turn to how Christian leaders perceived their relationship to traditional philosophers and how they dealt with the same problems of presenting philosophical discourse to the masses. By addressing

---

[3] A. Spira argues that most classical literature was essentially public, political, and pragmatic and that this phenomenon revived with the church as the new forum, see "Volkstümlichkeit und Kunst in der Griechischen Vaterpredigt des 4. Jahrhunderts," *JÖB* 35 (1985) 55–73. On the concern about simplicity and comprehensibility, see W. Kinzig, "The Greek Christian Writers" in *Handbook of Classical Rhetoric in the Hellenistic Period, 330 BC–AD 400*, S. Porter, ed. (Leiden, 1997) 633–70.

[4] Philostratus (*c.* 230) coined the term "Second Sophistic" and emphasized eloquence over philosophical tendencies. See J. Hahn, *Der Philosoph und die Gesellschaft: Selbstverständnis, öffentliches Auftreten und populäre Erwartungen in der hohen Kaiserzeit* (Stuttgart, 1989); R. Penella, *Greek Philosophers and Sophists in the 4th c.* AD: *Studies in Eunapius of Sardis* (Leeds, 1990); G. Anderson, *The Second Sophistic: A Cultural Phenomenon in the Roman Empire* (London, 1993); G. W. Bowersock, *Greek Sophists in the Roman Empire* (Oxford, 1969).

[5] On the problems of making neat distinctions among sophists, philosophers, rhetors, and "popular philosophers," see A. Brancacci, "Cinismo e predicazione popolare" in *Lo spazio letterario della Grecia antica*, vol. I.3, G. Cambiano et al., eds. (Rome, 1994) 433–55; G. R. Stanton, "Sophists and Philosophers: Problems of Classification," *AJPh* 94 (1973) 350–64; R. Hock, "Cynics and Rhetoric" in *Handbook of Classical Rhetoric in the Hellenistic period, 330 BC–AD 400*, S. E. Porter, ed. (Leiden, 1997) 755–73; Hahn, *Der Philosoph*, 12, 46–53; Bowersock, *Greek Sophists*, 11–13.

[6] The influence of the Second Sophistic on the style of Christian writers has been detailed elsewhere. See T. E. Ameringer, *The Stylistic Influence of the Second Sophistic on the Panegyrical Sermons of St. John Chrysostom* (Washington, DC, 1921); J. Campbell, *The Influence of the Second Sophistic on the Style of the Sermons of St. Basil the Great* (Cleveland, OH, 1983).

questions about the relationship between the popular and elite culture of this period, this chapter will highlight the ways in which both philosophers and preachers could act as ethical experts for the general population, with one setting the stage for the other. The continuity between traditional city life and Christian practices helps to explain the popularity of large church gatherings that featured preaching.

PUBLIC VERSUS PRIVATE PHILOSOPHICAL LIVES

When Maximus of Tyre (*fl. c.* 150 CE) attempted to attract new followers to the philosophical way of life, many were reluctant because they viewed philosophers as old, impoverished, and difficult to understand.[7] He assured them that this was not necessarily true and criticized those thinkers who did isolate themselves from the rest of the community. As citizens, philosophers were as integral to the city as a limb to a body, he argued. Any attempt to drop out of society was as destructive as a foot trying to live as an independent creature. Philosophy was not only for particularly intelligent people because almost all people were capable of learning higher truths. Therefore, social engagement mattered. In his own work, Maximus did not expect his students to be dedicated, full-time thinkers: he promoted philosophy as a basic need for all people, as well as a useful skill for certain careers.[8]

In discussions of the philosophical life, some thinkers idealized the reclusive life of contemplation; others promoted a life of public service. Members of the latter group were naturally more concerned about how they were perceived by non-philosophers and protested the bad reputation that their more antisocial counterparts earned for the entire discipline. This is illustrated in a set of two speeches by Maximus of Tyre, in which he voiced opposing arguments about the philosophical life. The active philosopher is comfortable appearing before crowds.[9] The reclusive philosopher, on

---

[7] Maximus, *Dia.* 1.9; cf. *Dia.* 22 and 25. See *Maximus of Tyre: The Philosophical Orations*, M. B. Trapp, trans. (Oxford, 1997). On philosophers as irrelevant: Lucian, *Bis accusatus* 11.

[8] *Dia.* 1.4–5, 1.7 and 5.1. Maximus presented himself as a "middle man" summarizing and clarifying the works of great thinkers such as Plato and Aristotle for people without the ability or inclination to understand them on their own, *Dia.* 11.1–6, 27.5. See G. Soury, *Aperçus de philosophie religieuse chez Maxime de Tyr, platonicien éclectique* (Paris, 1942); M. B. Trapp, "Philosophical Sermons: The 'Dialexis' of Maximus of Tyre" in *ANRW* II.34.3 (1997) 1945–76. Cf. Dio Chrysostom playing the same role, *Or.* 13.12–13.

[9] *Dia.* 15.2. Hahn notes that the second-century dream interpreter Artemidorus considered the sophist's relationship to the common folk as a way to distinguish sophists from philosophers, *Der Philosoph*, 48. On philosophy and public life, cf. Plutarch, *De liberis educ.* 7; Seneca, *Ep.* 7–9; J. L. Moles, "The Career and Conversion of Dio Chrysostom," *JHS* 98 (1978) 79–100.

the other hand, generates an atmosphere of mutual hostility: the people laugh at him when he presents his argument and his discourse includes a comparison of the passions – the lowest, undisciplined part of the soul – with the "lazy, undisciplined, and vulgar populace."[10] In his judgment of the two arguments, Maximus concludes with a compromise: philosophers should start off making speeches and being active in public life, and later as they grow old, they should withdraw from society if they wish.[11] The relationship with ordinary people is an important factor distinguishing the two types of the philosopher's life.

In the fourth century, the debate over the two ways of life continued. Although most pagan philosophers taught students and were charged with civic responsibilities, many still idealized the isolated life of contemplation.[12] The emperor Julian repeatedly emphasized that love of public acclaim was a vice, especially for those who claimed to be philosophers. He did not mean, however, that all true philosophers should withdraw from society. Rather, they should balance indifference to popularity with teaching fellow citizens how to improve themselves: true Cynics "benefited their fellow citizens not only as examples but also through their lectures."[13] Julian's writings demonstrate how the two conceptions of the philosophical life were not mutually exclusive. Even during his reign as emperor, setting a dramatic example of a public intellectual, he endorsed the reclusive life. In his letter to Themistius, another philosopher with an impressive public career, the emperor defended philosophers who concentrated on teaching and contemplation rather than public life. But, then again, the more isolated life was superior only because it benefited society at large. Julian flattered Themistius by telling him that he had more power than any king to influence society because he was training new philosophers who would contribute to society. Through their speeches and by setting good examples with their way of life, philosophers had a stronger impact on public

---

[10] *Dia.* 16.4. This was stock imagery guiding aristocratic views of the masses. See W. Barry, "Aristocrats, Orators and the 'Mob': Dio Chrysostom and the World of the Alexandrians," *Historia* 42.1 (1993) 82–103.

[11] *Dia.* 16.5.

[12] See G. Fowden, "The Pagan Holy Man in Late Antique Society," *JHS* 102 (1982) 33–59, esp. 39 and 50; P. Brown, *The Philosopher and Society in Late Antiquity* (Berkeley, 1978). On the variety of pagan views on the correct way of living, see G. Clark, "Philosophic Lives and the Philosophic Life" in *Greek Biography and Panegyric in Late Antiquity*, T. Hägg and P. Rousseau, eds. (Berkeley, 2000) 29–51; S. Elm, "Orthodoxy and the True Philosophical Life: Julian and Gregory of Nazianzus," *Studia Patristica* 38 (2001) 69–85.

[13] Julian, *To the Uneducated Cynics, Or.* 6.201D. Julian expresses concern about people who become Cynics harboring desires for luxury and popularity. He counsels them to reject social norms and expectations, but not to withdraw completely from society.

morality, Julian argued, than officials who ordered people to improve their behavior.[14]

As a philosopher who held public office, advised emperors, and gave public speeches in Constantinople, Themistius upset a number of his peers. His enemies criticized him for speaking to common people in the theater. They claimed this made him more of a sophist than a philosopher. In response to this accusation, Themistius defined "sophist" as someone whose speeches were pleasant to listen to but lacked intellectual content. He pled guilty to being pleasant to listen to, but countered that this quality did not preclude philosophical ideas. If rhetorical adornment made philosophy palatable to the masses rather than to only a few students, that was fine with him. Themistius wanted the masses to have access to philosophical teaching and considered rhetorical performances to be a means of accomplishing this. Themistius conceded that serious philosophers often had problems addressing crowds. When they spoke in public, they scared their listeners with harsh condemnations.[15] Echoing a similar remark by Dio Chrysostom (*c.* 40–*c.* 110), Themistius observed that people would not sit still for this – much of the audience would abandon an unpleasant, moralizing philosopher.[16]

Attacks on disengaged philosophers and increased admiration of rhetorical display during this period have led to the impression that philosophers were irrelevant to their broader society. The same sources that attack reclusive philosophers, however, reveal that others incorporated political virtue and responsibility in their world-views, even Neoplatonists such as Plotinus and Proclus, despite their otherworldly tendencies.[17] Distance from ordinary society was always a defining characteristic of the philosopher's image, and so their public actions, insofar as they were not purely philosophical

---

[14] Julian, *Letter to Themistius the Philosopher* 266A–B. Julian also encouraged priests of public cults to use their lives as an example of what they ought to preach to the people, *Fragment of a Letter to a Priest* 299B.

[15] Themistius, *Or.* 24.302a–c; cf. *Or.* 31.352. For a discussion of Themistius' views on how philosophy and rhetoric supported each other, see J. Vanderspoel, *Themistius and the Imperial Court: Oratory, Civic Duty and Paideia from Constantius to Theodosius* (Ann Arbor, MI, 1995) 7–10 and 44–8; L. J. Daly, "Themistius' Concept of *Philanthropia*," *Byzantion* 45 (1975) 22–40; R. Penella, "The Rhetoric of Praise in the Private Orations of Themistius" in *Greek Biography and Panegyric in Late Antiquity*, T. Hägg and P. Rousseau, eds. (Berkeley, 2000) 194–208.

[16] Themistius, *Or.* 33.364; Dio, *Or.* 72.7. See F. Brink, "Dio on the Simple and Self-Sufficient Life" in *Dio Chrysostom: Politics, Letters and Philosophy*, S. Swain, ed. (Oxford, 2000) 261–78. Cf. Plutarch, *De recta aud.* 12. On Dio's influence on fourth-century writers such as Synesius of Cyrene, Libanius, and Themistius, see A. Brancacci, *Rhetorike philosophousa: Dione Crisostomo nella cultura antica e bizantina* (Naples, 1985) 11–135.

[17] On the irrelevance of philosophers, see Fowden, "The Pagan Holy Man," 50–1 and 56. On the social responsibility of philosophers, see Brown, "Philosopher and Society," 2.

in nature, naturally overlapped with the territory claimed by other intellectual professions. The difficulty of drawing clear distinctions among rhetors, sophists, philosophers, and holy men is partially to blame for disagreements in the assessment of the public role of intellectuals in this period. It is telling that Themistius, who was unembarrassed about his fondness for pleasing rhetoric and public speaking, was labeled a sophist by his enemies (and many later commentators have agreed with them) but identified himself as a philosopher-statesman. Then and now, one observer's "popular philosopher" is another person's "sham philosopher" or "sophist" – the act of speaking in public and attempting to hold listeners' attention with rhetoric or humor often leads to a fall from the category of "philosopher." Making this type of distinction depends on the assumption that the moral and spiritual concerns of ordinary people were completely separate from those of the elite, which was not necessarily the case.[18]

Similarly, aristocratic condescension toward ordinary people is often cited as an indication of the gulf separating elite and mass culture. In many ways, though, expressions of snobbery can indicate all too much interaction with "the masses," rather than a life secluded to small circles of disciples. Remarks about "masses" usually indicate an unquestioned sense of superiority over ordinary people but not an inevitable lack of interest in their fates – this is an issue in both pagan and Christian works, which I will return to later in this chapter. Authors such as Dio, Maximus, Lucian, and Themistius, not to mention many Christian writers, criticized reclusive philosophers, demonstrating that they themselves did not belong to this group. Finally, even some of those who idealized the contemplative life often found themselves quite involved in the world. All of these considerations point to a less otherworldly role for philosophers in the Roman Empire and to more common ground with Christian approaches to teaching wisdom to the public.

PHILOSOPHERS IN PUBLIC

In addition to the debate over the philosophers' ideal way of life, Second Sophistic texts also provide indications about what these men actually did in public and how others perceived them. They often served as teachers, administrators, and ambassadors to imperial authorities on behalf of their home towns.[19] As well as private lectures to disciples, some spoke in

---

[18] On religious views cutting across society, see S. Mitchell, *Anatolia: Land, Men and Gods in Asia Minor*, vol. II: *The Rise of the Church* (Oxford, 1993) 48–9.
[19] Hahn, *Der Philosoph*, 54–5.

public, addressing people on the streets and in theaters. In this period, even Epicurean philosophy had a public presence. The philosophical writings of Diogenes Epikourios were originally an inscription in Oinoanda, Asia Minor, from the mid-second century CE. The inscription expresses concern with the general public, and a desire to promote this philosophy accordingly. Interestingly, the writer specifically chose to use an inscription in order to accomplish this.[20]

Rhetorical training helped many philosophers of this period hold the attention of large audiences. In a parody by Lucian, eloquence, combined with influences from comedy and Cynicism, could transform a traditional philosopher's esoteric style to "the same level as the common people."[21] This combination of literary and philosophical elements can be found in Dio Chrysostom's works. Dio emphasized ethics in his public speeches and, like others such as his Stoic teacher Musonius Rufus (*c*. 30–*c*. 100) and Maximus of Tyre, believed that all levels of society should listen to philosophical lectures.[22] Moreover, he claimed to be easy for ordinary people to understand. Recent studies on Dio agree, citing indications of his success with large audiences.[23]

Many of Dio's speeches are addressed to city assemblies, offering political or moral advice. He claims that, during his time as a wandering philosopher, people would recognize him as a philosopher, question him about good and evil, and invite him to speak to the general public.[24] The exact nature of these assemblies is unclear – we do not know whether these gatherings included the hoi polloi or a more limited audience. Dio posed, at least, as a speaker to an assembly of ordinary citizens, and performed in large theaters that could seat hundreds or even thousands of people – venues that could not have been overly exclusive. His comments about his listeners also indicate that he addressed the general public. In the *Euboicus*, an oration

---

[20] See J. Warren, "Diogenes Epikourios: Keep Taking the Tablets," *JHS* 120 (2000) 144–8, at 144. For more inscriptions regarding the civic activity philosophers, see M. N. Tod, "Sidelights on Greek Philosophers," *JHS* 77 (1957) 132–41.

[21] Lucian, *Bis accusatus* 33. Lucian depicts himself as under fire from the personifications of rhetoric and dialogue for having mixed the two together. See C. P. Jones, *Culture and Society in Lucian* (Cambridge, MA, 1986) 13.

[22] Dio, *Or.* 71.1. Dio's late antique biographer, the philosopher-bishop Synesius of Cyrene, approved of attempts to teach the general public: *Dion* 1.11. Dio's teacher, Musonius Rufus, taught that philosophers were the leaders of all people: Fragment 14. Both cited in Hahn, *Der Philosoph*, 55–6.

[23] Moles, "The career and conversion of Dio Chrysostom"; Hahn, *Der Philosoph*, 55–60 and 172–81. For Dio's claim to speak just like a mule-driver, see *Or.* 35.4.

[24] *Or.* 13.12–13. Lucian, in *Apologia* 3, claims that his composition had been admired in public by a large crowd and also by educated people who heard it in private. C. P. Jones considers Lucian's core audience to have been well educated, but acknowledges the influence from the general public in the content of his speeches, *Culture and Society in Lucian*, 13–15, 50.

within an oration, Dio depicts a city's assembly as a great crowd (πλῆθος, ὄχλος) whose lively members listened to some speakers and shouted down others. These scenes were influenced by Dio's vision of the classical Greek past, but as John Ma points out in his study of this speech, the *Euboicus* reflects the continuing practice of public discussion and debate by the citizens of Greek cities under Roman domination.[25] Dio's speeches reveal more than the classicizing tendencies of a Second Sophistic writer, since they were presented to the assemblies of various cities, large and small, as advice on politics and moral matters, and sometimes chiefly for entertainment. Although the images he projects should not always be taken at face value, rhetorical poses and classical topoi – such as his depictions of city assemblies – are not by definition unrelated to the society of the time.[26]

In an address to the people of Alexandria, Dio reveals that they were exposed to Cynics on the street corners, as well as to others who gave more formal speeches. But Dio complained that most of these speakers were too intimidated to rebuke the masses as philosophers should: "Only a few have been frank with you . . . they say one or two phrases, after railing at you rather than teaching you, they leave in a hurry, anxious about the possibility that afterwards you would make an uproar and send them away."[27] Dio's self-serving critique of his rivals should not obscure his revelation that others addressed the crowd as philosophers. Plutarch (*c.* 50–after 120) also observed the popularity of these speeches, noting that young men listened to philosophers as if they were actors in tragedies.[28] He criticized their tendency to seek entertainment rather than moral enlightenment because a typical philosopher's speech, in his view, should make people feel uncomfortable.[29] Plutarch also drew attention to similarities between the sophist, or popular speaker, and the philosopher: "In speeches on philosophy . . . a lot is without purpose. The grey hair of the speaker, his affectations, his

---

[25] J. Ma, "Public Speech and Community in the *Euboicus*" in *Dio Chrysostom: Politics, Letters and Philosophy*, S. Swain, ed. (Oxford, 2000) 108–24. Ma cites additional studies, inscriptions, and papyri indicating active participation of city assemblies in the Hellenistic period, 119–22. Cf. Dio, *Or.* 34.23, Dio's speech to the city of Tarsus, where he advises the assembly on political matters, critiques the city's leaders as if they are not present, and encourages them to allow linen-workers to become citizens, since carpenters, dyers, and shoemakers already have this status.

[26] For more on what rhetorical prose can tell us about social realities, see Barry, "Aristocrats, Orators and the 'Mob'."

[27] Dio, *Or.* 32.11. See A. Brancacci, "Cinismo e predicazione popolare," 433–55. In the fourth century, Themistius also complained about this type of speaker: "What they say is designed to be ingratiating . . . Since they are so courteous and agreeable to their audiences, their audiences salute and praise them in turn and consequently the earth and the sea are teeming with these men." (*Or.* 28.341; translation from *The Private Orations of Themistius*, R. Penella, ed., trans., and intro. [Berkeley, 2000] 175).

[28] Plutarch, *De recta aud.* 12.   [29] *De recta aud.* 16

eyebrows, his bragging, and especially the shouting and applause and the jumping of the audience . . ." Advising his students to be suspicious of smooth-talking philosophers, he switched to calling them sophists who use music and eloquence to persuade their listeners.[30] Plutarch's terms flowed easily from philosophers to deceptive philosophers, to sophists and singers, all while he was discussing one type of public performer. In the end, Plutarch considered philosophical discourses by such people to be dangerous, or, at best, a waste of time. Although his comments were clearly aimed at literate students, the difficulty of separating philosophers from entertainers indicates that their audiences would have also overlapped to some degree.

Maximus of Tyre is probably a good example of the type of speaker that Plutarch and Dio disapproved of. Maximus made entertainment integral to his works. In order to make his philosophical discourses more appealing to his students, he downplayed "verbs and nouns, or language skills, or refutations, debates and sophistry."[31] Taking it as his responsibility to adapt his teaching to the needs of listeners who were accustomed to being entertained, he pictured himself as a star – either an actor or an athlete – and presented his speech as a character from one of the episodes by "God, the dramatist."[32] This resemblance to public entertainment in performances and in listeners' reactions reveals that such speeches were intended to reach beyond the traditional confines of the philosopher's circle. As we will see, this tendency continued into the late antique period.

PHILOSOPHERS IN THE ATTIC

If a philosopher spoke in public, his ability to communicate with uneducated people depended on whether or not the Greek of the literary elite was intelligible to the general population in this period. Several recent studies have argued that rhetorical language was accessible to ordinary listeners because specialized vocabulary did not dominate the speaking of most "Atticizing" authors.[33] Second Sophistic writers were aware of the difference

---

[30] *De recta aud.* 7

[31] Maximus, *Dia.* 1.7–8. On Maximus' emphasis on practical questions at the expense of the theoretical, see Trapp, "Philosophical Sermons," 1947–50.

[32] *Dia.* 1.1–2; cf. *Dia.* 5.1.

[33] See Anderson, *Second Sophistic*, 86–100, esp. 91; S. Swain, "Reception and Interpretation" in *Dio Chrysostom: Politics, Letters and Philosophy*, S. Swain, ed. (Oxford, 2000) 13–50, at 39; W. Kinzig, "The Greek Christian Writers" in *Handbook of Classical Rhetoric in the Hellenistic Period, 330 BC–AD 400*, S. E. Porter, ed. (Leiden, 1997) 633–70, at 646–8; Trapp, "Philosophical Sermons," 1964–5. G. Kennedy argues that contemporary pronunciation made Attic Greek accessible to later Greek audiences, *Greek Rhetoric Under Christian Emperors* (Princeton, 1983) 48. In contrast, R. Browning emphasizes the gulf between Attic and Koine Greek in *Medieval and Modern Greek* (Cambridge, 1983) 44–50.

between Attic and contemporary Greek, but many of their comments indicate that the old dialect, or at least the way it was used in speeches, was comprehensible to ordinary Greek speakers.[34] Indeed, people apparently enjoyed listening to speeches that were slightly over their heads. Lucian mocked the speaker who overwhelmed crowds with Attic phrases in the hope of leaving the impression of being highly educated. In Lucian's satirical advice on how to be a successful sophist, rhetorical flourish and archaic language are presented as a way to show off one's learning to less educated listeners: "Choose fifteen or twenty Attic words from some place, learn them perfectly, have them ready at the tip of your tongue . . . Find secret and foreign words, which were rarely spoken by the ancients, and after collecting these and preparing yourself, shoot them at your audience. For the crowd will look up to you and consider you to be wonderful and more educated than them."[35] Lucian went on to explain that even fabricated or foreign words could be used, but that the speaker should claim that the phrase was ancient. The ridicule of old-fashioned Greek appears again in Lucian's biography of Demonax: the Cynic complains that an educated man answered one of his questions in "hyper-Attic" language, to which he retorted, "I asked you now, friend, but you answer me as if in Agamemnon's day."[36]

Several of Lucian's contemporaries agreed that archaic language was a flaw rather than an asset for any speaker, but especially in the case of a philosopher. Erudite authors such as Plutarch and Dio scoffed at overly complex or obscure speech. Even though unusual words could amaze an audience, they advised listeners and other speakers to value clarity. Plutarch complained that overemphasis on Attic Greek would cause "absence of mind and good sense, much foolery and produce a lot of drivel and wordiness in the schools."[37] He worried that students neglected philosophy, morality, and public conduct because of undue concentration on precise style. The philosopher should be able to communicate high-minded thoughts with clarity, even if tempted to use archaic language as an easy way to impress an audience. Perhaps as a result of this attitude, Dio does not appear to have used vastly different styles for his speeches in public theaters and the ones for select listeners, even though his

---

[34] Anderson, *Second Sophistic*, 86–91.
[35] Lucian, *Rhetorum praeceptor* 16. In another satire, Pan complains about the technical terms of philosophers, noting that common people are enchanted by them, *Bis accusatus* 11.
[36] *Demonax* 26.
[37] Plutarch, *De recta aud.* 9. Elsewhere, a Cynic character ridicules excessive concern for Attic Greek: Athenaeus, *Deipnosophists* 3.97–8.

audiences ranged from popular assemblies in provincial cities to the imperial court.[38]

In Late Antiquity, philosophers and sophists continued to have a public presence. Inscriptions attesting to their involvement in urban life record honors for intellectuals from government officials, as well as the honors they received from citizens, who praised them for their rhetorical skill, moral example, as well as their generosity in supporting civic projects.[39] Public life required the ability and the inclination to communicate with fellow citizens. Indeed, Eunapius (346–414 CE) evaluated philosophers and sophists of the fourth century CE not least on clear expression.[40] Even a Neoplatonist such as Porphyry could be praised for his clear presentation style. Plotinus, however, was known to be difficult to understand. Eunapius noted: "Even the masses, though they misunderstand some of his [Plotinus'] doctrines, are still swayed by them."[41] It is noteworthy, though, that Eunapius could claim that the masses had access to Plotinus' teaching and understood some, even if not all, of it. Elsewhere in this text, philosophers are praised for the simplicity of their words and depicted speaking to market women, while others are criticized for excessively difficult language.[42]

Like his predecessors, Themistius did not admire deliberately obscure language. He expressed his esteem for clarity when praising his father, also a philosopher: "Whenever other [devotees of philosophy] tried to say something philosophical – well, you would have a harder time grasping what they mean than understanding someone speaking Persian. But when my father spoke, even a vine-dresser or a smith had something he could take home with him. He would talk about government with an officeholder, about statesmanship with a statesman, and about any aspect of agriculture with a farmer."[43] Themistius also warned his listeners not to trust false philosophers who attempted to intimidate their audiences with antiquated words.[44] This statement is another hint at the appeal of difficult language,

---

[38] Moles, "The Career and Conversion," 96. Different audiences did not necessarily require vast changes in style, see L. Pernot, *La rhétorique de l'éloge dans le monde gréco-romain* (Paris, 1993) 439.

[39] See E. Sironen, *The Late Roman and Early Byzantine Inscriptions of Athens and Attica* (Helsinki, 1997) 72–85 and 114.

[40] See Penella, *Greek Sophists and Philosophers*, 41–2 and 76.

[41] Eunapius, *VP* 455. Porphyry remarks on Plotinus' lack of rhetorical style, *Vita Plotini* 18. See Penella, *Greek Sophists and Philosophers*, 41; Fowden, "Pagan Holy Man," 49 and 54–6.

[42] Chrysanthius' eloquence was designed to be suitable for everyone: Eunapius, *VP* 502. Aedesius was friendly to the woman selling vegetables, *VP* 482; Libanius was noted for his excessively Attic language, *VP* 496.

[43] Themistius, *Or.* 20.236; translation from Penella, *Private Orations*, 55. Elsewhere, Themistius speaks to his audience as farmers who possess knowledge of breeding livestock, *Or.* 21.248.

[44] *Or.* 21.253.

but in Themistius' view, if listeners could not easily understand the speaker, his lessons were probably not worth the trouble.

Like Maximus and Dio before him, Themistius argued against the stereotype of the philosopher as isolated from society, difficult to understand, and generally unpleasant. He claimed that the true philosopher was like Socrates, who spoke in a simple, ordinary manner, and would agree to talk to anyone, regardless of social status.[45] Themistius also criticized philosophers who refused to entertain their listeners, but only rebuked their audiences without any sort of pedagogical strategy. He found that one got better results when imitating a doctor who gave honey along with bitter medicine: "Perhaps you will let yourselves be more submissive to an oration that is therapeutic in a pleasurable way – an oration that one might liken to a skillful charioteer who uses the reins to control the chariot but does so without the goad or the whip. Now what can I say to benefit and, at the same time, to please you?"[46] Themistius spoke in this way because he did not want the content of his message to be dismissed due to an unpleasant presentation. It is worth noting that he expected rhetorical flair to entice the crowd, so long as it did not cross the line into obscure language. The objection many philosophers had to difficult language, as we have seen, was not that it drove listeners away, but that people were often wrongly impressed by it.

EVIDENCE FOR POPULAR APPEAL

Along with their claims that they spoke in a clear and popular style, there are other indications that philosophers, especially those influenced by Cynicism, interacted with the general population. Basic principles of Cynic philosophy – a virtuous life is the key to wisdom, book learning is not – made its adherents more accessible than other philosophers, not least because they lived and taught in public spaces.[47] Although Cynics viewed humanity as divided between the few wise people and the many foolish, they did not focus their attention on the former. At the same time, the roots of Cynic moral exhortations were, most likely, already familiar to listeners: Cynic teaching "often appears to be popular morality dressed up in philosophical garb."[48] Dio remarked that the masses remembered the sayings

---

[45] *Or.* 24.301.   [46] *Or.* 24.302; translation from Penella, *Private Orations*, 130.

[47] Although Cynicism has been called the "philosophy of the proletariat," most well-known Cynics came from distinguished families. See Downing, *Cynics and Christian Origins*, 96–7; Hahn, *Der Philosoph*, 172–82, esp. 180. On the numbers of people dressed as philosophers, see Dio, *Or.* 72.4, 32.9; cf. Lucian, *Fugitivi* 12, *Bis accusatus* 6, *Vitarum auctio* 11.

[48] Brink, "Dio on the Simple and Self-Sufficient Life," 276.

of Diogenes, which is not difficult to imagine – the dialogues, fables, and especially the simple sayings are easy to understand, if not to follow in practice.[49]

Cynic philosophers engaged people on the street with their observations on contemporary moral values and with their rejection of social customs. One of the purposes of Cynics' outrageous behavior – such as performing various bodily functions in public – was to call attention to themselves as spectacles, in order to draw listeners in for the moral. In one case, Dio caught the attention of a Roman army camp by stripping himself naked and jumping up onto an altar before persuading them not to rebel against the emperor.[50] As speakers, their primary goal was not to convince people to become Cynic philosophers but to educate them about virtue. They found their audiences on the streets, in front of temples, and in the theaters, even in relatively obscure cities of the provinces.[51] Contemporary descriptions of Cynics confirm their image as intellectuals concerned about the general public: they are referred to as teachers, doctors, and guardians.[52]

During his time as an itinerant Cynic, Dio rebuked philosophers who only lectured select audiences, since he believed that the general population needed to hear philosophical moralizing. Dio listed three categories of false philosophers that he observed in Alexandria: those who had good ideas but kept them away from the public; Cynics who, because of their begging, led the urban crowds to ridicule philosophers; and others who focused on amusing rather than edifying the crowd.[53] Aiming for a middle road between the reclusive thinkers and excessively entertaining speakers, Dio bragged about the wide reach and popularity of his own orations. He claimed that in Prusa, his home town, most people knew his speeches, in some cases well enough to reenact them among themselves like popular songs.[54] In Rome,

---

[49] Dio, *Or.* 72.11. On Cynic *chreia* collections and their importance in education, see Hock, "Cynics and Rhetoric," 755–73.

[50] Philostratus, *VS* 1.7.2. Hahn notes the prominence of Dio's charismatic and Cynic qualities, versus the rhetorical skill emphasized by Philostratus, *Der Philosoph*, 195–6. See also J. L. Moles, "'Honestius quam ambitiosius?' An Exploration of the Cynic's Attitude to Moral Corruption in His Fellow Men," *JHS* 103 (1983) 103–23, esp. 108; D. Krueger, "The Bawdy and Society: The Shamelessness of Diogenes in the Roman Imperial Culture" in *The Cynics: The Cynic Movement in Antiquity and Its Legacy*, R. B. Branham and M.-O. Goulet-Cazé, eds. (Berkeley, 1996) 222–39.

[51] Numerous anecdotes illustrate the broad appeal of Cynics to ordinary people: Epictetus' lamp and Peregrinus' walking stick became relics, see Lucian, *Adversus indoctum* 14; Demonax's gravestone, *Demonax* 67. The popularity of Cynic philosophy is clear in the case of cities, and possible in the case of countryside, see Hahn, *Der Philosoph*, 175–9; Anderson, *Second Sophistic*, 25.

[52] Moles, "Honestius quam ambitiosius," 112.   [53] Dio, *Or.* 32.8–10.

[54] Dio, *Or.* 42.4. In *Or.* 32.40, Dio lists the types of people in the Alexandrian theater: free citizens, women, children, and foreigners, including Greeks, Italians, Syrians, Libyans, Cilicians, Ethiopians, Arabs, Bactrians, Scythians, Persians, and Indians.

when people wanted to hear him speak, he waited until he gathered a large number together – he did not want to waste his words on a small group of people when he could speak to a crowd – and then proceeded to tell them that they needed to learn to live more simply in order to be happy.[55] We only have Dio's word on his own popularity. But even if he exaggerated the scope of his appeal (as is likely), his portrayal of himself as a man who could communicate with the masses indicates that this was something that men like him strove for.

Although he criticized the urban populace's love of entertainment, Dio's speeches often show signs of his sympathy with the poor, which would have been rooted in both Stoic and Cynic beliefs. His portrait of a noble, poor farmer, his defense of women and children forced into prostitution, and his condemnation of the wealthy who exploited their privileges all give indications of Dio's views of society and his potential appeal to ordinary listeners.[56] In certain instances there are clues about the social background of Dio's audience. In his home town of Prusa, part of the assembly had rioted over a grain shortage and attempted an attack on Dio's property. At the assembly the next day, he criticized their actions and defended himself as having had no role in the grain shortage. Although the rioters had aimed to kill him, Dio expressed concern for their problems, and offered them advice. He does not give any indication that he was unaccustomed to speaking to these people. On the contrary, he expected them to be familiar with him and his orations.[57]

Dio's moralizing sermons were not unique: "popular philosophers" were familiar figures in Roman cities and their informal speeches had a place among other types of rhetorical display. A treatise on public speaking from the late third or early fourth century describes the *lalia*, or informal talk, which appears to be the basic format of popular philosophical sermons of this period. In a *lalia*, the speaker was to give advice to an entire city and tell stories that the audience would enjoy, perhaps something from Herodotus or mythology. As for style, brevity and simplicity was best, along the lines of Xenophon and Dio Chrysostom.[58] This description of the *lalia* tells us

---

[55] *Or.* 13.31.
[56] On the poor farmer: *Or.* 7.5–20; on prostitution: *Or.* 7.133. See P. A. Brunt, "Aspects of Social Thought of Dio Chrysostom and of the Stoics," *PCPhS* 199 (1973) 9–34.
[57] He emphasized his good standing among the poor, *Or.* 46.7. Elsewhere, Dio demonstrates general good will towards the lower classes, *Or.* 34.21–3.
[58] *Menander Rhetor*, D. A. Russell and N. G. Wilson, eds., transl., and intro. (Oxford, 1981). On the *lalia*, see xxxi and 114–27. Menander mentions Xenophon and Dio Chrysostom, along with others, as examples. In their commentary on this section, Russell and Wilson cite Maximus of Tyre's dialexeis as examples of the *lalia*, along with works by Dio, Lucian, Choricius of Gaza, and

that Dio served as a good example of the simple style to rhetors in this later period and that advice to city assemblies was supposed to be brief, entertaining, and plain-spoken.

This treatise and references in our sources to street philosophers provide hints of a broader phenomenon of public philosophical preaching. One problem with sources such as Lucian and Dio, however, is their tendency to categorize less educated, less skilled, or lower-class speakers – whose speeches left no written record – as frauds.[59] But the contempt inspired by these "popular philosophers" indicates their visibility and general appeal. People were dismissed as sham philosophers on the basis of their humble social origins and lack of education and were accused of looking for easy money. In one of Lucian's satires, a Cynic explains the advantages of his school: "You will not need education and logic and nonsense: this road is your short-cut to fame. Even if you are a common man – a tanner, or a salted fish dealer, or a carpenter, or a banker – nothing will stop you from being marvelous, if only you are shameless and audacious and you learn how to rail at people properly."[60] Lucian voiced his suspicions about the motives of people who joined the Cynics, but did not dismiss the entire school of thought. In his insightful study of the philosopher's role in Roman society, Johannes Hahn observes that the ill will against fake philosophers went hand in hand with the importance of "true" philosophers – the bitterness aimed at people who did not meet expectations was rooted in the respect for the ideal philosopher.[61] Certainly, Lucian's admiration of the Cynics Diogenes and Demonax balanced his attacks on the ones he considered to be frauds.

Like the concern about sham philosophers, other statements illustrating the snobbery of the educated actually provide evidence for contact between the different classes. Quintilian's advice for orators in Rome was likely to be relevant in any part of the Empire: since speakers frequently addressed

---

Himerius. Cf. Trapp, "Philosophical Sermons," 1974. On the similarities of John Chrysostom's encomia to the *lalia*, see H. Hubbell, "Chrysostom and Rhetoric," *CPh* 19.3 (1924) 261–76, at 274–6.

[59] See Lucian's parodies of sham philosophers, *De morte Peregrini* and *Alexander*. Dio attacked so-called philosophers for claiming rather than earning the title (*Or.* 13.11), for not living up to their responsibilities as public advisers (*Or.* 32.8 and 20), and because they allowed themselves to be corrupted by luxury and fawned over wealthy people (*Or.* 77/78.34–5). On the problems with popular Cynics in particular, see *Or.* 32.9–10.

[60] Lucian, *Vitarum auctio* 11. Cf. Galen, *De peccatorum dignotione* 3.12. On the disapproval of philosophers profiting from their profession, see Hahn, *Der Philosoph*, 179. Dio notes that true philosophers would not want money or gifts in exchange for their lessons, *Or.* 13.33. Cf. Christian concerns about false prophets in the New Testament (*Mt.* 7:15).

[61] Hahn, *Der Philosoph*, 192–5.

assemblies of ordinary, uneducated people, they had to adapt their speeches in order to be comprehensible to such an audience.[62] In a similar vein, Dio complained that many sophists could not avoid adopting the attitudes of their listeners.[63] These authors' sense of superiority should not be looked at in isolation – often the same authors who lament the simple-mindedness of the common people are the same ones who elsewhere were concerned for the hoi polloi. For instance, when Lucian remarked that his teacher, the Cynic Demonax, occasionally "talked reason to excited multitudes," he meant this as a sign of his teacher's authority, clarity, and wisdom. Similarly, although Dio sometimes showed disdain for the lower classes, elsewhere, as we have seen, he sided with them and depicted the wealthy as immoral.[64]

In addition to his own suspicions about "so-called" philosophers, Dio's comments reveal a general aversion to philosophers (including "real" ones, such as himself) among the Roman people, because they criticized the common people for their love of diversions, and the wealthy for abusing their privileges. Their blunt assessments together with their distinctive appearance made philosophers open to attack on the streets.[65] Dio complained that the philosopher's cloak and long hair attracted people's attention to the degree that they went out of their way to heckle or harass intellectuals.[66] Not surprisingly, many people disliked the philosophers' moral superiority. They suspected that philosophers laughed at them in private, ridiculing all of the things that they cherished in life and worked hard for, such as physical comfort, popularity, and honors. According to Dio, the crowds "abuse and jeer at them [philosophers] as being wretched and foolish, knowing that if they establish them as senseless and mad, they will prove themselves to be

---

[62] Quintilian, *Inst.* 3.8.2, cited in Downing, *Cynics and Christian Origins*, 104, along with additional references from Quintilian on the influence of applause on court cases.

[63] Dio, *Or.* 35.8. For instances of class snobbery, namely the view expressed by Themistius, Eunapius, Ammianus, and Julian that humble birth was correlated with low intelligence, see Fowden, "Pagan Holy Man," 49.

[64] Lucian, *Demonax* 9. For Dio, see Brink, "Dio on the Simple and Self-Sufficient Life," 265–8 and J. L. Moles, "Cynic Cosmopolitanism" in *The Cynics: The Cynic Movement in Antiquity and Its Legacy*, R. B. Branham and M.-O. Goulet-Cazé, eds. (Berkeley, 1996) 114–20. Julian was capable of such statements as "The gods are not the cause of their poverty, but rather the greediness of us men of property . . .," *Fragment of a Letter to a Priest* 290A.

[65] Appian, a Roman official and historian, condemned those who were dressed as poor philosophers, and attacked the rich and powerful, *Mithridatica* 28, cited by Hahn, *Der Philosoph*, 174. Cf. Julian's remarks about Cynics flattering the lower classes and insulting the upper classes, *To the Cynic Heracleios* 223D. On the philosopher's freedom of speech (parrhesia), see P. Brown, *Power and Persuasion in Late Antiquity: Towards a Christian Empire* (Madison, WI, 1992) 61–70; P. Heather and D. Moncur, *Politics, Philosophy, and Empire in the Fourth Century: Select Orations of Themistius* (Liverpool, 2001) 4–5 and 19–42.

[66] Dio, *Or.* 72.1.

self-controlled and intelligent."[67] Dio's complaints about bad philosophers and bad listeners fit well together. The likely reactions of public speakers to these attacks – softening criticism with pleasing images and jokes or simply abandoning public orations on morality – turned speakers into precisely the types Dio condemned.

In contrast to those who attacked philosophers, some people admired them enough to use their images on sarcophagi. Paul Zanker's study of this phenomenon among "lay" followers in Rome demonstrates that interest in philosophy had spread among the "prosperous middle classes" by the third century CE. Men depicted themselves either as philosophers or among philosophers, often with their wives standing by as Muses. In one example, a Roman centurion wearing the philosopher's *pallium* is surrounded by itinerant Cynic philosophers. A number of lower-end sarcophagi also display this theme, whose popularity was rivaled only by hunting and pastoral scenes in the late third century. Zanker argues that these images illustrate the admiration of people outside the formal schools for philosophers and their association of philosophers with spirituality.[68] Strong feelings about philosophers, stemming from either frustration or awe, point to the important role intellectuals played in the public imagination.

In the fourth century, Cynics still figured prominently in discussions of the philosopher's public persona. The emperor Julian shared many of the views expressed by his predecessors: he admired the lives and teachings of the earliest Cynics, but believed that his contemporaries used this as a short-cut to achieving the privileges of a philosopher.[69] His critique also highlights the popular appeal of these men. When men dressed up as Cynics, they expected to attract admiring crowds. Julian accused his contemporaries of gathering large audiences for public speeches and entertaining them with pleasant stories.[70] Again, Julian did not condemn public appearances per se, but rather the willingness to water down philosophical principles in order to enjoy popular acclaim.

---

[67] *Or.* 72.7–8 and 34.2. Cf. Themistius' complaint that the philosopher is judged by other philosophers, but also by orators, teachers, physical trainers, and soldiers, *Or.* 26.312.

[68] The number of these sarcophagi indicates that these were not for actual teachers and scholars. See P. Zanker, *The Mask of Socrates: The Image of the Intellectual in Antiquity*, A. Shapiro, trans. (Berkeley, 1995) 267–76 and 282–4.

[69] Julian considered false Cynics to be rhetoricians who spread a prejudice against real philosophers among the multitude, *Or.* 7.224–5 and 6.197D. On Julian and the Cynics, see P. Athanassiadi, *Julian: An Intellectual Biography* (New York, 1992) 128–39. On fourth-century CE Cynics, see Downing, *Cynics and Christian Origins*, 275.

[70] *Or.* 7.216C–D. Julian approved of bringing moral exhortation to a wide audience and encouraged priests to preach to the public, *Fragment of a Letter to a Priest* 288B and 299B.

The statesman and philosopher Themistius was not a Cynic, but his entertaining public speeches might have annoyed Julian's sensibilities in the same way. Themistius modeled himself on Plato and Aristotle and spoke in theaters crowded with people who, he claimed, shouted out their approval and frequently jumped up from their seats.[71] He admits that he "does not sit quietly in his room and converse solely with his pupils; instead, he comes out into the public arena, does not hesitate to appear in the very heart of the city, and ventures to speak before all sorts of people."[72] When attacked by his peers for doing so, he defended himself by citing Plato. According to his definitions, the statesman (πολιτικός) addressed the masses out of concern for them, but the popular speaker (δημολόγος) did so seeking fame and applause. Themistius also observed that Plato spoke and taught people in banks, workshops, and wrestling schools, and Aristotle taught that writings for the general public should be easy to understand.[73]

In addition to calling on precedent as a defense of public speaking, Themistius argued that large audiences were the most efficient way to help as many people as possible. Unlike doctors, who could only benefit one person at a time, the philosopher who used clear, understandable rhetoric in the theater could help thousands of people at once, by persuading listeners to care for their souls and place less emphasis on their material possessions. Themistius envisioned a program of moral education for the masses, required by law:

> These philosophical pronouncements would make anyone at all better and more courageous in the practice of virtue, whether a rhetor or an average citizen or a general, whether rich or poor, young or adult or elderly. For they are aids and benefits that are equally applicable to all . . . people should heed them regardless of their financial status. If the law ordained that the whole citizenry, with their wives and children, should gather in assembly every year, then on that occasion the speaker who organizes the meeting should be obliged to set forth in his oration such principles for the people.[74]

Themistius went on to explain additional practical reasons why moral instruction for a large mixed audience was preferable to a small group:

---

[71] Themistius describes the enthusiasm he inspired in a large crowd (πολὺν ὄχλον) at the theater, *Or.* 26.311. Cf. *Or.* 22.265 and 23.282–3. See L. Méridier, *Le Philosophe Thémistios: devant l'opinion de ses contemporains* (Paris, 1906), and Penella, "The Rhetoric of Praise," 198–200.

[72] Themistius, *Or.* 26.313; translation from Penella, *Private Orations*, 142. Cf. *Or.* 21, *passim*, for another defense of speaking to large audiences.

[73] On definitions of statesmen and sophists: *Or.* 26.314–15. On the popular audiences of Plato and Aristotle: *Or.* 26.318–19. Cf. Dio, *Or.* 13.14.

[74] Themistius, *Or.* 26.321; translation from Penella, *Private Orations*, 152. This idea is similar to Julian's expectations of the pagan priest as moral exemplar and teacher depicted in *Fragment of a Letter to a Priest*. On the relationship between the two men, see T. Brauch, "Themistius and the Emperor Julian," *Byzantion* 63 (1993) 79–115.

For the larger and more inclusive the audience is, the more effective and trustworthy the speaker will seem to them. When people are praised, they enjoy it less if they are praised as part of a large group. But the situation is different if they are being given injunctions or admonitions. In this case, being part of a crowd lessens much of the irritation and ill will that any words of censure or admonition naturally bring on.[75]

Themistius faced the same problem as earlier speakers: they needed to circumvent the anger caused by their advice by planning ways to capture the attention of ambivalent listeners. Despite his time spent on panegyrics, court politics, as a patron to other intellectuals, and as an administrator, Themistius pictured the ideal philosopher as focused on advising the public on practical ethics.[76]

CHRISTIAN AND PAGAN INTELLECTUALS: COLLEAGUES AND COMPETITORS

As learned men addressing broad audiences, Christian preachers often had much in common with their pagan counterparts. Their adaptation of pagan *paideia*, though, led to numerous conflicts. When Emperor Julian banned Christians from teaching rhetoric, some Christians actively fought against him, claiming their fair share of the classical heritage. Others condemned traditional education as vanity, yet relied on their rhetorical training in order to couch their critiques. This tension between their satisfaction in the simple wisdom of fishermen and their desire to demonstrate brainpower added new dimensions to the old problems of the intellectual's role in society.[77] Here, the focus is on the conversion of the philosopher's identity – his moral authority, rhetorical training, and public appeal – for the practical needs of a Christian preacher. As we will see, Christian claims on these traits marked preachers as members of the elite, but also helped them communicate with and impress their congregations.

The overlap between traditional philosophical ideals and Christian teachings was obvious to both sides. Christians agreed with many traditional ethical insights, especially the Cynic rejection of wealth, and embraced a

---

[75] *Or.* 26.321–2; translation from Penella, *Private Orations*, 152–3. He also advises that philosophers should not avoid large audiences just because of the dim-witted people who do not benefit from it, *Or.* 26.323.

[76] Themistius emphasized ethics throughout his speeches, even when he addressed the imperial court, see Penella, "The Rhetoric of Praise," 194–208.

[77] On the similarities between the pagan and Christian "philosophical life" in contrast to their different attitudes toward the poor, see Clark, "Philosophic Lives and the Philosophic Life," 46–8. On Christian efforts to transform pagan intellectual life, see S. Rappe, "The New Math: How to Add and to Subtract Pagan Elements in Christian Education" in *Education in Greek and Roman Antiquity*, Y. L. Too, ed. (Leiden, 2001) 405–32.

number of the philosopher's attributes.[78] Similarities in their appearances were not accidental. Self-conscious remarks by pagan philosophers, as well as satirical depictions of them, illustrate that the meaning of their garb was common knowledge. Perhaps the most important influence of this "look" can be seen in late antique images of Christ, which passed on the prestige of this bearded, long-haired style to later eras.[79] Along the same line, Tertullian wore the philosopher's cloak as a sign of his moral gravity. Origen of Alexandria cited Cynics as precedents for Christian preaching in public. From the other point of view, Galen observed that Christians, although unschooled, lived like good philosophers.[80] Direct comparisons between Christian teachers and philosophers were not very problematic in the second and third centuries. Later, when more Christians became increasingly concerned with dividing themselves off from all aspects of "pagan" culture, they still pointed out these similarities, if only to underline the superiority of the Christian wise man. More often, though, Christian and pagan commentators aimed traditional attacks on false philosophers against each other. For example, Christian preachers expressed admiration for the Cynic Diogenes in some instances, but also criticized Cynics for indecency and dismissed their volunteer poverty as attention-seeking, echoing complaints made by Lucian and Julian about Cynics.[81]

Similarly, from a pagan perspective, Christians seemed unappealing in familiar ways. Lucian pictured Christ as a sophist, categorizing him among sham philosophers and his followers as dupes.[82] Later, Julian compared Cynics to Christian monks, meaning this as an insult to both groups. For him, the signature cloak, staff, wallet, and long hair were signs of the same hypocrisy and self-indulgence, regardless of creed. By calling contemporary

---

[78] Downing, *Cynics and Christian Origins*, 290–5. On the similarity of the appearance of pagan and Christian holy men, see P. Brown, "Asceticism: Pagan and Christian" in *CAH*, vol. XIII (1998) 601–31, at 604.

[79] Zanker, *Mask of Socrates*, 109. On the effect of the popularity of the philosopher theme on Christian iconography: 287–8 and 296. Cf. Dio, *Or.* 72.

[80] Tertullian, *De Pallio* (CCSL 2.733–50); Origen, *Contra Celsum* 3.50 (SC 136.118–20). On Galen's views of Christians, see R. Wilken, *The Christians as the Romans Saw Them* (New Haven, 1984) 79–80. On Tertullian and Dio Chrysostom as speakers, see Anderson, *Second Sophistic*, 208. On similarities between monks and pagan philosophers and pagan reactions to monks, see Brown, "Asceticism: Pagan and Christian," 601.

[81] See D. Krueger, *Symeon the Holy Fool: Leontius' Life and the Late Antique City* (Berkeley, 1996) 79–84; G. Dorival, "L'image des Cyniques chez les Pères grecs" in M.-O. Goulet-Cazé and R. Goulet, eds. *Le Cynisme ancien et ses prolongements: actes du colloque international du CNRS* (Paris, 1993) 419–43; P. R. Coleman-Norton, "St. Chrysostom and the Greek Philosophers," *CPh* 25 (1930) 305–17. On pagan and Christian critique of Cynics, see Downing, *Cynics and Christian Origins*, 286–97. Cf. Chrysostom, *Adv. Jud.* 5.3 (PG 48.886), where his dismissal of Apollonius of Tyana as a fraud is similar to Lucian's satires of sham philosophers.

[82] Lucian, *De morte Peregrini* 13.

Cynics "monks," Julian claimed that both groups made a public display of tattered clothes in order to receive public support and honors.[83] In all of these cases, the perceptions of Christians' and philosophers' shared qualities and the attacks each group made on one another revolved around the public image of moral experts.

In other instances, similar training and mutual admiration bound fourth-century Christian leaders to well-known pagan rhetoricians and philosophers. Their letters reveal affectionate relationships, especially between pagan teachers and Christian students, which were, to a great extent, built on shared experiences with public speaking. Basil and Libanius' correspondence illustrates a relationship based on the enjoyment of rhetorical display – they impressed each other by trading transcripts of their speeches.[84] Trained by both pagan and Christian teachers in Athens, Gregory of Nazianzus openly admired both Themistius and Libanius.[85] For his part, Gregory of Nyssa's letters to Libanius are thick with praise for the pagan rhetorician. He even encouraged Libanius to force a reluctant young man to study rhetoric because it was for his own good. In a particularly striking letter, Gregory appears to have written to two of Libanius' students in order to encourage them to show his treatise against a heretic to their teacher: "If some part of this work seems worthy of the sophist's ear, choose the parts, especially from before the debates, which have a style suitable for speaking, and bring it to him. Similarly, you will find that some passages from the dogmatic sections are explained not without grace."[86] If

---

[83] Julian, *Or.* 6 (224C) and 7 (224B–D); cf. Aelius Aristides, *Or.* 402d, on the resemblance of Christians and Cynics.

[84] Among Libanius' many rhetoric students, at least five went on to become bishops and gained good reputations as preachers, including Basil, Amphilochius of Iconium, and John Chrysostom. See P. Petit, *Les étudiants de Libanius* (Paris, 1957) 40. On Basil's rhetoric teachers in Athens, see P. Rousseau, *Basil of Caesarea* (Berkeley, 1994) 29–35. Letters 351–9 in Basil's collection include messages back and forth between Basil and Libanius, in which they compliment each other's rhetorical skill. Although their authenticity is questionable, some scholars count at least part of the correspondence as genuine; see R. Pouchet, *Basil le Grand et son univers d'amis d'après sa correspondance: une stratégie de communion* (Rome, 1992) 151–75. Rousseau maintains reservations as to their authenticity, see *Basil*, 57–60.

[85] His teachers included the pagan Himerius and Christian Prohaeresius. On Libanius and Themistius, see G. Naz., *Ep.* 236 and 24, respectively. On the life of philosophy, see R. R. Ruether, *Gregory of Nazianzus, Rhetor and Philosopher* (Oxford, 1969) 19–29; Elm, "Orthodoxy and the True Philosophical Life."

[86] G. Nys., *Ep.* 15, to John and Maximianus, who were most likely students of Libanius (SC 363.210). For Gregory of Nyssa's relationship with Libanius, see G. Nys., *Ep.* 13 and 14 (SC 363.194–206). Elsewhere, especially in his *Life of Macrina*, he promotes a Christian alternative to traditional *paideia*. See S. Rubenson, "Philosophy and Simplicity: The Problem of Classical Education in Early Christian Biography" in *Greek Biography and Panegyric in Late Antiquity*, T. Hägg and P. Rousseau, eds. (Berkeley, 2000) 110–39.

the addressees of this letter were indeed students of Libanius, then Christian friends could expect the rhetorician to read their theological compositions, as long as they were skillfully composed. These friendly anecdotes contrast with the sharp divisions emphasized in the "triumphal narrative" of Christian over pagan that has dominated much of the historiography of this period from the fifth century on.[87]

The obvious similarities between themselves and philosophers sometimes caused Christians to clarify their distinctions. After a riot in Antioch, John Chrysostom pointed out that Cynics with their long beards and staffs had abandoned the city, but the monks had entered it in order to help. This juxtaposition was intended to emphasize the differences between the two groups: despite the resemblance between the Cynics and monks, Chrysostom argued, the monks were motivated by a superior philosophy.[88] "Philosophy" was clearly perceived as the highest attainment of pagan culture, which added to the satisfaction Christian preachers found in pointing out how easily philosophers had been surpassed. The prestige of philosophers was a target to knock down and to redefine at the same time. This is why Chrysostom, when introducing rural, Syriac-speaking monks to his urban congregation, announced that these men were now the real philosophers.[89] Pagans who claimed that title had been merely acting like wise men, in costumes of beards, staffs, and cloaks.

Elsewhere, advising members of his congregation to raise their sons to become philosophers (that is, Christian philosophers), Chrysostom suggested that people too poor to afford higher education should consider the Cynics: "For if some Greeks (worthless men, dogs) put many to shame by taking up their worthless philosophy (for such is Greek philosophy), or rather not philosophy itself but only its name, by putting on a worn-out cloak and growing out their hair, how much more impressive would an actual philosopher be?"[90] Chrysostom set the Cynic up as the poor man's philosopher who could impress the crowds, in order to promote a Christian version of this calling. As an example, he describes a poor rural man who

---

[87] See P. Brown, *Authority and the Sacred: Aspects of the Christianisation of the Roman World* (Cambridge, 1995) 1–26.

[88] *De stat.* 17.2 (PG 49.174) and 19.1 (PG 49.189–90). Chrysostom was aware of the characteristics shared by Christians and philosophers, and told his listeners to excel over the pagans, *Hom. in Mt.* 15.9 (PG 57.235) and 21.4 (PG 57.300). Cf. *Hom. in Gen.* 28.5 (PG 53.258), on the triumph of fishermen over philosophers.

[89] *De stat.* 19.1 (PG 49.189). Sozomen refers to monks as "philosophers"; he considered them particularly important in the conversion of Syria, *HE* 6.34. Cf. Antony of Egypt's ability to recognize philosophers from their appearance; see P. Rousseau, "Antony as Teacher in the Greek *Life*" in *Greek Biography and Panegyric in Late Antiquity*, T. Hägg and P. Rousseau, eds. (Berkeley, 2000) 89–109, at 96–8.

[90] *Hom. in Ephesians* 21.3 (PG 62.152–3).

had captivated urban audiences with his wisdom: "When he burst into the cities (and this rarely happened), there was never such a lively crowd, not when orators, sophists, or anyone else rode in."[91] Chrysostom offers the rustic, uneducated saint as the Christian answer to the Cynic, that is, as a role model for the philosophically ambitious poor. Like the Cynic, the uneducated ascetic would be able to hold his own against the orators and sophists. In this instance, the Christian adaptation of the philosopher's image and cultural cachet was not only for the sake of the cultured elite, but also for the ordinary laity, who were already accustomed to being impressed by these figures.

Claims to a superior – if not less shabbily dressed – counterpart to the Cynics were not always enough. Some educated Christians needed to demonstrate that they had real philosophers, according to the traditional definition, in their ranks. In his catalogue of impressive Christians, Jerome defiantly countered pagan critics of his religion by publicizing its intellectual achievements. Jerome had no problem compiling a list of Christian philosophers and orators, because, by his time, many Christian leaders had been trained in traditional schools of rhetoric and philosophy.[92] Jerome's brief biographies present evidence for Christians who had excelled in public speaking and philosophy, and who sometimes even wore the traditional philosopher's clothing. In a couple of cases, while praising the eloquence of Christian leaders, he remarks on their ability to communicate with the crowds. For Jerome and the men he describes, part of the tradition they claimed was the public persona and popularity of the philosopher.[93]

CHRISTIAN SPEAKERS AND THE CROWDS

The debate over worldly and isolated philosophical lives reemerged when Christians attacked pagan thinkers for their elitism because it had prevented them from spreading their lessons to many people. Among Christians, Chrysostom boasted, the fishermen, tax collectors, and tent-makers had

---

[91] *Hom. in Ephesians* 21.3 (PG 62.153). When addressing pagans, Chrysostom attempted to convince them of the honor of the monastic life by pointing out that the simple life was a virtue in pagan traditions of wisdom, *Adv. oppug.* 2.4–5 (PG 47.336–40).

[92] Jerome, *De viris illustribus* 6. Eight of the men described in this work held the title of either "philosopher" or "rhetorician." Jerome remarks on the rhetorical skill of almost all of the others. On the Christian acceptance of elements of pagan *paideia*, see Rubenson, "Philosophy and Simplicity," 135–6; Rappe, "Pagan Elements in Christian Education."

[93] On Christians wearing the philosopher's garb: *De viris illustribus* 20 and 23; popularity with crowds: 54.8 and 91; public readings: 23.3; 71; 76; 115; 127. Victorinus the Rhetorician is singled out as being difficult to understand, 101.

turned numerous farmers and herdsmen into philosophers.[94] In this matter of accessibility, it was easy for Christians to claim the upper hand. But
educated Christians faced the same basic choice between retreating from
society and embracing it in order to try to teach the less knowledgeable.
Gregory of Nazianzus pondered the value of the Christian philosophical
life, weighing the different advantages of public service and pure contemplation. Regarding secular careers, though, there was no contest – public life offered only vanities.[95] Numerous educated men such as Gregory
hoped to avoid the responsibilities of priests and bishops, claiming, at least,
to prefer concentrating on their own souls.[96] But even if they had been
successful in avoiding official roles, they probably would not have been
simply left alone. Just as reclusive philosophers found themselves serving
the public, Christian ascetics could not avoid interacting with would-be
disciples and people seeking their help.[97] John Chrysostom's life offers
a different example of how these conflicting impulses – to serve and to
retreat – could resolve themselves. According to Palladius' account of his
life, he lived among the monks in the mountains outside of Antioch until
the ascetic life ruined his health, forcing him to return to the city. But
he accepted his role as a priest and later as bishop with enthusiasm. To
judge from his descriptions of the distractions and frustrations of normal society contrasted with the peace and solitude of monastic life, it is
likely that he considered being a pastor to be even more of a spiritual
challenge.[98]

   As was the case with philosophers, the active life for a Christian thinker
would require contact with a wide range of people. Despite their religion's
emphasis on the care of the poor, most upper-class Christians still retained
some customary contempt for the masses. Basil of Caesarea, well known
for his concern for the souls of laypeople, complained that his regular
contact with the public had "soiled" him, making him unfit to write to a

---

[94] Chrysostom, *De stat.* 19.2 (PG 49.190).

[95] Elm, "Orthodoxy and the True Philosophical Life"; Ruether, *Gregory*, 136–46.

[96] Although the rejection of public service was a trope – good Christian leaders could not seem too
eager for power, just as philosophers could not openly seek power and retain their privilege of free
speech – it seems in many cases to have been sincere. See A. Sterk's study of the ascetic element in
the ideal bishop, in *Renouncing the World Yet Leading the Church: The Monk-Bishop in Late Antiquity*
(Cambridge, MA, 2004).

[97] P. Brown, "The Rise and Function of the Holy Man in Late Antiquity," *JRS* 61 (1971) 80–101 and
Authority and the Sacred, 57–78.

[98] For instance, Chrysostom describes how the monks were free from the ordinary worries and temptations that plagued laypeople, *De Laz.* 3.1 (PG 48.991–2). See A. Hartney, *John Chrysostom and the
Transformation of the City* (London, 2004) 23–32.

sophist.[99] False claims of unworthiness are de rigueur in correspondence among educated writers, but this reference to the common people represents one aspect of Basil's views: to him, the laity *was* vulgar. Yet with this in mind, he did not abandon them to their vices, but planned to explain religious doctrine to them. Again, aristocratic contempt did not necessarily lead to an unbridgeable gap between elite and mass culture. For Christian writers and speakers, Basil advocated the simple style, because their goal should be to educate listeners and not to show off their skills.[100] He believed that homilies should be fit for their primary audience, that is, for simple and uneducated people.[101] Similarly, John Chrysostom could complain about his congregation and call attention to their ignorance and bad manners, but also tell with pride how illiterate fishermen had triumphed over philosophers.[102]

Just as philosophers dismissed ornate style and complicated reasoning as tools of deception, orthodox Christians accused heretics of being sophists who confused the laity with their deceptive reasoning.[103] Chrysostom describes the Gospel written by John, who used simple words and images so that his teaching would be accessible to all men, women, and children, which he contrasted sharply with the deceptive nonsense of teachers such as Pythagoras who deliberately used obscure speech.[104] Convoluted style, condemned by numerous philosophers since Socrates, now verged on being positively evil. But still, some situations called for a sort of orthodox sophistry. Gregory of Nazianzus could call a friend's love of sophisticated rhetoric a foolish pastime, but also admitted using rhetorical devices and complex arguments himself. Although he might have preferred the simplicity of the apostles, he was not a fisherman and possessed no miraculous

---

[99] Basil, *Ep.* 20. On Basil's range of views from disdain to sincere concern for the less educated members of his congregation, see Rousseau, *Basil*, 40–4.

[100] Basil, *Ep.* 135. Basil wrote in both styles: Rousseau, *Basil*, 46 and Anderson, *Second Sophistic*, 213.

[101] For Basil's views on simplicity of speech, see Rousseau, *Basil*, 125–9. Several of his contemporaries also promoted a simple style, see P. Auksi, *Christian Plain Style: The Evolution of a Spiritual Ideal* (Montreal, 1995) 144–73; R. Van Dam, *Becoming Christian: The Conversion of Roman Cappadocia* (Philadelphia, 2003), esp. 101–4.

[102] Chrysostom often commented on his audience's difficulty learning his lessons, which he attributed primarily to a lack of enthusiasm, e.g. *De stat.* 5.7 (PG 49.80); *Hom. in Mt.* 2.5 (PG 57.30), 37.6 (PG 57.426), 88.4 (PG 58.780–1). On the simplicity of the apostles and biblical texts: *Hom. in Gen.* 28.5 (PG 53.258); *Hom. in I Cor.* 7.1 (PG 61.53–5).

[103] Gregory of Nazianzus blamed the heretics for bringing elaborate and frivolous discourse into Christian theological discussions, see Auksi, *Christian Plain Style*, 164–70.

[104] *Hom. in John* 2.2 (PG 59.31–2). Cf. Jerome's claim that he spoke with rustic simplicity like the apostles, rather than in evil rhetoric: Jerome, *Hom. in Psalmos*, 1.91, cited in Auksi, *Christian Plain Style*, 171.

powers. Realistically, he needed rhetoric and arguments in order to face his opponents.[105]

Despite their condemnations of sophistry and promotion of the *sermo humilis*, many Christian leaders spoke in a more or less elevated style. Even though Basil of Caesarea spoke to everyone from aristocrats to laborers and expected them to understand him, he used formal language.[106] Comments about the reception of sermons indicate that their rhetorical style was acceptable to the laity. It is important to remember that these men had strong motivations compelling them to speak to ordinary people in an accessible way. In Italy, Ambrose advised other clerics not to bore their audiences: if preachers lost their people's attention, by speaking too long or failing to use clear and simple language, they risked their own salvation as well as that of their listeners.[107]

A CASE-STUDY: A LESSER-KNOWN CAPPADOCIAN

As we have seen, the continuity between the pagan Second Sophistic writers and the Christian preachers can be found in their personal relationships, their education, and their activities as public speakers. It is not possible to look into all of the illustrations of these relationships here, but a case-study can show how the different individuals and themes discussed in this chapter are tied together in a fourth-century individual's intellectual life and his relationship with both ordinary and extraordinary people. The career of Amphilochius of Iconium, a cousin of Gregory of Nazianzus and student of Libanius, provides a particularly good example of how a Christian bishop preserved the attributes of the traditional sophist and how rhetorical skill mattered even in a relatively obscure city.[108] Although he was

---

[105] On the necessity of sophisticated rhetoric, see G. Naz., *Or.* 36.4 (SC 318.248–50); against rhetorical sophistry: see G. Naz., *Ep.* 233, to Ablabius, a sophist and later Novatian bishop of Nicaea. Socrates describes Ablabius as an impressive orator, whose sermons remained in circulation and who continued to be a sophist after he became a bishop, *HE* 7.12.

[106] Basil, *Hexaemeron* 3.1 (SC 26.190). See M. Cunningham, "Preaching and Community" in *Church and People in Byzantium*, R. Morris, ed. (Birmingham, 1986) 29–46, at 33. Cf. Dennis Trout's view that Paulinus of Nola meant for his speeches to be understood by both the educated and uneducated listeners, "Town, Countryside and Christianization at Paulinus' Nola" in *Shifting Frontiers in Late Antiquity*, R. Mathisen and H. Sivan, eds. (Aldershot, 1995) 175–86, at 184. On the Christian adoption of the art of rhetoric, see Averil Cameron, *Christianity and the Rhetoric of Empire: The Development of Christian Discourse* (Berkeley, 1991) 120–54.

[107] Thomas Graumann, "St. Ambrose on the Art of Preaching" in *Vescovi e pastori in epoca teodosiana: XXV incontro di studiosi dell'antichità cristiana* (Rome, 1997) 587–600, at 590–2. Cf. Chrysostom, *De sac.* 4.9 (SC 272.278–80); Klingshirn, *Caesarius of Arles*, 76–81 and 149.

[108] *Amphilochii Iconiensis opera*, CCSG 3, C. Datema, ed. (Turnhout, 1978). Jerome and Theodoret admired Amphilochius but most modern authors have not been impressed, see Datema in

not necessarily a typical bishop, his career illustrates how the connections of *paideia* between pagans and Christians played out in a preacher's contact with the public.

Amphilochius studied with Libanius in the 350s and then went to Constantinople as a rhetor and lawyer. When he ran into financial troubles, his cousin Gregory intervened by asking Themistius (among others) to help him out.[109] Subsequently, Amphilochius moved to the Cappadocian countryside to take care of his aging father, who was a friend of Libanius and a rhetor well known in his home town. Amphilochius had intended to isolate himself from the world in order to live an ascetic life, but soon his friend, Basil, pressured him into becoming the bishop of Iconium in 374. His correspondence with Basil and Gregory of Nazianzus reveals the tension between his desire for retreat and contemplation, and the public demand for his expertise – a dilemma shared by both philosophers and educated Christians.[110]

Although Amphilochius, like many of his contemporaries, had been reluctant to become a bishop, his pagan rhetoric professor, surprisingly, was thrilled at the news of his ordination. Despite Libanius' attacks on some Christians – namely, monks who destroyed ancient shrines in the countryside – he enthusiastically congratulated Amphilochius on his new position, because the episcopal throne gave him an opportunity to display his talent as a public speaker:

When I found out that you had become a great steal [stolen from the rhetoricians by the Church, presumably] and you were on the throne and had been given some base of operations for making speeches, I rejoiced and I praised the ones who had seized you and I considered that your soul bears fruit again. For I hear how you move the crowd, how wonderful it is, how the shouts are resounding, and I don't doubt it.[111]

Amphilochii Iconiensis opera, xxvii–xxx, and K. Holl, *Amphilochios von Ikonium in seinem Verhältnis zu den Grossen Kappadoziern* (Tübingen, 1904). On the relationship between Amphilochius and the Pseudo-Chrysostom, see Holl, *Amphilochios*, 59 and 89; C. Datema, "Amphiloque d'Iconium et Pseudo-Chrysostom," *JÖB* 23 (1974) 29–32.

[109] G. Naz., *Ep.* 22–4.

[110] Basil, *Ep.* 150 and 161. On Basil's relationship with Amphilochius, see Rousseau, *Basil*, 258–63; R. Van Dam, *Families and Friends in Late Roman Cappadocia* (Philadelphia, 2003) 142–5, 151–2. The better-known Cappadocians clearly influenced his choices. After Gregory of Nazianzus helped Amphilochius with financial troubles, he urged him to leave his secular career for a religious life. When the people of Iconium asked Basil to find a bishop for them, Basil chose Amphilochius (Basil, *Ep.* 138 and 161). Both Amphilochius and his father, Amphilochius the elder, resisted at first (Basil, *Ep.* 161; G. Naz., *Ep.* 63).

[111] Libanius, *Ep.* 1543, to Bishop Amphilochius. In their commentary in *Libanios: Briefe*, G. Fatouros and T. Krischer, eds. and trans. (Munich, 1980) 467–9, G. Fatouros and T. Krischer observe that Foerster and Seeke at one point considered this letter to be fake, but that Foerster later revised his

The bishop and the rhetorician's chair were one and the same in this case, as Libanius saw it, and the reactions of the crowd confirmed this.[112] Basil also remarked on the bishop Amphilochius' skill as a popular speaker. When inviting Amphilochius to Caesarea to speak at a saint's festival, Basil asked him to come early because his people liked him the best, even though they had listened to many visitors.[113] When taken together with Libanius' comment that he had heard how his student was able to "move the crowds," Basil's comments appear to be more than mere politeness.

Local men were inspired by Amphilochius' appointment and, according to Libanius, "compete diligently in rhetoric, since they have before their eyes what their city has for an advocate."[114] These rhetors of Iconium are otherwise unknown – Libanius does not mention their religious background, only their excitement over having a prestigious rhetor in their home town. This comment indicates that Amphilochius was expected to continue playing the role of rhetor, to perform and impress, but also to allow ambitious locals to exploit his education and connections. Additionally, Amphilochius wrote a treatise giving advice on the Christian life, which appears to have been for young men who were under his instruction. Borrowing some of the content from Basil's *Address to Young Men*, he wrote his advice as a poem.[115] This poem was aimed at young men and written in a style meant to capture their attention (i.e. to entertain men such as the ones who annoyed Gregory of Nazianzus with their concern for literary style). Such Christian treatises on proper education for young men – in addition to Amphilochius' and Basil's works, John Chrysostom also wrote one – demonstrate the continuation of some of the sophist's pedagogical responsibilities which were handed over to the clergy.

The style and content of Amphilochius' homilies indicate that his popularity in Iconium and Caesarea could have easily been with a general audience. They are filled with repetitions and striking imagery, demonstrating that the praise from Basil and Libanius was probably based on relatively simple and straightforward but dramatic speeches. His description and

---

opinion. They also note that Libanius' use of robbing/stealing imagery here regarding Amphilochius' role in the Christian Church adds authenticity to Sozomen's report that Libanius complained that the Christians "stole" John Chrysostom, *HE* 8.2.

[112] On chairs as attributes of philosophers, see Zanker, *Mask of Socrates*, 118. Libanius refers to another student who became a rhetoric teacher as having a "thronos" in *Ep.* 1048.

[113] Basil, *Ep.* 176, written in 374. Cf. Amphilochius' *Hom.* 8, where he was invited to speak somewhere else, probably at Basil's. See Datema's introduction to the text, xix.

[114] Libanius, *Ep.* 1543. For additional evidence of philosophers and other intellectuals in small cities of central Asia Minor, see Mitchell, *Anatolia*, 85.

[115] For an introduction, text, and German translation, see E. Oberg, "Das Lehrgedicht des Amphilochios von Ikonium," *JbAC* 16 (1973) 67–97.

interpretation of the resurrection of Lazarus is particularly outstanding in this regard. Amphilochius took advantage of the topic of resurrection to catch his audience's attention with a description of Lazarus' decomposing body, which lingers over the details of his flesh, entrails, and bones. Later, he returns to this image in reverse for the recomposition of the body after Jesus' intervention. Also, his concern for ordinary listeners emerges in the prominent role of "the crowd" in his narrative: the "faithful crowd" stands by and watches Jesus' miracles, and they are the ones the Pharisees try to lead astray. Amphilochius' homily depicts "the entire city" observing or participating in every scene, which would encourage his congregation to identify with the story. The bishop also engaged his listeners by repeating key phrases from the Scriptures. In a short section, he voiced Jesus' commands "roll away the rock" and "Lazarus, come here" five and seven times respectively.[116] In this lucid description of a dramatic event, it is easy to imagine the congregation repeating these lines along with him.

Amphilochius' popularity as a speaker points to the continuity between the sophist and preacher. His vocation as a preacher, teaching Bible lessons to his congregation, utilized his traditional education. Given Libanius' enthusiasm, Amphilochius could still pass as a good sophist. Libanius' comments and Amphilochius' popularity also tell us something about the expectations for popular pagan speakers. Libanius' approval of Christian homilies, and his delight at their popularity, indicate that this type of writing appealed to him – they must not have seemed entirely unfamiliar in style or purpose. Private letters also reveal connections among most of the fourth-century authors discussed in this chapter: Libanius, the rhetoric professor of Antioch, wrote to Basil, Themistius, Amphilochius, and Julian, among many others, and, as was mentioned earlier, Gregory of Nazianzus wrote to Themistius on behalf of Amphilochius. All of these figures, pagan or Christian, dealt with issues of speaking in public and fulfilling their responsibilities to the people of their cities as philosophers, sophists, or bishops. John Chrysostom is notably absent from Libanius' correspondents. Having stayed in Antioch, he apparently distanced himself from his teacher, but he did not disassociate himself from the prominent and popular role that rhetoricians and sophists held in his society. Like his predecessor Dio, he later earned the name Goldenmouth for his eloquence.[117]

---

[116] Amphilochius, *Hom.* 3.4. Amphilochius' exegesis was literal, clearly influenced by the Antiochene school. See Datema's introduction to Amphilochius, *Opera*, xxix.

[117] Possibly, their lack of correspondence was due to Chrysostom's relative apathy for the Classics. See Saddington, "The Function of Education according to Christian Writers," 90–2; Hubbell, "Chrysostom and Rhetoric," 267.

CONCLUSIONS

Public speakers – who could be counted in one or more of the overlapping categories of philosophers, preachers, holy men, sophists, and orators – were often influenced by a sense of responsibility to the general population. In many ways, Christian preachers modeled themselves on previous – ultimately, biblical – Christian teachers, but they were also aware of their counterparts among pagan philosophers. In both pagan and Christian contexts, the appeal of some types of philosophical discussions reached well beyond highly educated circles, and found listeners from the prosperous middle classes, as well as the artisans and workers of the urban population. It is clear that a philosophical subject or a degree of rhetorical eloquence of a text can no longer be taken as a sure sign of an exclusively upper-class, educated audience.

The embrace of classical education eased the transition of many elites from pagan to Christian circles, but in addition to this, Christian leaders also simply needed to use rhetorical training in order to communicate with their audiences. Although the origins of the sermon as part of the liturgy and its focus on exegesis owe more to Jewish traditions than to genres of classical rhetoric, pagan learning influenced the ways in which educated preachers talked about the Scriptures.[118] Likewise, the public speaking of pagan philosophers and orators shaped the expectations of the congregations who listened to the sermons. Widespread interest in rhetorical speaking and the speakers' ability to convey information appropriately to a broad audience were at the root of the popularity of sermons.[119] In this context, several studies have described the bishop as taking over the traditional role of the philosopher and the pulpit as a new stage for rhetorical performance.[120] As we have seen, Christian preachers shared several concerns with other Second Sophistic intellectuals: the tension between public and contemplative life, their ambivalence toward the lower-class crowd, and the love of rich rhetoric versus their practical embrace of a plain style.

---

[118] On the Jewish origins of the sermon, see F. Siegert, "Homily and Panegyrical Sermon" in *Handbook of Classical Rhetoric in the Hellenistic Period, 330 BC–AD 400*, S. E. Porter, ed. (Leiden, 1997), 421–43. On the overemphasis in scholarship on the influence of Cynic diatribe on Christian preaching, see C. Schäublin, "Zum paganen Umfeld der christlichen Predigt" in *Predigt in der Alten Kirche*, E. Mühlenberg and J. van Oort, eds. (Kampen, 1994) 25–49, at 26–8. On the broader influence of classical ideas on Christian approaches to teaching and learning, see P. Kolbet, "The Cure of Souls: St. Augustine's Reception and Transformation of Classical Psychagogy," Ph.D. dissertation, University of Notre Dame (South Bend, IN, 2002).

[119] Anderson, *Second Sophistic*, 42–4 and 205–13.

[120] Vanderspoel, *Themistius and the Imperial Court*, 17; Brown, *Power and Persuasion*, 48; R. Wilken, *John Chrysostom and the Jews: Rhetoric and Reality in the late 4th Century* (Berkeley, 1983) 101.

A Christian preacher could use Second Sophistic skills as a way to captivate his congregation, which was especially important given the threat of competing Christian sects. John Chrysostom indicated what might be at stake: if the clergy did not speak persuasively – even if their arguments were based on divine truth – ordinary laypeople would fall into heresy. Chrysostom warned his fellow preachers that "the simple multitude" attended debates over doctrine and if heretics could outargue orthodox priests, the listeners would assume the problem was with the doctrine. This meant that poor rhetorical performance could lead both listener and speaker to face harsher punishments from God.[121]

The long-standing tradition of philosophers who attempted to teach morality to the public helps us to make sense of the Christian preacher's role in late antique society. In addition to studies of the liturgical function of sermons and the literary origins of this genre, it is also necessary to examine the reasons for the popularity of sermons. By looking at their ways of thinking about interaction with different ranks of society, we can better understand the ties between pagan and Christian intellectuals and how they related with the rest of society. To emphasize further the importance of the cultural context of preaching, the next chapter will focus more closely on the urban environment of John Chrysostom and his congregation in Antioch. It is important to try to understand the extent to which people were exposed to public speaking, whether it was philosophical, religious, political, or simply entertaining. Close attention to the social context of these events – the purpose of the occasions, the types of people who gathered, where they gathered – contributes to our understanding of the popularity of Christian preachers. This, in turn, allows us to appreciate the information sermons provide about ordinary Christians.

---

[121] Chrysostom, *De sac.* 4.9 (SC 272.278–80). On public theological debates, see R. Lim, *Public Disputation, Power and Social Order in Late Antiquity* (Berkeley, 1995).

CHAPTER 2

Rhetoric and society: Contexts of public speaking in late antique Antioch

Christians in Antioch were well acquainted with public speaking outside of their churches. In addition to moralizing speeches by Cynics and other philosophers, other types of oratory such as political discourse and entertainment shaped the social milieu in which Christian preachers flourished. This culture of public speaking helps to explain how and why ordinary people listened to sermons such as John Chrysostom's. Although most of Chrysostom's listeners were less educated than their preacher, they lived in one of the most vibrant cities of the late Roman Empire, where numerous civic events featured rhetorical speaking. The world outside the church affected the interactions within it: the urban setting was where the laypeople developed their taste for eloquence, where preachers acquired rhetorical skills, and where these skills acquired prestige.

Ordinary people talked about politics. Chrysostom compared the calm, spiritual conversations held by monks to the constant political discussions carried on by members of his congregation.[1] These conversations seemed like pointless trivia to Chrysostom, but ordinary people were interested in facts about the failures, successes, and scandals of public figures. Likewise, they also memorized lyrics they heard in the theaters.[2] In order to have these discussions and sing the songs in the barbershops and marketplace, they had to listen to political announcements and attend theatrical performances. Although Chrysostom dismissed these concerns as distractions from the Christian life, experiences in political and theatrical contexts helped to prepare laypeople to listen to and understand rhetorically crafted speeches such as his own sermons.

While the political influence of orators had declined from earlier eras, late Roman cities continued to offer a number of occasions for public speaking.

[1] Chrysostom, *Hom. in Mt.* 69.3 (PG 58.651–3).　　[2] *Hom. in Mt.* 1.7–8 (PG 57.22–3).

42

Professional rhetors became famous throughout the Empire by competing with one another in public for prizes. Speakers served as advocates in trials, often with crowds listening and shouting opinions to the judge. The theater also played a vital part in city life and still included dramatic readings as one of its features.[3] In these various public gatherings, the audience's response – applause, acclamations, and even riots – illustrates a high level of popular attention and participation. This chapter will examine these different types of public speaking that took place in Antioch, which will provide a broader context for the popular appeal of Christian sermons. Because of all of the ways in which rhetoric permeated urban culture, when laypeople encountered eloquence in church, even the uneducated could be experienced listeners.

ORATORS: DECLAMATIONS, PANEGYRICS, AND FESTIVALS

Traditionally, the Athenian democracy and the Roman Republic have been considered the only contexts in the ancient world in which deliberative rhetoric truly mattered, when orators such as Demosthenes and Cicero changed, or at least attempted to change, the course of history. But the art of speaking remained fundamental long after participatory forms of Greek and Roman government had left the stage. The pinnacle of ancient education was the school of rhetoric, and the skill continued to be an important element of elite identity throughout the later Roman Empire.[4] During the imperial period, the *demos* of Greek cities still gathered to listen to rhetoricians demonstrate their skills at civic festivals. Public ceremonies and contests put the achievements of the most accomplished rhetors on display for the general population.[5] In Constantinople, Libanius observed: "People who had been so excited over horse races and theatrical spectacles had switched their attention to rhetorical performances."[6] As is the case in all performances, the spectators could enjoy and judge the achievements of others, without necessarily having any training or ability in the field themselves. Far from being confined to the educated elite, the regular

---

[3] Most of the theater performances at this time, however, were pantomimes. See T. D. Barnes, "Christians and the Theater" in *Roman Theater and Society*, W. J. Slater, ed. (Ann Arbor, MI, 1996) 161–80, at 166–78; R. C. Beacham, *The Roman Theatre and Its Audience* (London, 1991) 193–8.

[4] For a discussion of the role of literary education in the making of elite identity, see R. Kaster, *Guardians of Language: The Grammarian and Society in Late Antiquity* (Berkeley, 1988) 14; M. W. Gleason, *Making Men: Sophists and Self-Presentation in Ancient Rome* (Princeton, 1995).

[5] S. Alcock, *Graecia Capta: The Landscapes of Roman Greece* (Cambridge, 1993); T. Whitmarsh, *Greek Literature and the Roman Empire: The Politics of Imitation* (Oxford, 2001).

[6] *Or.* 1.37 and 2.24–5.

performance of rhetoric in public provided links between the various social groups within cities.

Public speaking by trained rhetoricians attracted crowds in late Roman cities on numerous occasions: imperial birthdays, *adventus* ceremonies, religious festivals, dedications of buildings, and the arguments in the lawcourts. The general population, including men and women, would attend many of these events.[7] Public orators were popular, even glamorous figures, who were known for their loud voices, gestures, and eye-catching appearance.[8] One type of rhetorical performance in particular, the declamation, shared the same themes with the more fanciful theater productions: adulterous wives, pirates, young lovers, and shipwrecks.[9] Speeches on these themes were learning exercises for students and/or competition pieces. Young orators used imaginary dramatic situations in order to practice rhetorical devices and master the art of making arguments. The structure of these declamations was similar to that employed in Greek legal practice where litigants pleaded their own cases.[10] Orators designed the fictitious situations in the declamations in order to make the argument interesting for the hearer and difficult for the speaker, allowing the maximum opportunity for the speaker's display of cleverness.

Of the fifty-four declamations by Libanius that survive, some deal with situations from classical Athenian history and mythology, but many are based on the everyday conflicts between the rich and poor, among family members, and between lovers.[11] Some declamations, such as the story of a freeloader who had missed a free dinner due to horse problems, focused on humor and stock characters of comedy.[12] The legal format of these speeches also reveals a public interest in court speeches as entertainment, a topic that will be discussed in more detail below. Declamations were recited in theaters and temples primarily to other students of rhetoric, as well as

---

[7] S. MacCormack, *Art and Ceremony in Late Antiquity* (Berkeley, 1981) 1–15.

[8] Lucian, *Rhetorum praeceptor* 15; D. A. Russell, *Greek Declamation* (Cambridge, 1983) 82; *Libanius: Imaginary Speeches: A Selection of Declamations*, D. A. Russell, ed. and trans. (London, 1996) 7–8. See Themistius' description of rhetors addressing theaters and festival assemblies, dressed up, with cosmetics and flower garlands, *Or.* 28.341.

[9] Russell, *Imaginary Speeches*, 5–11.

[10] Ibid., 7. Most of the evidence concerning declamations comes from the fourth through sixth centuries CE.

[11] Russell, *Imaginary Speeches*, 8.

[12] Libanius, *Declamation* 28.22–4, in Russell, *Imaginary Speeches*, 173–4. On the educational value of lurid declamations which focused on sexual crimes, see R. Kaster, "Controlling Reason: Declamation in Rhetorical Education at Rome" in *Education in Greek and Roman Antiquity*, Y. L. Too, ed. (Leiden, 2001) 317–37.

in formal displays and contests, which could entertain a thousand listeners or more.[13]

In addition to the declamations composed for practice and competition, rhetoric teachers trained their students in the art of panegyric, an important element of public festivals, both religious and civic, and of other political events.[14] The presentation of this type of oratory with its eloquent flourishes was always a social act, and was usually aimed at a wide audience. The recipients of the panegyrics were not always privileged individuals – entire cities were often praised.[15] Speakers such as Libanius were keenly aware of how to craft such a speech for the general public. In a revealing case, Libanius had to present different versions of a funeral oration to two audiences because of the politically sensitive nature of his critique of imperial policy. He mentions in his *Autobiography* that he excised the controversial political statements from his public speech, but does not indicate that he changed his rhetorical style for the different audiences.[16]

During festivals, orators announced the games and honored the people who had sponsored the events. Libanius' oration in praise of the city of Antioch was presented at the Olympic games of 356. In this speech, Libanius described eloquence as a natural element of the city that was available to all of its inhabitants, comparable to the favorable climate and abundant water resources.[17] Occasions such as the Kalends of January, dedications of public buildings, imperial accessions, visits, birthdays, and anniversaries were all regularly marked by orations of praise from local rhetors. Panegyrics were required so often that rhetoric professors taught students formulae for writing praise for different events. The frequency of these civic panegyrics is clear from the handbooks for orators.[18]

Panegyrics, like declamations, were also given in contests. D. A. Russell points out that although no specific competition piece survives, hundreds

[13] Russell, *Greek Declamation*, 75–6. Cf. Dio Chrysostom's audiences, such as in *Or.* 32. Teaching lectures were also sometimes public, Eunapius, *VP* 483.

[14] M. L. Clarke, *Rhetoric at Rome: A Historical Survey* (New York, 1996) 43; R. Penella, "The Rhetoric of Praise in the Private Orations of Themistius" in *Greek Biography and Panegyric in Late Antiquity*, T. Hägg and P. Rousseau, eds. (Berkeley, 2000) 194–208.

[15] On the social nature of epideictic speeches, see L. Pernot, *La rhétorique de l'éloge dans le monde gréco-romain* (Paris, 1993) 438. For panegyrics that praised the official and the city at the same time, see Libanius, *Or.* 59, 12, and 13. Cf. D. A. Russell, "The Panegyrists and Their Teachers" in *The Propaganda of Power: The Role of Panegyric in Late Antiquity*, Mary Whitby, ed. (Leiden, 1998) 17–50. On imperial *adventus*, see MacCormack, *Art and Ceremony in Late Antiquity*, 1–61.

[16] Libanius, *Or.* 1.111–12.

[17] *Or.* 11.192. Although clearly exaggerated, this passage indicates that a rhetor might wish that *all* people in the city enjoy and understand rhetoric.

[18] For panegyric formulae, see *Menander Rhetor*, D. A. Russell and N. G. Wilson, eds., trans., and intro. (Oxford, 1981) *passim*.

of them must have been written and much of rhetoric teaching was aimed at winning these contests.[19] Teachers of rhetoric were conscious of the general public and did not teach their students to write only to please other rhetoric experts. For example, Menander Rhetor advised students to be very clear about the structure of their speeches so as not to lose their listeners' attention. Aside from civic displays, rhetors also found audiences in family ceremonies such as weddings, birthdays, farewells, and funerals.[20]

Because of the classical references and elevated prose of rhetoricians such as Libanius, the high regard for rhetorical speeches is often attributed solely to the tastes of highly educated listeners or readers.[21] But references by Libanius and his peers about their own audiences indicate that stylized rhetoric appealed to a wider range of people. Although he often displayed a customary disdain for the lower classes, Libanius' interests were not confined to literary conversations in the parlors of the city's elites. He took up the causes of the city's bakers and the peasants of the countryside and proudly referred to the laborers having a high opinion of him when he walked by their workshops.[22] His role as public advocate does not in itself mean that his rhetoric was popular among bakers and peasants, but this aspect of his career indicates that the rhetor was concerned with the world beyond sophists and upper-class students. Although it is risky to take a rhetorician's words at face value, especially when he is describing his own popularity, his work as a public advocate lends credence to his claim that when he spoke in public, many people came to listen and, like Chrysostom, he faced the task of quieting too much applause.[23] In other words, it is significant that he wished to be seen as popular.

Rhetors' presentations were, of course, affected by what people wanted to hear. Without admitting to doing this themselves, speakers criticized their rivals for playing to their audiences. Plutarch had warned young men against speaking to large audiences because "to please the multitude is

---

[19] Russell, "Panegyrists and their Teachers," 23; Pernot, *Rhétorique de l'éloge*, 49.

[20] *Menander Rhetor*, 372.14; D. A. Russell, "Panegyrists and their Teachers," 18, 28–9 and "Rhetors at the Wedding," *PCPhS* 205 (1979): 104–17.

[21] On ornate rhetoric as an indication of an elite audience, see P. Petit, "Recherches sur la publication et la diffusion des discours de Libanius," *Historia* 5 (1956) 479–509; J. H. W. G. Liebeschuetz, *Antioch: City and Imperial Administration in the Later Roman Empire* (Oxford, 1972) 25–31. Liebeschuetz also remarks that Libanius' orations are simpler than those of other orators, 24.

[22] Libanius, *Or.* 30.50 and 2.5. H.-U. Wiemer, "Der Sophist Libanios und die Bäcker von Antiocheia," *Athenaeum* 84 (1996) 527–48. On the other hand, for Libanius' snobbery toward the lower classes, see B. Leyerle, *Theatrical Shows and Ascetic Lives: John Chrysostom's Attack on Spiritual Marriage* (Berkeley, 2001) 27 n. 77.

[23] On applause, see *Or.* 2.24.

to displease the wise."[24] Later, Themistius observed about such speakers: "Since they are so courteous and agreeable to their audiences, their audiences salute them in turn and consequently the earth and sea are teeming with these men."[25] Claims that rivals won popularity by diluting the content of their speeches or by flattering their audiences can be interpreted as further evidence that speakers wanted to be popular, and that they were envied when they succeeded in gaining popularity.

PUBLIC SPEAKING IN JULIAN'S *MISOPOGON*

Evidence of several specific occasions of public speaking in Antioch can be found in Emperor Julian's (361–3) *Misopogon* ("Beard-Hater") and the writings that it inspired. The scandal began after some Antiochenes composed parodies of the philosopher-emperor, making fun of his restrained habits and unkempt appearance, which they recited in the marketplaces. Julian, in his response, seemed particularly unsettled by the Antiochenes' suggestion that he should twist rope from the strands of his long beard. The satires also compared him unfavorably with the previous emperor Constantius II (337–61), mocked him for fighting against Christ, and ridiculed his choice of Helios the sun-god as the image for his coins.[26] Libanius, in an oration criticizing the Antiochenes for their disrespectful behavior, reveals that the parodies were part of holiday festivities of the Kalends of January.[27] The rhetor acknowledged that the expectation of satires during the holiday provided a possible excuse for the writers and audience of the offensive material. But their insults, he explained, were too bitter for good-natured holiday jokes. Libanius defined the proper limits to this fun according to how his own slaves insulted him during the festival, and how he expected them to do so only in good humor.[28]

---

[24] Plutarch, *De liberis educ.* 6.

[25] Themistius, *Or.* 28.341; translation from *The Private Orations of Themistius*, R. Penella, ed., trans., and intro. (Berkeley, 2000) 175.

[26] Julian, *Misopogon*: regarding his beard, 338B–339A; on Constantius and Christ, 357A; on the coins, 355D. For other accounts of the parody, see Socrates, *HE* 3.17; Sozomen, *HE* 5.19; Amm. Marc. 22.14.1–3.

[27] Libanius expected the Antiochenes' excuses for the parodies would involve their careful adherence to traditional holiday celebrations of the Kalends, which was consistent with Julian's wishes, *Or.* 16.35. The fact that the satires of Julian included references to his persecution of Christians is interesting. Either Christians who were offended by the pagan emperor were themselves taking part in a traditional festival or pagans were attacking Julian for his anti-Christian policies. For an excellent discussion of the traditions of popular satire during holidays and how authority figures responded to them, see M. W. Gleason, "Festive Satire: Julian's *Misopogon* and the New Year at Antioch," *JRS* 76 (1986) 106–19.

[28] Libanius, *Or.* 16.36.

These satires gave voice to the agitation in the city caused by the emperor's policies. Julian had attempted to resolve a dispute over high grain prices by mandating a lower price, which in the end drove the grain dealers out of the city and led to a scarcity of food. This crisis, coupled with the festival allowing satires, led to the expression of widespread discontent with the emperor. Julian himself described how the populace was unhappy with his abstemious ways, particularly his neglect of the theater, and acknowledged that the general population disliked him.[29] Not surprisingly, the Christians held an even greater grudge against him for his policies attacking their religion.[30]

The poems, or songs, were performed in anapaestic verse among the crowds in the marketplace. Julian reminded the Antiochenes: "You abused me in the marketplace, in front of the general population, with the help of enough citizens who were witty enough to compose such things."[31] Julian was not specific about what sort of person composed the offensive poems. Presumably, the authors were literate but not especially well known in the city, or else they would have been singled out by either Julian or Libanius. It was not merely the composition of the poems that bothered Julian, but the performances of them that spread the ridicule to the entire city via the crowded streets of the marketplace. The emperor stated his beliefs about the audience's role in the offense: "You know perfectly well that all of those who recited these sayings are partners with those who listened to them. The one who listened with pleasure to the slander shares the same pleasure as the speaker, even though he went to less trouble. Both are equally to blame."[32] The poems were written to amuse large crowds and to give voice to widespread sentiments about the emperor. Their inspiration and audience were popular, but they were presented in a form that required a certain level of literary education. Significantly, the fact that the poems required some training to compose did not mean that they reflected only the concerns of the educated elite. Julian's comments indicate as much when he makes the distinction between the composers of the verses and the people who enjoyed listening to them.

---

[29] Julian, *Misopogon* 357D. It is interesting to note that Julian counts Christians as his main critics, but here his critics are theater enthusiasts. Clearly, the two groups overlapped. Julian also forbade pagan priests to go to the theater, *Fragment of a Letter to a Priest* 304.

[30] For responses to Julian's policies, see "Gregory Nazianzen's Two Invectives against Julian the Emperor" in *Julian the Emperor*, C. W. King, trans. (London, 1888) 1–121; S. N. C. Lieu, ed., *The Emperor Julian: Panegyric and Polemic* (Liverpool, 1989) 41–128.

[31] *Misopogon* 364A.   [32] Ibid.

The emperor's description of his dealings with the Antiochenes reveals other instances of public speaking that reached the ears of the populace. Disappointed at the lack of enthusiasm the Antiochenes showed for traditional religious celebrations, the emperor arranged an assembly at a temple. The people met him with shouts and applause similar to their behavior in the theaters.[33] Julian complained, though, that their enthusiasm was not directed to the gods. He proceeded to lecture the people gathered in the temple, rebuking them for their irreverence.[34] Also, during his ill-fated stay in Antioch, Julian was known to address the senate on various occasions and to spend time presiding over and speaking in the lawcourts.[35] He displayed his rhetorical abilities most famously, however, in the *Misopogon* itself, which he had posted outside of the imperial palace, where people were accustomed to reading or listening to the edicts and letters from emperors.[36]

RHETORIC IN THE COURTS

As we have seen, public speaking did not lose its prominence in Greek cities under Roman domination. Likewise, the courts continued to provide opportunities for speakers attempting to impress and persuade large audiences, even though they functioned without formal juries.[37] The appeal of the courtroom drama was not confined to the upper classes. This was a litigious world, where people from all levels of society could have their day in court.[38] Libanius' advocacy on behalf of the bakers and peasants in Antioch confirms that this was true in fourth-century Antioch.

In the Roman world, people seeking legal assistance placed more importance on the skill of speaking than on knowledge of the law. John Crook observes that this preference for rhetorical skill was a manifestation of the general cultural emphasis on eloquence. The ability to make persuasive arguments and communicate them in clear and careful language was one of the most respected and well-honed skills known to the Greeks and

---

[33] *Misopogon*, 344B.   [34] *Misopogon*, 344B–C.

[35] Libanius, *Or.* 16.27 and 18.182. Ammianus emphasizes Julian's unusual sense of justice, Amm. Marc. 22.10.5.

[36] Gleason points out that both literate and illiterate people would have had access to these documents, "Festive Satire," 106. See also her analysis of the relationship between imperial edicts, letters, and the *Misopogon*, 116–18.

[37] See E. Fantham, "The Contexts and Occasions of Roman Public Rhetoric" in *Roman Eloquence: Rhetoric in Society and Literature*, W. J. Dominik, ed. (London, 1997) 111–28, at 122–3. On the admiration of the power of the advocates' rhetorical skills, see J. Harries, *Law and Empire in Late Antiquity* (Cambridge, 1999) 107.

[38] J. A. Crook, *Legal Advocacy in the Roman World* (London, 1995) 125.

Romans.[39] Litigants hired professional speakers because they were trained in the best ways of making arguments, convincing the judge, and capturing the emotions of the crowd if necessary. Like festival orators seeking a prize, the lawyer had to meet his audience's expectations.[40] These concerns underline the common ground of the legal advocate and actor, the courtroom and theater – not to mention the preacher's pulpit and the orator's bema. The advocate's skill stemmed from the same training as that of the competitor in panegyric contests. In fact, the two could have been the same men at different stages in their careers, or merely on different days.[41] Among the careers that Libanius' students followed after completing their education, there were many legal advocates among the rhetoric teachers, imperial officials, and bishops.[42] The skills of speaking and gesturing were necessary in all of these different contexts because their goal was to win and keep the attention of a large group of people through performance and language.

While the legal advocates' speeches would have been of immediate interest to the litigants and judge, other people gathered at the courts either out of personal concern or for entertainment. When Libanius praised the eloquence of Antioch's senators, he added that when these men served in the courts, they attracted crowds: "Their minds are so sharp, their words so concise and ever-flowing, that many of the people who love to listen to these things meet at the lawcourts, as though at schools, to listen to the speeches presented before ruling magistrates, which they compose on the spot with more confidence than if they had been already prepared."[43] Since the courts brought in people from outside the city, the speeches presented spread the city's fame for the art of speaking throughout the land.[44]

---

[39] Ibid., 196–7.
[40] See Quintilian's advice to lawyers on speech writing, personal appearance, and gestures: *Inst.* 4.1, 54; 11. 2, 17; 12. 9, 16. Cited in Crook, *Legal Advocacy*, 137–8.
[41] Educated men practiced law at the beginning of their public careers, while professional advocates came from a lower social status, although still one with access to rhetorical education; cf. A. H. M. Jones, *The Later Roman Empire, 284–602: A Social, Economic and Administrative Survey*, vol. 1 (Baltimore, MD, 1992) 507–16. See Crook, *Legal Advocacy*, 102 for the continuity of legal rhetoric in the later Roman Empire.
[42] P. Petit, *Les étudiants de Libanius* (Paris, 1957) 154–69. Petit lists the information regarding the careers of 104 of Libanius' students in a table: 39.4 percent government officials; 21.1 percent *curiales*; 29.8 percent advocates; 9.6 percent professors (bishops, for some reason, are included with the advocates). Petit remarks that, out of these professions, the professor's was the least desirable, and suggests that Libanius would have followed a different path, if his father had not died early.
[43] Libanius, *Or.* 11.139. On the eloquence of lawyers compared to both preachers and actors, see Chrysostom, *De sac.* 5.1 (SC 272.282).
[44] Libanius, *Or.* 11.191–2.

Accounts of Christian martyrs show quite clearly the drama of court proceedings and how they attracted crowds to listen to the interrogations and judge's rulings. In some cases, verbatim court records reveal the process of the hearings. Such records from fourth-century Donatist martyr trials in North Africa describe the judges, advocates, witnesses, and litigants engaged in the arguments.[45] Earlier accounts of martyrs also give relevant details about the actual process and setting of the trials: the defendant went up on the *gradus*, a low platform about one step up, and the judge would preside from the bema, a higher platform. The function of the *gradus* was to make it easier for the crowd to see the accused.[46] People not directly involved in the trials were clearly present, and presumably the same was true for many trials not involving Christian martyrs. The information provided in the acts of the martyrs reveals that the very structure of the court reflects the expectation of an audience.

The people who gathered to watch the trials sometimes influenced, or at least attempted to influence, the judge's decision. The audience let the judge know its thoughts about how long the questioning of a defendant should last, and whether the person should be condemned or set free.[47] David Potter's examination of martyrdoms as spectacles highlights the presence of the crowd and its participation in trials. Trials and executions were more than displays of power from the top meant to intimidate the rest of the society. Rather, they provided opportunities for the crowd to exercise its clout.[48]

THE THEATER

As another context in which ordinary people attended performances, the theater served as a meeting place between the community's leaders and the larger population and as a site for the diffusion of culture.[49] Performers expected and prized reactions from their audiences, to the extent that a silent audience was literally a curse wished upon enemies, as one inscription tells us.[50] In general, the same groups of people who attended church

---

[45] Harries, *Law and Empire*, 74–5, 99, and 129–30.

[46] D. Potter calls attention to the similarities between entertainment and court trials, in "Performance, Power and Justice in the High Empire" in *Roman Theater and Society*, W. J. Slater, ed. (Ann Arbor, MI, 1996) 129–59, at 146–7.

[47] Ibid., 150.   [48] Ibid., 159.

[49] See P. Rey-Coquais, "La culture en Syrie à l'époque romaine" in *Donum Amicitiae: Studies in Ancient History*, E. Dabrowa, ed. (Krakow, 1997) 139–60, at 152–5.

[50] See C. Roueché, *Performers and Partisans at Aphrodisias in the Roman and Late Roman Periods* (London, 1993) 28.

also went to the theater.[51] Chrysostom assumed this when he complained that his listeners' behavior in church was all too similar to their behavior at the theater. In advice to another preacher, he warned: "Most people have become accustomed to listening not for profit, but for pleasure, sitting like judges of tragic actors and harpists."[52] Gregory of Nazianzus had a similar complaint: "They are not looking for priests, but for orators."[53] When laypeople applauded the speeches they heard in church, Chrysostom responded by emphasizing that they were *not* at the theater. Such applause was not unique to the church in Antioch or to this preacher: congregations throughout the Roman world in Late Antiquity often responded enthusiastically, accustomed to this from their experiences with rhetoric as public entertainment.[54] Because everyone was well aware of this connection, popular expressions of enthusiasm for sermons inspired suspicion among church authorities.[55]

Christian leaders' reactions to the spectacles provide much of our information for the content of productions in Late Antiquity, as well as unmistakable proof that they were still quite popular among Christians and pagans alike.[56] Critical of all types of traditional public entertainment, Christian writers were most disturbed by the female dancers and the males who performed as females.[57] The most popular theatrical performances of this period, the pantomimes, acted out familiar stories through dancing, often comedies about adultery, but the content could also include parodies of current events.[58] According to Eusebius, even the doctrinal disputes of the

---

[51] For inscriptions by various groups of people in the theater in late antique Aphrodisias, see Roueché, *Performers and Partisans*, 83–128.
[52] Chrysostom, *De sac.* 5.1 (SC 272.282). On the depictions of the crowds in art and literature, see R. Lim, "In the 'Temple of Laughter': visual and literary representations of spectators at Roman games" in *The Art of Ancient Spectacle*, B. Bergmann and C. Kondoleon, eds. (New Haven, 1999) 343–65. On the overlap between theater crowds and Christian congregations, see N. McLynn, "Seeing and Believing: Aspects of Conversion from Antoninus Pius to Louis the Pious" in *Conversion in Late Antiquity and the Early Middle Ages: Seeing and Believing*, K. Mills and A. Grafton, eds. (Rochester, NY, 2003) 224–70, at 226–7.
[53] G. Naz., *Or.* 42.24 (SC 384.106).
[54] A. Olivar discusses references to applause from the sermons of both Latin and Greek Church Fathers, *La predicación cristiana antigua* (Barcelona, 1991) 834–67.
[55] H. Stander, "The Clapping of Hands in the Early Church," *Studia Patristica* 26 (1993) 75–80.
[56] For evidence from inscriptions and mosaics for theatrical performances and competitions in Roman Syria, see Rey-Coquais, "La culture en Syrie," 153–4.
[57] For an in-depth examination of Chrysostom's treatment of this subject, see Leyerle, *Theatrical Shows*, *passim*.
[58] Cf. Libanius' topics for declamations that included situations from mythology as well as everyday life: Russell, *Imaginary Speeches*, 8. See Libanius, *Defense of the Dancers*, and Barnes, "Christians and the Theater," 166–78 for descriptions of different types of pantomime performance. It is also noteworthy that the pantomime in Rome was believed to have been Syrian in origin.

Christians became subject matter for the theater. During the Arian controversy, "the solemnity of divine teachings endured the most shameful ridicule in the midst of the theaters of the unbelievers."[59] Later pantomimes were accused of parodying the sacraments, especially baptism.[60]

In addition to dancers, the theater still had a place for performances more closely related to those of the orator, advocate, and preacher: the tragic actor. In this period, actors recited excerpts from tragedy. Inscriptions recounting prizes that were awarded reveal that tragic actors performed as competitors in contests that were held in almost every Greek city in the second and third centuries.[61] Augustine also mentions that the theater included these performers along with comedians and mimes.[62]

From early on, Christians did not approve of the theater. In the second century, Tertullian counted giving up the theater as part of the renunciation of the devil in the baptismal rites. To him, all public entertainment was suspect because of its roots in pagan festivals.[63] On the other hand, many pagan writers also condemned spectacles on moral grounds.[64] Chrysostom's condemnations centered on entertainment as a waste of time that could lead to more serious sins such as lust and drunkenness.[65] Despite their complaints about the theater, Christians did not attempt to destroy these buildings as they did the pagan temples. Chrysostom faced resistance from his congregation when he condemned the theater unconditionally. They pointed to the laws that supported the theater and asked incredulously whether the whole building should just be shut down because of their preacher's objections.[66] In any case, while the spectacles

---

[59] Eusebius, *Vita Constantini* 2.61.5. Either the actors were imitating the quarreling bishops, or else this did not actually happen, but was an expression of the worst possible humiliation in Eusebius' mind.

[60] See R. Lim's discussion of the conversion and martyrdom of mimes Porphyry and Gelasinus, "Converting the Un-Christianizable: The Baptism of Stage Performers in Late Antiquity" in *Conversion in Late Antiquity: Seeing and Believing*, K. Mills and A. Grafton, eds. (Rochester, NY, 2003) 84–126, at 91–4.

[61] Barnes, "Christians and the Theater," 169.

[62] Augustine, *Confessions* 3.2.2 and *Sermon* 198.3 (PL 38.1026). Cf. Barnes, "Christians and the Theater," 171–2. Barnes, with the help of a CD-ROM, counted almost 200 references by Augustine to the theater.

[63] Barnes, "Christians and the Theater," 173–8.

[64] Tertullian, *De spectaculis* (SC 332). Cf. Clement of Alexandria, *Paedagogus* 3.11.76–7 (SC 158.148–50). For pagan critiques of spectacles, see Dio, *Or.* 32; Libanius, *Or.* 16.43; Julian, *Letter to a Priest*, 304. See Lim, "In the 'Temple of Laughter'," 356–60; Leyerle, *Theatrical Shows*, 42–74.

[65] Chrysostom, *Hom. in Mt.* 67.3 (PG 58.635–7).

[66] *Hom. in Mt.* 37.6 (PG 57.427). Imperial legislators still treated the theater and other spectacles as necessary components of urban life, although some concession was made to Christian moral outrage. Laws were decreed forbidding the Maiouma, a show that involved naked women cavorting in water: *Codex Theodosianus* 15.6.1.2; cf. Barnes, "Christians and the Theater," 174–5. On the evidence for this festival, see G. Greatrex and J. Watt, "One, Two, or Three Feasts? The Brytae, the Maiuma and the

of Christian liturgical processions were gaining popularity and prestige, older forms of entertainment continued to be definitive aspects of urban life.[67]

Despite the predominantly negative view of the theater presented in Christian sermons and treatises, the similarities between performances of preachers within the churches and those of the actors were apparent to everyone.[68] Blake Leyerle's examination of Chrysostom's use of theatrical imagery and vocabulary in sermons and treatises illustrates how deeply embedded these performances and stories were in this culture. The sound of applause in the church was disturbingly similar to that inspired by the actors, which the preachers noticed and commented on. But the similarity between the crowd's behavior in the theaters and churches is not surprising, given the ways in which audiences were accustomed to expressing themselves to performers as well as to authorities.[69]

BUILDINGS FOR PUBLIC SPEAKING AND PERFORMANCE

The size and centrality of the public buildings in late antique Antioch and comparable cities support the literary evidence for the popularity and accessibility of performances. In the city centers, numerous places were available for gatherings, both formal and informal. These locations created a "rhetorical infrastructure," reflecting the importance of oratory and other performances.[70] Theaters were the most prominent places for public gatherings, but the wide streets, the marketplaces, and the baths set the scene for less organized types of public speaking, such as the parodies of Julian discussed earlier.

Theaters were particularly prominent features of cities in late Roman Syria, even more so than in other parts of the Empire. The Antiochenes

---

May Festival at Edessa," *Oriens Christianus* 83 (1999) 1–21. On lay resistance to the condemnation of spectacles, see Lim, "In the 'Temple of Laughter'," 359.

[67] See J. F. Baldovin, *The Urban Character of Christian Worship: The Origins, Development and Meaning of Stational Liturgy*, Orientalia Christiana Analecta 228 (Rome, 1987) 253–65; O. Pasquato, *Gli spettacoli in S. Giovanni Crisostomo: paganesimo e cristianesimo ad Antiochia e Costantinopoli nel IV secolo* (Rome, 1976) 287–363.

[68] An exception to these negative views of the theater is Choricius of Gaza's sixth-century treatise *On Behalf of Those who Represent Life in the Theater of Dionysus* (*Or.* 8, in *Opera*, R. Foerster, ed. [Stuttgart, 1972], 344–80). Also, Palladius describes Porphyry, the bishop of Antioch in 404, as holding a more sympathetic view of spectacles, *Dial.* 16 (SC 341.304–6).

[69] On the popular awareness of theatrical plots, see Leyerle, *Theatrical Shows*, 27–9; Pernot, *Rhétorique*, 461; N. Adkin, "A Problem in the Early Church: Noise during Sermon and Lesson," *Mnemosyne* 4.38 (1985) 161–3.

[70] Pernot, *Rhétorique*, 440–1.

enjoyed music, dancing, and acting in at least one theater: that of Dionysus founded by Julius Caesar and Augustus on the slopes of Mt. Silpius at the edge of the city. Unfortunately, the physical remains of this building have not survived. Based on what survives in other cities, though, we can assume that this imperial capital had a large theater. Not far away, the smaller city of Apamea could boast of one of the largest theaters of the entire Empire. Also, Daphne, the nearby suburb of Antioch, had a theater, built by Emperor Hadrian for the Antiochene Olympic games. This theater had room for 6,000 people and is depicted on the mid-fifth-century Yakto mosaic as a major feature of the town.[71] In contrast to Italy, all of the Syrian theaters were public buildings and were often located in the most central quarter of the city or in its immediate periphery. The theater was the principal building in large cities – its presence conferred the status of a "city" upon a settlement in this period. Also, all of the important cities, as well as many of the less significant ones, in the East had theaters, while the presence of other large public buildings was less consistent.[72]

Some scholars, influenced by the writings of Ammianus and others on this subject, have described a particular love of entertainment as characteristic of Antioch. They, like Chrysostom, interpreted the Antiochenes' fondness for spectacles as a childish weakness.[73] Yet, however taken they were by the theater's productions, Syrians in general did not share the Western appreciation for blood spectacles.[74] Edmond Frézouls speculates that this was the case not because the Syrians had more refined tastes in entertainment than Westerners, but because the theater was often the only building they had for spectacles.[75] Whatever the reasons for the theater's popularity, it was an important gathering place for political reasons, as we shall see shortly, in addition to being a source of entertainment.

References to performances and gatherings in other buildings of late antique cities also give us an idea of the frequency of public speaking. Libanius mentions that imperial edicts were read aloud outside the *bouleterion*.[76] Also, by the mid- to late fourth century, Christian churches were prominent buildings that played a role in public life. Both Libanius and Chrysostom remarked on gatherings around or in churches, or at the

---

[71] D. Levi, *Antioch Mosaic Pavements*, 2 vols. (Princeton, 1947) 326–37.

[72] E. Frézouls, "Recherches sur les théâtres de l'Orient Syrien," *Syria* 38 (1961) 54–86, at 61; Pasquato, *Spettacoli*, 59–70.

[73] Pasquato, *Spettacoli*, 65; P. Petit, *Libanius et la vie municipale à Antioche au IVe siècle après J.-C.* (Paris, 1955) 245.

[74] L. Robert found that there were few references to gladiators in the inscriptions from this region, *Les gladiateurs dans l'Orient grec* (Paris, 1940) 241.

[75] Frézouls, "Recherches sur les théâtres," 85.   [76] Libanius, *Or.* 1.157.

bishop's residence, such as when, in the aftermath of the Riot of the Statues, an imperial prefect spoke to the people in the church, announcing that their city would not, after all, be destroyed because of its disrespect to the emperor.[77]

People also assembled in the marketplace and the baths, although less formally than in the theater. In his panegyric to Antioch, Libanius spoke at great length about the charm of the city's marketplace and the colonnades. Although the large open markets of late antique cities would fade away in the fifth century, Libanius could boast of the wide, crowded streets of the marketplace of his day.[78] The orator ended his description of the colonnaded main street by remarking on the covered walkways throughout the city that protected pedestrians from sunshine and rain. This convenience, he claimed, allowed more interaction among the city's inhabitants than in most places, bringing them closer together as neighbors and friends.[79] He then proceeded to describe the theater, hippodrome, and baths as the public buildings with the most importance to the life and identity of the city.

In general, the late antique city was a place for public life. In his article on the transformation of late antique cities into medieval Islamic cities, Hugh Kennedy emphasizes the conversion of public space into private space.[80] He argues that this development was not caused by the transition to Islam, for it began in the last years of Byzantine rule. The stark contrast that Kennedy demonstrates between Syrian cities before and after this transformation (which took place well after Chrysostom's time) underlines the importance of the public life in Late Antiquity.

INTERACTION: ACCLAMATIONS AND RIOTS

Festivals, public spectacles, and court trials were occasions when municipal, provincial, and imperial authorities faced the broader population of the cities. These authorities, whether they were local elites who funded a spectacle or a visiting emperor, expected to be acknowledged by the people gathered around them. The urban population used these opportunities to express their gratitude or anger and to make requests through the organized chanting of acclamations. Sources attest to acclamations

---

[77] Libanius, *Or.* 19.25–8; Petit, *Libanius et la vie municipale*, 224; Chrysostom, *De stat.* 16.1 (PG 49.161).
[78] Libanius, *Or.* 11.173.   [79] *Or.* 11.217.
[80] The mosque and its courtyard became the center for political ceremonies, court trials, and education. See H. Kennedy, "From *Polis* to *Madina*, Urban Change in Late Antique and Early Islamic Syria," *Past & Present* 106 (1985) 3–27, at 15–16.

in the High Empire, but the majority of surviving evidence, including the texts of the chants themselves, is from the fourth and fifth centuries CE.[81] Eastern cities in particular produced many records of citizens' acclamations of praise to cities and to important people.[82] Looking at this aspect of public spectacles can also help us to understand the background to the dynamics between church authorities and laypeople during sermons.

Theater claques helped in organizing the shouting, although their importance is debated. Some scholars have pointed to these groups as agents of factions who manipulated the masses by composing acclamations that the rest of the audience followed blindly.[83] Libanius provides support for this view by blaming disturbances in the theaters on a particular group of troublemakers.[84] Because of the frequency and sophistication of the acclamations, however, Charlotte Rouché concludes that audiences in Roman theaters probably did not passively chant sayings composed by others.[85] Rouché's work investigates the texts of acclamations found inscribed on columns in the marketplace of Aphrodisias. These acclamations celebrated the finished portico and honored the man who had paid for the building. Other acclamations were found in Aphrodisias on the walls in the baths, theater, and on the bases of statues, sometimes painted one on top of another. These inscriptions and painted words confirm what the narrative histories describe as an important aspect of public gatherings in Late Antiquity.[86]

Acclamations in the Roman Empire are found in the early history of Christianity as reported in the Gospels. Jesus stood before a potentially lenient judge, but the shouts from the spectators changed Pilate's mind (John 19:12). In the Acts of the Apostles, the silversmiths in Ephesus started the chant in the theater in favor of Artemis and against Paul, with the rest of the theater-goers joining in (Acts 19:23–41). The martyrs faced equally vociferous crowds during their trials and punishments. A crowd demanded the flogging of the North African martyr Perpetua (d. 203) and her

---

[81] C. Rouché, "Acclamations in the Later Roman Empire: New Evidence from Aphrodisias," *JRS* 74 (1984) 181–99, at 183; Liebeschuetz, *Antioch*, 208–19 and Petit, *Libanius et la vie municipale*, 219–45. On first- and second-century acclamations, see Potter, "Performance, Power and Justice," 144.
[82] Harries, *Law and Empire*, 66.
[83] See Rouché, "Acclamations," 183–4, for a discussion of the various interpretations of theater claques. Cf. Liebeschuetz, *Antioch*, 212–17.
[84] Libaniaus, *Or.* 41.9. As Petit points out, this was probably the rhetor's wishful thinking at work, *Libanius et la vie municipale*, 222–7. On the political importance of the theater assemblies, see Leyerle, *Theatrical Shows*, 36–41.
[85] Rouché, "Acclamations," 184.   [86] Ibid., 197.

companions. When the women were forced to enter the arena naked, the same crowd demanded that they be allowed to wear clothes. A similar intervention takes place in the *Acts of Paul and Thecla*.[87] In all of these narratives, the voice of the crowd was influential or even decisive. As David Potter has pointed out, such violent events reinforced the authority of the state because there was an agreement that justice was being done. The opinion of the audience was vital to the entire act.[88] Because popular approval legitimized authority, power was never monopolized by the rulers. Without exaggerating the freedom and power of ordinary people under imperial rule, it is clear that people, in the cities at least, voiced their opinions and the rulers often responded to them. The emperors kept track of the enthusiasm, or lack thereof, as well as requests made in these acclamations, for they were recorded and sent to the imperial court. Unpopular officials were replaced or punished based on this information.[89]

Acclamations from crowds in an imperial capital's theater were usually events for emperors to enjoy. Eunapius described Constantine's excessive desire for praise from his audiences in the theaters, a comment meant as a critique of both the Christian emperor and the people assembled in the theaters.[90] In Antioch, acclamations greeted the emperor and the governor of the province whenever they entered or left the city, when they were in the streets, and especially when they attended the theater.[91] Ammianus describes an encounter in Antioch between Julian and a crowd that had condemned one of the emperor's personal enemies. Surprisingly, the emperor did not take the opportunity to kill the man. The historian presents this as an example of Julian's gentle nature, implying that any execution supported by popular acclamations would usually have been considered justified.[92] All of these examples support the view that the ordinary people, when assembled together, played an active, if limited, role in political events.

---

[87] Potter, "Performance, Power and Justice," 152–4.

[88] Potter argues that the study of spectacles can provide a more nuanced view of Roman politics because it reveals that the aristocrats were not entirely dominant. See "Performance, Power and Justice," 155–9. Cf. Lim, "In the 'Temple of Laughter'," 348. On the importance of the crowd's approval in both pagan and Christian contexts, see J. Harries, "Favor Populi: Pagans, Christians and Public Entertainment in Late Antique Italy" in *Bread and Circuses: Euergetism and Municipal Patronage in Roman Italy*, K. Jones and T. Cornell, eds. (London, 2003) 125–41.

[89] *Codex Theodosianus* 1.16.6, cited in Harries, *Law and Empire*, 59. On acclamations, requests, and riots in Antioch, see Liebeschuetz, *Antioch*, 208–18; in Eastern cities: J. Colin, *Les villes libres de l'Orient grec-romain et l'envoi au supplice par acclamations populaires*, Collection Latomus 82 (Brussels, 1965); Alan Cameron, *Circus Factions: Blues and Greens at Rome and Byzantium* (Oxford, 1976) 157–92 and 271–96.

[90] The pagan writer implies that Constantine's desire for acclamations more than anything else motivated his establishment of a new capital, Eunapius, *VP* 462.

[91] Liebeschuetz, *Antioch*, 209.   [92] Amm. Marc. 22.9.16.

In troubled times, acclamations could be the start of more intense demonstrations. During Julian's difficult stay in Antioch, he heard the shouts of "everything plentiful, everything dear" in the theater and responded by trying to enforce a lower grain price. As we have seen, his price edict created even worse conditions and led to the public mockery of his beard.[93] Other authority figures sought out positive acclamations from the Antiochenes by giving in to their demands.[94] But when the demands of the populace were not met, there was always the chance of a riot.

Ammianus described a number of riots that took place in the imperial capitals of Rome, Antioch, and Constantinople between 353 and 368. The first full description in this work of an urban disturbance is a riot in Antioch in 354. While in Antioch, Emperor Gallus enjoyed attending games in the hippodrome, which is probably where the citizens approached him, asking him to prevent an imminent grain shortage. Instead of attempting to help, Gallus openly blamed the provincial governor for the problems and then left town. A day or two later, the crowd set fire to the house of a local aristocrat and then attacked and killed the governor. In his account, Libanius adds that five metalworkers led the crowd.[95] After this riot and murder, the city was not punished as a whole, but a few people from the crowd, presumably the metalworkers mentioned by Libanius, were picked out and executed. Ammianus spoke for the ruling class when he wrote: "After [the governor's] pitiful death, each person considered the ruin of one person to be an image of his own danger and dreaded something similar to the recent example."[96] The riot demonstrated the upper classes' vulnerability as a small privileged minority: it was a threat telling them that they must listen whenever the crowd at the circus spoke to them, particularly about food shortages.[97]

Both Libanius and Chrysostom witnessed and wrote about the Riot of the Statues, which occurred in 387 in Antioch. The announcement of new taxes spurred the first protests, which were made by the town council and then spread, culminating in the toppling of imperial statues. According to Libanius, theater claques magnified or led the disturbance. Both Libanius and Chrysostom wrote about the fear that permeated the city in the days following the riot and the attempts to persuade authorities to be lenient with the city.[98] The people of Antioch were afraid of a punishment that would affect the entire city, and the wealthy feared widespread property

---

[93] Julian, *Misopogon*, 368C; Libanius, *Or.* 18.195 [94] See Liebeschuetz, *Antioch*, 215.
[95] Libanius, *Or.* 19.47; Amm. Marc. 14.7.3–5. [96] Amm. Marc. 14.7.6.
[97] On food riots, see H. Kohn, *Versorgungskrisen und Hungerrevolten im spätantiken Rom* (Bonn, 1961).
[98] Libanius, *Or.* 19–23. See F. van de Paverd, *St. John Chrysostom, the Homilies on the Statues: An Introduction* (Rome, 1991) 38–106.

confiscation. In the end, though, the authorities picked out only a few individuals to arrest and execute.

All of these instances, from acclamations recorded during the dedication of a building to riots over food shortages, demonstrate that people expressed themselves and attracted the attention of the authorities. In the theater and courts, the crowd's evaluation of economic and legal situations figured into the decision-making of emperors, governors, and local officials. As we will see in later chapters, when people responded to government officials and expected that their complaints would be listened to in the theater, they would not be afraid to question and disagree with their preacher in church.

CHRISTIAN ORATORS AND AUDIENCES

Urban Christian preachers in Late Antiquity had much in common with other public figures. Chrysostom's connection with Libanius is unusually obvious: Chrysostom studied rhetoric under Libanius and both wrote speeches in reaction to the same event, the Riot of the Statues.[99] A comparison of their writings on the riot reveals how both speakers used the same arguments and rhetorical devices, reflecting their shared educational backgrounds.[100] Despite Libanius' traditional religious beliefs, he welcomed Christian students. Libanius' works indicate the religion of eighty-eight students: seventy-five pagans, twelve Christians, and one Jew, the son of the Jewish patriarch Gamaliel. His correspondence reveals the religious identity of many of his friends and acquaintances: the rhetor wrote to at least 76 Christians and 102 pagans.[101] In addition to the philosophical ideals discussed in the previous chapter, rhetorical training was part of the shared culture of the educated elite, regardless of religion.

As part of his program to revive pagan worship and divert attention from the Christian Church, Emperor Julian forbade Christians the right to teach rhetoric. Educated Christians were furious. Even the pagan historian Ammianus, an admirer of Julian in most respects, condemned this insult to

---

[99] Chrysostom mentioned studying with Libanius in *Ad Viduam* 1.2 (PG 48.601) and attacked him in *Liber in Sanctum Babylam* 18–20 (PG 50.560–5). Cf. Sozomen, *HE* 8.2.

[100] Liebeschuetz, *Antioch*, 37–8. On common rhetorical devices used by both pagan and Christian speakers, see R. Wilken, *John Chrysostom and the Jews: Rhetoric and Reality in the Late 4th Century* (Berkeley, 1983) 95–125; Paverd, *Homilies on the Statues*, 16–18.

[101] Petit, *Les étudiants de Libanius*, 196. For Gregory of Nazianzus' and Gregory of Nyssa's connections with Libanius, see G. Nys., *Ep.* 13 and 14; G. Naz., *Ep.* 192 and 236. Cf. Theodoret's correspondence with a pagan sophist, see *Ep.* 17, 28, 44, 19, 20, 22. See also R. Van Dam, "Emperors, Bishops and Friends in Late Antique Cappadocia," *JThS* 37 (1986) 53–76.

the Christians.[102] The last pagan emperor reasoned that those who denied the traditional religion had no business professing traditional education. Educated Christians vehemently disagreed with this view and, despite a few cases of ambivalence, generally embraced the study of classical literature and rhetoric as preparation for studying the Scriptures, for writing treatises, and, of course, for preaching in churches.[103] This last view, not Julian's, was the one that prevailed in Late Antiquity. Pagan teachers accepted Christian students while most Christian intellectuals acknowledged the value of rhetoric for their own goals.[104]

The audience's behavior in church reflected the similarities they perceived between public speaking within the church and in other social settings. In Ephesus in 431, the Christian crowd responded to the church council with acclamations. The proceedings from the "robber synod" at Ephesus in 449, the Council of Chalcedon, and later councils also include acclamations from the bishops that established the legitimacy of the decisions.[105] Like dancers in the theaters and public orators competing during festivals, some bishops also hired claques to lead their audiences' applause.[106] Vocal reactions to the church councils clearly spread beyond the circles of the bishops. In his *Life of Constantine*, Eusebius points out that "it was possible to see not only church leaders sparring in debates, but congregations were divided, with people leaning toward one group or another."[107]

Augustine's letters provide us with an example of a bishop listening to and valuing his congregation's opinion by paying attention to their acclamations. Toward the end of his career, Augustine announced the name of his successor and his congregation accepted him with acclamations. The bishop reminded them that their demonstration was official, and that shorthand writers (*notarii*) were recording it in the public record.[108] A number of bishops, including Ambrose and Augustine, were chosen by popular acclamation. In situations like this, bishops clearly followed the pattern set by the secular authorities who sought out

---

[102] Amm. Marc. 22.10.7.
[103] On Christian acceptance of pagan education in the East, see W. Jaeger, *Early Christianity and Greek Paideia* (Cambridge, MA, 1961). The most famous example of ambivalence is Jerome's dream about being an adherent to Cicero rather than Christ: Jerome, *Ep.* 22.30; J. N. D. Kelly, *Jerome: His Life, Writings, and Controversies* (New York, 1975) 41–4.
[104] See book 4 of Augustine's *De doctrina Christiana*, where he views eloquence as a neutral skill, regardless of its pagan past.
[105] Roueché, "Acclamations," 184. On the techniques by which these acclamations were recorded: ibid., 184–7; Lim, *Public Disputation*, 225. For examples of acclamations and the Church, see Harries, *Law and Empire*, 67–9.
[106] Roueché, *Performers and Partisans*, 29; Liebeschuetz, *Antioch*, 217–18.
[107] Eusebius, *Vita Constantini* 2.61.5.   [108] Harries, *Law and Empire*, 68.

acclamations in the theater in order to gauge popular approval of their actions.

While discussing the requirements of a good preacher in his treatise *On the Priesthood*, Chrysostom exclaims: "Do you not know what a love for speeches has burst into the minds of Christians these days?"[109] Much of his advice in this treatise to a fellow preacher involved coping with the congregation's reaction to sermons. Chrysostom emphasized that a preacher should say what was necessary rather than what would make him popular among the laity, and above all should try not to be affected by applause or lack thereof. He acknowledged the appeal of an audience's enthusiastic acclamations, but maintained that the preacher should not seek the same rewards as the public orator. Also, Chrysostom's treatment of this topic provides yet another indication that the Christian congregation's reaction to the preacher's performance resembled their behavior in the audience of secular orators.[110] Despite his complaints about the audience's enthusiasm for eloquence and his professed belief that popularity should not be an issue for a preacher, Chrysostom himself was well known to be popular precisely because of his eloquence.[111]

In Late Antiquity, church controversies were often public concerns. In addition to acclamations made before the bishops and preachers, congregations could and did turn to rioting for specifically Christian reasons. Chrysostom's episcopal career is a case in point. As bishop of Constantinople, he faced more intrigue and rivalries than in Antioch but enjoyed the same widespread popularity. After a synod of bishops deposed him and banished him from the city, many people gathered at the church and shouted out that a council should be convened to change this decree. While this crowd prevented imperial officers from taking Chrysostom into exile, he slipped away and left town early in order to prevent further disturbances. The populace then gathered at the churches, marketplaces, and the emperor's palace, and "many insulting speeches were uttered against the emperor and the council."[112] Finally, with their enthusiastic support for the bishop and their critique of his enemies, these Christians convinced the empress and, in turn, the emperor to recall their bishop.

Later, when Chrysostom hesitated before reentering the city, the people began shouting and making speeches against the imperial family again,

---

[109] Chrysostom, *De sac.* 5.8 (SC 272.302).   [110] *De sac.* 5.1 (SC 272.284).

[111] Socrates, *HE* 6.2. T. Urbainczyk, "Vice and Advice in Socrates and Sozomen" in *The Propaganda of Power: The Role of Panegyric in Late Antiquity*, Mary Whitby, ed. (Leiden, 1998) 299–310. See also Wilken, *John Chrysostom and the Jews*, 101.

[112] Sozomen, *HE* 8.18.

which persuaded their bishop to hasten his return. Singing psalms and carrying torches, they led him to the church and compelled him to take the episcopal throne and give the usual benediction. The crisis ended with Chrysostom giving a speech that he composed on the spot, which was interrupted by the applause and acclamations of his listeners.[113] These events of Chrysostom's first exile and his return reflect the power of popular opinion and acclamations at every step. Speeches were made on both sides, from the crowd's insults directed at the imperial family to Chrysostom's speech once he was returned to his episcopal chair. In this case, the Christian congregation acted like the general population would during times of secular crisis such as food shortages.

CONCLUSIONS

All of the different forms of public speaking prevalent in Late Antiquity were related phenomena, deeply rooted in the urban culture of the time. The orator, legal advocate, actor, and preacher all fed and were fed by the general enthusiasm for eloquence. In addition to providing information about the performances, literary sources describe ways in which listeners responded to these speakers. Examining how audiences reacted to these performances improves our understanding of how ordinary people interacted with authority figures.

Scholars have pointed out the links among the orator at the public ceremonies and rhetorical contests, the advocate in the courts, the actor in the theater, and, finally, the preacher in the church. But the implications of these connections have not yet been fully examined, especially with regard to Christian preachers.[114] In all of these contexts, the inclination to listen to and value eloquence was not limited to the upper-class men who studied how to produce eloquence. For pagans and Christians alike, the appreciation of rhetoric depended more upon access to a lively urban culture than upon social class. The familiarity of local audiences with particular speakers such

---

[113] Ibid.; cf. Socrates, *HE* 6.16. On the role of the people in church controversies, see T. E. Gregory, *Vox Populi: Popular Opinion and Violence in the Religious Controversies of the Fifth Century* AD (Columbus, OH, 1979); M.-Y. Perrin, "A propos de la participation des fidèles aux controverses doctrinales dans l'Antiquité tardive: considérations introductives," *AntTard* 9 (2001) 179–99.

[114] For a comparison of preacher and orator, see Wilken, *John Chrysostom and the Jews*, 101–25. On advocates and the actors, see Crook, *Legal Advocacy*, 137–8. Potter calls attention to the similarities between entertainment and court trials, in "Performance, Power and Justice." Clarke notes the qualities bishops shared with grammar teachers, philosophers, and orators, in *Rhetoric at Rome*, 153. Leyerle's *Theatrical Shows* takes these connections among orators, actors, and preachers as its starting point, 61–7. Harries notes that bishops were also entertainers in "Favor Populi," 133.

as Libanius and Chrysostom must have also broadened their appeal. In Late Antiquity, city people had a taste for rhetoric, and as we will see in chapter 4, Chrysostom did his best to adapt his sermons in order to appeal to them. As we turn to look closely at Chrysostom's sermons, this broader perspective helps us to ask and answer questions about these sources: what segments of society were present at church services? Why and how did ordinary people listen to these sermons? How did laypeople react to the demands of the clergy? The examination of the social context of this encounter allows us to understand the ways in which the congregation and preacher interacted, and how this contact affected the manner of Christianization.

CHAPTER 3

John Chrysostom's congregation in Antioch

When John Chrysostom preached to his congregation, he addressed men and women, rich and poor, and also artisans and laborers. But the question of the social and economic backgrounds of those who listened to his sermons is more difficult to answer than this, for when Chrysostom referred to the "artisans," "laborers," and "the poor" in his audience, some of his terms are misleading, at least some of the time. Similarly, the presence of women in the congregation does not inevitably mean that the preacher spoke to them. A closer look at the sermons' language and its implications, as well as other contemporary sources, is necessary in order to gain a better understanding of who was in the preacher's audience.

Since the study of late antique sermons has grown rapidly in recent years, it is necessary to summarize and assess this scholarship before examining Chrysostom's congregation here. Scholars have interpreted the composition of the preacher's audience in Late Antiquity with vastly different results. In some cases, the listeners are pictured as social and cultural peers of their well-educated preachers; in other studies, the diverse congregation includes men and women from various social and economic backgrounds. Since quotations can be found in late antique sermons to support either view, assumptions about late antique society and the role of rhetorical speaking in this culture have guided scholars to privilege certain passages over others. For example, Chrysostom's remarks to the wealthy in his congregation, which focus on their particular sins and their potential to give alms, have been emphasized by those arguing that the sermons were aimed primarily at elite listeners. But at other moments, the preacher spoke directly to women, the poor, artisans, and laborers. A diverse audience, though, presents problems similar to the ones that, as we have seen, concerned philosophical speakers: would ordinary people follow the arguments and imagery of well-crafted oratory, not to mention the more abstract theological concepts? Did the condescension current in upper-class sentiments prevent Christian leaders from truly communicating with their social inferiors?

In a provocative and often-cited article, Ramsey MacMullen argues that Chrysostom's concentration upon the wealthy as well as his "rhetoric pitched at a high level" confirms that the preacher faced a congregation filled with members of the upper classes.[1] Ordinary people, such as artisans and farmers, as well as a "sprinkling of the pious poor" showed up for church primarily for important holy days, but the sermons were not aimed at them. The typical congregation, in this case, would be composed of the urban elite, predominately the male half: either the women did not come in the same numbers or the sermons simply were not addressed to them.[2] Carrying the prejudices of their social class into their ecclesiastical careers, church leaders did not think it was necessary to speak to their inferiors.

Some have disagreed with this account, arguing that the preacher's audience in Late Antiquity was more representative of the entire Christian community.[3] Wendy Mayer points out that the attention focused on the wealthy stemmed from their social rather than numerical dominance, and compares this with the use of masculine pronouns and direct addresses to men, even when women were present. In either case, disproportionate attention to socially dominant groups does not prove that other types of people were absent.[4] Philip Rousseau articulates his "more optimistic view"

---

[1] R. MacMullen, "The Preacher's Audience (AD 350–400)," *JThS* 40 (1989) 503–11, at 504. He also cites references to the wealthy in the sermons of Basil, Jerome, Gregory of Nazianzus, and Asterius of Amaseia, 507. Cf. R. MacMullen, *Christianizing the Roman Empire, AD 100–400* (New Haven, 1984) 59–67. For an overview of the scholarship on John Chrysostom and his audiences, see W. Mayer, "John Chrysostom: Extraordinary Preacher, Ordinary Audience" in *Preacher and Audience: Studies in Early Christian and Byzantine Homiletics*, P. Allen and M. B. Cunningham, eds. (Leiden, 1998) 105–37, at 109–14.

[2] MacMullen, "The Preacher's Audience," 508–10. On the elite audience of sermons, see E. McLaughlin, "The Word Eclipsed? Preaching in the Early Middle Ages," *Traditio* 46 (1991) 77–122; J. Dumortier, "Une assemblée chrétienne au IVe siècle," *Mélanges de Science Religieuse* 29 (1972) 15–22; J. H. Barkhuizen, "Proclus of Constantinople: A Popular Preacher of Fifth-Century Constantinople" in *Preacher and Audience: Studies in Early Christian and Byzantine Homiletics*, P. Allen and M. B. Cunningham, eds. (Leiden, 1998) 179–200.

[3] For scholars arguing for a wider audience, see M. B. Cunningham, "Preaching and Community" in *Church and People in Byzantium*, R. Morris, ed. (Birmingham, 1986) 29–46; W. Mayer, "Who Came to Hear John Chrysostom Preach? Recovering a Late Fourth-Century Preacher's Audience," *Ephemerides Theologicae Lovanienses* 76 (2000) 73–87; "Female Participation and the Late Fourth-Century Preacher's Audience," *Augustinianum* 39 (1999) 139–47; J. H. W. G. Liebeschuetz, *Barbarians and Bishops: Army, Church and State in the Age of Arcadius and Chrysostom* (Oxford, 1990) 173–4 and 182–3; S. Ashbrook-Harvey, "Antioch and Christianity" in *Antioch: The Lost Ancient City*, C. Kondoleon, ed. (Princeton, 2000) 39–49, at 44; A. Hartney, *John Chrysostom and the Transformation of the City* (London, 2004) 43–5; J. A. Munitiz, "Catechetical Teaching-Aids in Byzantium" in *ΚΑΘΗΓΗΤΡΙΑ: Essays Presented to Joan Hussey for Her 80th Birthday*, J. Chrysostomides, ed. (Camberley, Surrey, 1988) 69–83.

[4] Mayer views Chrysostom's congregation as including women as well as men, their slaves, clergy, artisans, and soldiers, but not necessarily the extremely poor, "John Chrysostom: Extraordinary Preacher, Ordinary Audience," 123–6; "Who Came to Hear?" 80–7; *John Chrysostom*, 34–40.

in an essay focused on evidence from the late antique and early medieval West. He argues that these sermons reached listeners far beyond the educated elite.[5] Jerome, Ambrose, Gregory of Tours, and Gregory the Great captured the attention of crowds of people, influenced their beliefs, and did so in plain, generally comprehensible language. Rousseau concludes: "Only a member of the elite could have developed such vivid discipline; but the invitation to understanding and social inclusion was visibly broader in its address."[6]

Such analyses draw strength from the consistency of late antique writers' theories of preaching with the sermons that they delivered. Rousseau demonstrates that church leaders wanted to reach as many people as possible and were reputed to have done so. The advice they gave to others about reaching a broad audience should at least serve as a caveat to modern hypotheses concerning what was easy and what was difficult for ordinary people to understand. In treatises touching on this matter of communicating with a mass audience, Jerome, Augustine, Ambrose, and Chrysostom all promoted an accessible style of preaching that would reach as many people as possible.[7] Likewise, as we have seen, the historians from this period described the influence of sermons upon urban crowds. The evidence that is available, in other words, demonstrates that sermons were written in the way that they were planned – comprehensible and even pleasant for people to listen to. With these points in mind, this chapter will examine the composition of Chrysostom's congregation in Antioch, focusing on his references to his listeners' economic status, specific professions, and his advice and exhortations to women. Although the exact proportions of different types of people among lay Christians cannot be known for certain, the content of the sermons clearly points toward a diverse audience.

SOCIAL AND ECONOMIC ASPECTS OF THE CONGREGATION: THE "MIDDLING CLASSES"

Ordinary laypeople in this period were known for their interest in church matters. The church historian Socrates reports that there were theological

---

[5] P. Rousseau, "'The Preacher's Audience': A More Optimistic View" in *Ancient History in a Modern University*, vol. II: *Early Christianity, Late Antiquity and Beyond*, T. W. Hillard and E. A. Judge, eds. (Grand Rapids, MI, 1998) 391–400.

[6] Rousseau, "'The Preacher's Audience'," 400.

[7] Chrysostom, *De sac.* 5.1–3 and 5.6 (SC 272.280–6 and 294); Augustine, *De catechizandis rudibus* (CCSL 46.121–78). See T. Graumann, "St. Ambrose on the Art of Preaching" in *Vescovi e pastori in epoca teodosiana XXV: incontro di studiosi dell'antichità cristiana* (Rome, 1997) 587–600; Cunningham, "Preaching and Community," 33; Rousseau, "'The Preacher's Audience'," 393.

disputations in every household. In the same period, Gregory of Nyssa made his well-known remark that merchants and moneychangers kept the marketplace noisy with their discussions of theology.[8] But such theological inclinations did not mean that the average Christian was educated. Among non-Christians, the stereotype of the pious Christian was the opposite: detractors claimed that they were drawn from the ranks of "slaves, women, nurses, midwives, and eunuchs."[9] This was an old accusation, initiated by early pagan critics of Christianity, which implied that the religion would only appeal to groups of people prone to making bad judgments. In response to this caricature, Chrysostom did not deny that his community included people of such low status, but protested that they were not the *only* ones.

Clearly, the Church's ideal was to be inclusive. During a sermon just before Easter, Chrysostom addressed the catechumens who would be baptized together and ordered them to forget their earthly differences: "The rich man may not show contempt for the poor man, the poor man may not think he has any less than the rich man: for in Jesus Christ there is neither male nor female, no Scythian, no barbarian, no Jew, no Greek, all types of inequalities are taken away, even those of age and family origin."[10] The biblical origin of much of this statement does not undermine its relevance for the reality of the fourth-century church. Although social divisions remained, when the preacher encouraged his listeners to ignore their differences, he indicated that different groups were gathered together in the church. As we have seen, this kind of social contact may not have been that unusual in cities.

Numerous sermons indicate that "artisans," "laborers" and "the poor" were listening, but the case has been made that all of these groups were in fact members of relatively elite classes – "artisans" were really prosperous merchants, and "the poor" were upper-class people who had come down in the world. Variations in class and status among the members of the congregation, then, would be confined to the most privileged part of society. But this interpretation depends on the assumption that late antique society was starkly divided between an affluent minority and a wretchedly poor

---

[8] Socrates, *HE* 2.2; G. Nys., *De deitate filii et spiritus oratio* (PG 46.557). On the social context of these popular discussions, see R. Lim, *Public Disputation, Power and Social Order in Late Antiquity* (Berkeley, 1995) 149–81; M.-Y. Perrin, "A propos de la participation des fidèles aux controverses doctrinales dans l'Antiquité tardive: considérations introductives," *AntTard* 9 (2001) 179–99.

[9] Chrysostom, *Hom. in I Cor.* 7.8 (PG 61.66). For an account of Celsus' attack, see Origen, *Contra Celsum* 2.55 (SC 132.414).

[10] *Cateches.* 3.4 (SC 366.228–30).

majority, which is far from certain. Commenting on the population of Antioch, John Chrysostom counted ten percent of society as wealthy, ten percent as poor, with the rest in between these two extremes. He projected that if the majority of people gave alms properly, each poor person could easily be taken care of.[11] Although his account seems somewhat optimistic, recent studies indicate that "middling classes" were more prominent in late antique society than is usually assumed. In his study of poverty in Late Antiquity, Peter Brown emphasizes the importance of these groups, which scholars have largely ignored in favor of the extremely wealthy and (less often) the extremely poor.[12] Most people were neither impoverished nor completely safe from falling into poverty. This is why Chrysostom could refer to someone who was clearly not starving – someone who had slaves or owned a business, for instance – as poor.[13]

"THE POOR"

"The poor" in Late Antiquity included upper-class people fallen on hard times, but obviously this term did not apply to them alone – it also named the situation or potential situation of the vast majority.[14] In some instances, it is quite clear that "the poor" refers to the destitute. The terrible suffering of beggars was unmistakable: all Christians – even those with meager resources themselves – were expected to give alms to help them.[15] The category of "the poor" shifted according to context and the "middling classes" could go either way: "the poor" could refer to everyone except the wealthiest landowners and at the same time everyone except for the penniless were enlisted to help "the poor."

[11] He also estimated that the church's property was roughly equal to an individual who ranked low among the wealthy, yet could support 3,000 widows and virgins, as well as prisoners, travelers, sick and maimed, servants of the church, and also supply food and clothes each day to anyone who asked, *Hom. in Mt.* 66.3 (PG 58.630).

[12] Archaeological evidence does not show an increase in poverty in this period. The attention focused on the poor by church leaders was due to a change in ideology, not in living conditions. See P. Brown, *Poverty and Leadership in the Late Roman Empire* (Hannover, NH, 2002) 47–8. On the changes in views of society from "citizens and non-citizens" to the "rich and the poor," see E. Patlagean, *Pauvreté économique et pauvreté sociale à Byzance 4e–7e siècles* (Paris, 1977) 9–35. Also, see A. Parkin, "Poverty in the Early Roman Empire: Ancient and Modern Conceptions and Constructs," Ph.D. dissertation, Cambridge University (2001). I was unable to obtain a copy of this at the time of writing.

[13] See MacMullen, "The Preacher's Audience," 506 n. 6.

[14] MacMullen argues that when Chrysostom speaks to "the poor," these could not have been truly poor because they were expected to give tithes as alms, or had household slaves, "The Preacher's Audience," 506–8. Mayer acknowledges the same difficulty in interpreting these terms, "Who Came to Hear?" 81–4.

[15] Commands to give alms were not addressed only to the well-to-do, see Chrysostom, *De eleem.* 3 (PG 51.265).

In many instances, Chrysostom discussed the distinctions within his audience in economic terms, contrasting the rich and the poor while addressing both groups. After admonishing the wealthy for their love of luxury, he revealed that he was also speaking to those without the chance to experience luxury in the first place. He noted that he hoped the hungry and sick were comforted by his sermons and could look forward to God's compensation for their suffering.[16] In his sermons on the story of Lazarus and the rich man, he addressed both the rich and the poor within his audience, pointing out the lessons of the story for both groups.[17] Speaking to the poor as well as those who wished to become rich, he explained that poverty was advantageous for everyone as a source of blessings, and preferable to both luxury and power.[18] His praise of poverty could function to soothe people who had little or nothing, and also to shame the wealthy for their extravagance. Church gatherings provided an opportunity to address the rich and the poor at the same time. According to tradition, the wealthy invited the poor to funeral feasts. Chrysostom encouraged them to establish additional customs that involved sharing their wealth, such as regularly inviting the poor to communal meals.[19] Contact among different social classes clearly occurred in church, but its effects were fleeting. Wealthy people took communion alongside the poor, but then later disassociated themselves from their less fortunate brethren: "Let us listen to these words, all of us who approach the holy table here with the poor but when we leave, we do not seem to have seen them, but we are drunk and we hurry past those who are hungry."[20] In this case, in addition to a general tendency to address the wealthy directly because of their social dominance, the preacher simply found more to criticize in their way of life. The only trouble Chrysostom found with the poor in particular was that they complained about their poverty.[21]

Repeated demands to the audience to give alms to the poor could be interpreted to mean that the poor themselves were not in the church. Even the poor, though, were singled out and told to give alms: "Are you poor, even poorer than anyone else? . . . Are you lacking even sufficient food? But

---

[16] *De Laz.* 7.5 (PG 48.1052–3). Similarly, in her article focusing on the thirty-four homilies on Paul's letters to the Hebrews, P. Allen notes the presence of rich widows, elderly people, married men and women, the wealthy and the poor, and both the literate and illiterate, "The Homilist and the Congregation: A Case Study of John Chrysostom's Homilies on Hebrews," *Augustinianum* 36 (1996) 397–421, esp. 409–11.

[17] *De Laz.* 2.1 (PG 48.981) and 6.3 (PG 48.1031).   [18] *Hom. in Mt.* 90.3 (PG 58.791).

[19] *Hom. in I Cor.* 27.1–3 (PG 61.223–8).   [20] *Hom. in I Cor.* 27.5 (PG 61.230–1).

[21] Hartney also emphasizes this point in *John Chrysostom and the Transformation of the City*, 44–5. On the view that the wealthy committed most of the sins, see Sozomen, *HE* 8.2.11.

you are not needier than the widow of Sidon."²² All were expected to help support those with even less, men and women, free people and slaves, the wealthy and the poor.²³ It is important to remember that Chrysostom was not merely raising funds. Almsgiving did not only serve to help the poor recipients but also the donors, in which case a small contribution from a poor person was significant enough to benefit his or her soul.

At times, he referred to the poor who waited outside the doors of the church. More fortunate people were expected to appreciate beggars, because they were preferable to thieves and because their example reinforced the values taught by the preacher.²⁴ When telling women to forget about fancy jewelry and give alms instead, Chrysostom spoke of the guilt that they should feel when they were all dressed up for church and paraded past the poor who crowded the church's steps.²⁵ He also compared the basins outside the church, where people washed their hands before entering, to the poor, who allowed laypeople to cleanse their souls by giving alms, if only they would take the opportunity.²⁶

Some of the poor outside the church were elderly people, who had once been successful and strong.²⁷ The sad condition of many of these people inspired the sermon *On Almsgiving*, which admonished Christians for allowing the beggars to suffer. On the way to church, Chrysostom had seen "many lying in the middle of the streets, some with their hands cut off, others with eyes missing, others covered in incurable sores and wounds."²⁸ The more fortunate Antiochenes dismissed these wounded people as fugitives and foreigners, who came to the city for an easier life.²⁹ Chrysostom agreed that they were not all natives to the city, but maintained that this did not lessen their worthiness for alms. He criticized the almsgivers who were too careful about deciding who deserved their charity. The poor responded to such judgments by simulating, or even creating, additional wounds: blinding their children, putting nails in their heads, and other self-inflicted miseries.³⁰

If the beggars outside the church were baptized Christians, or planning to eventually join, they would have been required to attend the catechetical lessons during Lent. Also, considering Chrysostom's tendency to speak

---

²² *De incomp.* 8.2 (PG 48.771). For other particularly strong exhortations for almsgiving, see *Hom. in Mt.* 88.3–4 (PG 58.778–80) and *De eleem.* (PG 51.261–72).
²³ *De eleem.* 3 (PG 51.265). ²⁴ *Hom. in I Cor.* 30.4 (PG 61.255).
²⁵ *Hom. in Mt.* 89.3 (PG 58.784–5). ²⁶ *De poen.* 3.2 (PG 49.294).
²⁷ *Hom. in I Cor.* 30.4 (PG 61.255). ²⁸ *De eleem.* 1 (PG 51.261).
²⁹ *De eleem.* 6 (PG 51.269–70); *Hom. in Mt.* 35.3–4 (PG 57.409–10).
³⁰ *De eleem.* 6 (PG 51.269); *Hom. in I Cor.* 21.6 (PG 61.177–8).

about poverty and almsgiving, and to criticize the rich energetically, who would have appreciated these words more than the poor waiting for the end of the church service? The daily activities of the poverty-stricken gave Chrysostom little to complain about. Even if they were aggressive or deceitful in their begging, Chrysostom placed all of the blame for their misfortunes upon tight-fisted Christians. On the other hand, if the poor did stay outside and were absent from the sermons and ceremonies, it would not have been due to any lack of sympathy or interest on the part of the priest.

ARTISANS AND WORKERS

Although it is likely that some of the artisans addressed in the sermons were prosperous members of the "middling classes," these people clearly did not identify themselves as members of the elite. Chrysostom addressed manual laborers and sympathized with their obligations and insecurities about interacting with the city's elites. He also spoke to the elites about the workers, to try to persuade them to respect social inferiors as religious equals. The details of these discussions indicate that the workers in the congregation were more likely to have belonged to the majority of the population than to the ranks of the wealthy elite.

Speaking directly to artisans, Chrysostom contrasted them with the more affluent Antiochenes: "You often sit in your workshops observing the rich people with flatterers and fancy clothes, who seize the things of everyone, while having more than their share."[31] In another instance, Chrysostom warned overly confident Christians against attending pagan festivals, because their actions would confuse those who would be unable to socialize with pagans while keeping their own beliefs secure. Apparently addressing the upper classes, he told them to be considerate of their fellow Christians, even if they were shoemakers or dyers.[32] Their social lives were organized more along lines of status than religion – upper-class Christians preferred to associate with Jews and Hellenes of their own class, rather than with

---

[31] *In Kalen.* 3 (PG 48.957). On early Christian epitaphs in Greece that mention occupations, see E. Sironen, *The Late Roman and Early Byzantine Inscriptions of Athens and Attica* (Helsinki, 1997) 401–2. Sironen encounters the same difficulty as those who study the preacher's audience: he cannot know whether an artisan was a business-owner or a manual laborer, or both. Christian occupations included church officials (thirty-two male and three female priests), a grave-digger, doorkeeper, night watchman, steward, archive keeper, a palace official, and soldiers. Cf. Caesarius of Arles' congregation, which included businessmen, salesmen, goldsmiths, craftsmen, physicians, artisans, government officials, and servants. See W. Klingshirn, *Caesarius of Arles: The Making of a Christian Community in Late Antique Gaul* (Cambridge, 1994) 172.

[32] Here, Chrysostom shares an upper-class view that the lower classes would be less able to make fine distinctions, *Hom. in I Cor.* 20.5 (PG 61.168).

lower-class Christians.[33] The preacher responded to the social divisions within the congregation by urging his listeners to ignore these distinctions: "Do not say 'so and so is a blacksmith, a shoemaker, he is a farmer, he is a fool,' and look down upon him."[34] These concerns voiced by the preacher indicate that different social groups encountered each other at church, even if they were not entirely comfortable with this contact.

Chrysostom also singled out groups according to their type of work in order to explain that they all belonged in the congregation despite their differences. Chrysostom expected all of them to have time to worship in the morning before work: "Make a serious effort to come here at dawn to offer prayers and confessions to the God of all things . . . after leaving here filled with awe, let each one take up his own tasks, one hurrying to his manual labor, another rushing to his military post, and yet another going off to deal with political matters."[35] Chrysostom also reassured the artisans and the poor in his audience by reminding them that Paul worked as a humble tent-maker.[36] When people needed to be reminded of the contents of previous sermons, the preacher understood why his listeners had been distracted: the women had been taking care of children and their homes, while the men were occupied with their crafts, but they attended church each Sunday despite their worldly obligations.[37] When discussing the Sermon on the Mount, Chrysostom pointed out that Jesus' audience had included everyone, even the lowliest of people. Later, he addressed the poor and the workers in his own audience and reassured them that their lowly status did not affect their identities as Christians.[38]

Discussions of the manner of life among the monks also brought the status distinctions within his congregation to the fore. Chrysostom observed that the monastic life seemed unpleasant and harsh to his listeners, even though, in his view, the time passed in the theater by artisans and soldiers brought them more pain in the end than the ascetic life.[39] Since the monks did not generally judge people according to social position, visiting them could bring down the pride of the powerful and reassure the more lowly of their worth. Chrysostom pictured the gathering of various types of people at a monk's hut: a simple laborer and a powerful military officer would sit

---

[33] *Hom. in Mt.* 59.5 (PG 58.581).

[34] *Hom. in Mt.* 59.4 (PG 58.579). Elsewhere, in order to convince the wealthy to be considerate to the less privileged, he compared the latter to the apostles and the earliest Christian communities, *Hom. in I Cor.* 20.5 (PG 61.168).

[35] *Cateches.* 8.17 (SC 50.256–7). [36] *De stat.* 5.2 (PG 49.71). [37] *De poen.* 3.1 (PG 49.291).

[38] *Hom. in Mt.* 15.1 (PG 57.223) and 15.11 (PG 57.237). Elsewhere, he claims that everyone could understand his sermons, *Hom. in Mt.* 1.5 (PG 57.20).

[39] *Hom. in Mt.* 67.3 (PG 58.635–7).

together on straw pallets with the monks.[40] If the laity could not erase or ignore their social distinctions in the city, at least they could visit monastic communities, where virtue and poverty counted for more than high rank and wealth.

The subject of work and status also emerged in discussions of the typical sins of various professions. Chrysostom began to discuss sinful activity in general, and then proposed to tailor his discussion to each type of listener: "So where do you want me to begin? With slaves? With the free? With the soldiers? With the civilians? With the rulers? With the ruled? With the women? With the men? With the old men? With the young? With what age group? With what tribe? With what rank? With what occupation?"[41] He went on to describe the particular sins of several of these groups. Soldiers were prone to robberies, frauds, false accusations, and filthy language. Workmen and artisans were likely to fall into sins directly related to their work: dishonesty in their business deals, oaths and perjury, as well as a general preoccupation with material possessions.[42] Then the preacher turned to landowners and focused in on their particular faults. Asking who could be more unjust than these men, he blamed them for treating their laborers like mules and for leading them into debt.[43] Wealthy landowners gave high-interest loans to their workers, taking advantage of the workers' misfortunes without considering their obligations to their wives and children, or even their basic humanity. Chrysostom ended this striking discussion by calling for the cancellation of debts.[44]

But were these workers relatively poor or fairly comfortable owners of workshops? Naturally, it depends upon one's perspective. Most of these workers – butchers, tanners, smiths – while not beggars, would be considered impoverished by today's standards, and by those of the wealthy Antiochenes.[45] Libanius pointed to the many burdens that had been placed upon the artisans and shopkeepers of Antioch. They were required by law to clean drains and maintain public buildings, and to supply room and board to government officials. Even the cost of keeping lamps lit outside their shops could affect their livelihood.[46] Although some families built up considerable wealth and power from crafts and trades, most of them

---

[40] *Hom. in Mt.* 69.3 (PG 58.653–4).   [41] *Hom. in Mt.* 61.2 (PG 58.590).

[42] He speaks of δημιουργῶν and χειροτεχνῶν, *Hom. in Mt.* 61.2 (PG 58.591).

[43] *Hom. in Mt.* 61.3 (PG 58.591).   [44] *Hom. in Mt.* 61.3 (PG 58.592–3).

[45] A. H. M. Jones gives examples of extremely successful craftsmen and merchants, but holds that most were small-time, *The Later Roman Empire, 284–602: A Social, Economic and Administrative Survey* (Baltimore, MD, repr. 1986) 858–61. Cf. P. Brown, *Power and Persuasion in Late Antiquity: Towards a Christian Empire* (Madison, WI, 1992) 91.

[46] Libanius, *Or.* 46.19–21.

depended upon family members and perhaps a few hired laborers in order to survive.

Finally, there should be no disagreements about whether or not one line of work should be grouped with the elite: the pickpockets. They were present in the congregation, at least occasionally. The thieves most likely hoped to pass by unnoticed, but they did not always succeed in this: "He [the devil] had some robbers and purse snatchers mixed into the crowd to steal the money that many of the people who are often gathered here have on them. And this has happened here often, and to many people. So that this does not happen, so that the loss of money which many have suffered does not eventually extinguish your enthusiasm for listening, I exhort and advise all of you not to come in here carrying money."[47] Chrysostom comforted his law-abiding listeners with the story of how the devil took Job's money. He assured them that if they stopped worrying about theft, the devil would quit using it as a means to bother them. If they were aware of Chrysostom's highly critical views of personal property, Antiochene thieves must have felt quite comfortable in his congregation, for reasons other than the crowds of people with spare change. Chrysostom blamed the victims: "Aren't you the ones who make them robbers? Aren't you the ones who make fugitives and conspirators, setting your wealth before them just like bait?"[48]

Comparisons to other preachers of this era also attest to a range of people in the congregations, demonstrating that the relationship between Chrysostom and his congregation in Antioch was part of a wider phenomenon. Basil of Caesarea described people who were far from wealthy listening to his five Lenten sermons on the Creation: "Many artisans, employed in manual labors and who earn just enough at their daily work to provide for their own nourishment, are surrounding me and obliging me to be brief, so I shall not keep them too long from their jobs."[49] In the fifth century, a Carthaginian bishop, Quodvultdeus, spoke to an audience comprised of Berber and Punic artisans, along with some farmers, fishermen, and wealthy people.[50] From the fourth century on, Eastern writers often cited the *Apostolic Constitutions*, a set of ecclesiastical guidelines for Christian worship compiled near Antioch. The *Constitutions*, although mainly directed at clergy, also addressed the laity and demanded that Christians be

---

[47] Chrysostom, *De incomp.* 4.446–54 (SC 28.264).   [48] *Hom. in I Cor.* 21.5 (PG 61.176).

[49] Basil, *Hexaemeron* 3.1 (SC 26.190), cited by Cunningham in "Preaching and Community," 33. Basil also expected former prostitutes and thieves to show up at a martyr shrine where he spoke. See Cunningham, "Preaching and Community," 33.

[50] See T. Finn, "Quodvultdeus: Preacher and the Audience. The Homilies on the Creed," *Studia Patristica* 31 (1997) 42–58, at 49.

treated the same regardless of their different places in society.[51] From what we can tell from these descriptions of church services, only the sick and prisoners tended to be missing, with good reason, from liturgical gatherings.[52] None of the documents present the homily as a sort of seminar for the highly educated.

SLAVES

There is no disagreement that slaves accompanied the wealthy to church services – the question is whether the sermons were addressed to them as well. In order to be full members of the church, though, slaves, like everyone else, had to undergo catechism and baptism, and the baptismal homilies attest to their presence at these services.[53] Whether or not wealthy people brought slaves to church primarily as a display of their wealth, slaves heard the same sermons. Also, as we will see, the preacher noted the presence of slaves and spoke directly to them on occasion.

Ideally, the religious education of slaves extended beyond church services. The heads of households were instructed to watch over their slaves' behavior and correct them when they strayed from Christian precepts. In this matter, slaves are grouped with wives and children.[54] The low status of slaves did not exempt them from Christian expectations. Indeed, the religion added to their duties – slaves were expected to monitor the behavior and beliefs of other slaves.[55] When giving instructions on how to break bad habits of behavior, Chrysostom advised listeners to employ the help of their slaves, who would keep watch over them and chide them when

---

[51] Address to the laity: *Const. apost.* 2.26 (SC 320.234); all people to be treated the same: 2.58.6 (SC 320.322). On the complexity of these sources, as well as their importance, see P. Bradshaw, *The Search for the Origins of Christian Worship: Sources and Methods for the Study of Early Liturgy*, 2nd edn. (Oxford, 2002) 73–97.

[52] *Const. apost.* 8.10.14–15 (SC 336.170). See E. Braniste, "The Liturgical Assembly and Its Functions in the *Apostolic Constitutions*" in *Roles in the Liturgical Assembly: the 23rd Liturgical Conference*, M. O'Connell, trans. (New York, 1981) 73–99, at 90–1.

[53] Numerous avowed Christians would have delayed baptism, but there is no reason to assume that slaves would have been more likely to do this than others. For references to slaves being baptized, see *Cateches.* 1.27 (SC 50.122) and 7.10 (SC 50.234); *Hom. in I Cor.* 1.2 (PG 61.14) and 19.4 (PG 61.156–7); *De eleem.* 3 (PG 51.265). See G. Kontoulis, *Zum Problem der Sklaverei (ΔΟΥΛΕΙΑ) bei den kappadokischen Kirchenvätern und Johannes Chrysostomus* (Bonn, 1993) 315–78. Most slaves were domestic servants: Jones, *Later Roman Empire*, 792–4 and 851–5. On delayed baptism, see M. Dujarier, *A History of the Catechumenate*, E. Haasl, trans. (New York, 1979) 81–4.

[54] Wives and slaves are to be prevented from joining Jewish celebrations: Chrysostom, *Adv. Jud.* 4.7 (PG 48.881). If children, servants, or wives swore oaths, Chrysostom instructed the man of the house to send them to bed without supper, *De stat.* 5.7 (PG 49.79).

[55] Chrysostom, *De stat.* 16.6 (PG 49.170).

they fell back into their old ways.[56] Playing on the assumption that slaves were generally immoral, Chrysostom offered examples of pious slaves, in order to shame free people into better behavior. But these models could also have been meant to encourage the slaves. For example, Chrysostom noted that slaves often stood by soberly while free men got drunk, and they were the ones who literally followed Christ's example by knowing how to turn the other cheek. The preacher also referred to the shame that slave-owners felt when their slaves observed them engaging in unwholesome behavior: men were ashamed to visit prostitutes if a respectable servant observed such actions.[57]

In a straightforward discussion about the nature of slavery, Chrysostom explained his attitude toward the slaves in his congregation and to slavery as a human condition. He claimed that a sermon was worthwhile if only one person in the church listened to it, and even if that one person were a slave.[58] Later in the same sermon, the preacher announced that one's character determined true status, and that a slave could be nobler than a free person, while the rich could belong to the lowest class if their souls were enslaved to material desires. Immediately following this statement, Chrysostom explained the origins of slavery, from Noah's son Ham – slavery came from sin. But, as the runaway slave who was baptized and joined Paul demonstrated, slaves could become free.[59] The mere fact that slaves could be more virtuous than their masters proved that slavery and freedom were mere names that ultimately meant nothing. Christians should learn to transcend the usual definitions of personal status:

I say this [about slavery], and I will not stop saying it, so that you may understand the true nature of things and not be led astray by the same fraud as most people, so that you may know what a slave is, what a poor person is, what a low-born person is, what a blessed person is, and what suffering is.[60]

Slavery was like death, insofar as both were not as bad as they seemed. Because of Christ, both were reduced to mere names that no longer described reality. "Sleeping and dreaming" rather than "death" described

---

[56] *Hom. in Mt.* 17.7 (PG 57.264).

[57] Sober slaves contrasted with drunken free men: *De Laz.* 6.8 (PG 48.1039); embarrassment of sins observed by virtuous slaves: *De stat.* 13.3 (PG 49.139); people should learn from their servants to turn the other cheek: *Hom. in Mt.* 87.4 (PG 58.773). Regarding Salome's dance, Chrysostom observes that Christian servant-girls were more respectable than pagan princesses, *Cateches.* 2.9 (SC 366.202).

[58] *De Laz.* 6.2 (PG 48.1029)

[59] *De Laz.* 6.6–8 (PG 48.1036–9). Cf. *Hom. in Gen.* 29.6 (PG 53.270), where Chrysostom explains that sin introduced slavery in order to provide constant instruction for people.

[60] *De Laz.* 6.8 (PG 48.1039).

the next stage of existence more accurately. Likewise, "slavery" had more to do with sinfulness than with a particular person's legal status.[61]

Chrysostom did not propose an end to slavery, but he did urge the wealthy to treat their slaves well.[62] Again grouping slaves along with wives and children, the preacher emphasized that heads of such households should interact with their charges with restraint and kindness.[63] Chrysostom considered it shameful to own too many slaves, and referred to the fact that Adam and Eve did not possess a single one. One could own one or two slaves and still be virtuous, as long as they learned a craft and were eventually set free. This particular advice provoked a negative reaction from the audience, certainly from the slave-owning portion, but the preacher maintained his position: "I know that I am burdensome to my listeners. But what can I do?"[64]

FARMERS

The congregation, with its artisans, soldiers, landowners, laborers, thieves, and slaves did not often include members of the majority of the region's population: the farmers. Even when people from the countryside did appear in church, many spoke Syriac, while Chrysostom spoke only Greek. Nevertheless, Chrysostom welcomed them to his church and pointed out their rustic virtues to the rest of the congregation.[65] His view of the farmers had much in common with the traditional romanticizing of simple, wholesome country life, which overpowered any traditional urban or upper-class snobbery that he might have inherited. For instance, when monk-priests arrived from the countryside in order to help the city after the Riot of the Statues, Chrysostom praised them because they did not waste their time with such things as horse races and rioting.[66] As naturally virtuous as the country people might have been, Chrysostom believed they could benefit from his sermons when they were able to attend church assemblies in the city. During a saint's festival, when peasants joined the congregation to visit

---

[61] *Hom. in Gen.* 29.6 (PG 53.269–70). Cf. *Hom. in I Cor.* 32.6 (PG 61.272).

[62] On Christianity and the continuity of slavery, see R. MacMullen, "What Difference did Christianity Make?" *Historia* 35 (1986) 322–43, esp. 324–5.

[63] *Hom. in Gen.* 38.7 (PG 53.359–60). Elsewhere, Chrysostom compared the master's duty to punish servants to God's duty to punish humans and assumed that masters would beat their slaves as well as disobedient children, *Adv. Jud.* 8.6 (PG 48.936–7).

[64] *Hom. in I Cor.* 40.5 (PG 61.354).

[65] *Cateches.* 8.2 (SC 50.248–9). See S. Brock, "Greek and Syriac in Late Antique Syria" in *Literacy and Power in the Ancient World*, A. K. Bowman and G. Woolf, eds. (Cambridge, 1996) 149–60.

[66] *De stat.* 19.2 (PG 49.188). See F. van de Paverd, *St. John Chrysostom, the Homilies on the Statues: An Introduction* (Rome, 1991) 260–93.

the martyrs' tombs, the preacher worked in an exhortation against oaths into his praise of the martyrs, so that the country people would be certain to hear the warnings.[67]

The way Chrysostom took special note of their presence in the city reveals that they did not often join the congregation. This, along with the language differences, provides considerable proof that Syriac-speaking farmers were not often present. It is worth noting here, however, that the distinctions in wealth between the urban and rural populations were probably not as stark as many have assumed. Archaeologists have remarked on the surprisingly prosperous peasantry in Northern Syria during this period. The abundant archaeological evidence – the remains of 700 agricultural villages – provides yet another indication that this region was not stratified simply between the wealthy landowners and the destitute poor.[68]

WOMEN IN THE CONGREGATION

Chrysostom's attitude toward women is usually defined by his conflict in Constantinople with Empress Eudoxia and his friendship with Deaconess Olympias. His pastoral duties during his days in Antioch, though, frequently brought him into contact with more ordinary women.[69] Direct addresses to women and passages about women – both their sins and their virtues – attest to their presence in the congregation.

Many of the regulations in the *Apostolic Constitutions* involve laywomen and deaconesses. Women were expected to sit separately from the men in church and were divided into widows, wives, and virgins. The compiler of the constitutions expected the church building and the clergy to be prepared to accommodate females: women were to arrive in church through separate doors and be watched over by deaconesses.[70] These instructions

---

[67] *De Anna* 1.1 (PG 54.634). Cf. Basil's concern for country bishops and their laity and the ambitions of villagers to hold church office, see S. Mitchell, *Anatolia: Land, Men and Gods in Asia Minor*, vol. II (Oxford, 1993) 69–72.

[68] G. Tate, "Expansion d'une société riche et égalitaire: les paysans de Syrie du Nord du IIe au VIIe siècle," *Comptes Rendus de l'Académie des Inscriptions et Belles-Lettres* 3 (1997) 913–41.

[69] On the bishop's relationship with the empress and the deaconess, see W. Mayer, "Constantinopolitan Women in Chrysostom's Circle," *VChr* 52 (1998) 1–24; E. Clark, *Jerome, Chrysostom and Friends: Essays and Translations* (New York, 1979); K. Holum, *Theodosian Empresses: Women and Imperial Dominion in Late Antiquity* (Berkeley, 1982) 48–78.

[70] *Const. apost.* 2.57.10 (SC 320.314). Cf. Augustine, *Sermon Dolbeau 2/Mayence 5.5* in *Vingt-six sermons au peuple d'Afrique*, F. Dolbeau, ed. (Paris, 1996) 330. J. Lassus notes that churches in Syria typically had multiple entrances, probably for this reason, *Sanctuaires chrétiens de Syrie: essai sur la genèse, la forme et l'usage liturgique des édifices du culte chrétien, en Syrie, du IIIe siècle à la conquête musulmane* (Paris, 1947) 186.

went into great detail on the specific functions for deaconesses, while an entire book is devoted to the care of widows.[71] Chrysostom's sermons support these indications that women composed a considerable portion of the congregation.[72]

As we have already seen, Chrysostom knew of a negative stereotype of churchgoers as being predominately female and elderly. He responded by saying that other people showed up as well, but not that such a statement was completely false.[73] Along with the juxtaposition of the wealthy and the poor, he also noted the presence of both men and women in church together, and emphasized that ritual actions such as baptism and fasting during Lent brought all people to an equal level, women as well as men.[74] Although he usually spoke as if he were addressing a male audience, a number of sermons include passages directed specifically at women. In some cases, he spoke to women as an afterthought in order to remind them that his lessons applied to them as well as the men, indicating the presence of women even when he had not been speaking directly to them.[75]

In a particularly revealing passage, Chrysostom explained that even when women were not explicitly addressed in the Scriptures, the message was still directed to them. When preaching on the Gospel of Matthew, Chrysostom explained that Jesus had addressed women: "The laws which He gives are always general, even if He seems to address Himself to men only. For in conversing with the head, He makes His exhortation common to the whole body as well. For He knows woman and man as one living creature, and never divides the species."[76] The same was true of Paul's letters and missionary work. Chrysostom explained that Paul's words were aimed at both men and women, even if this was not spelled out in the text. When assuring his female listeners that they would be rewarded for raising their children well, he stressed that the Scriptures were addressed to women

---

[71] On widows, see the third book of the *Apostolic Constitutions* (SC 329.120–65). Deaconesses are mentioned throughout the *Constitutions*, especially in the second book, on the ecclesiastical hierarchy, and in book 8 on the blessings, ordinations, and Eucharistic assemblies.

[72] See Mayer's view that women might even be considered Chrysostom's "core audience," "Female Participation," 139–47. See also R. Taft's discussion of women's church attendance and their space in the church, "Women at Church in Byzantium: Where, When – and Why?" *DOP* 52 (1999) 27–87. Some have made the assumption based on speculation that women did not attend church. See Dumortier's conclusions that women would have been too busy taking care of their children and households to attend church, "Une assemblée chrétienne au IVe siècle," 20, and MacMullen's estimation that women were either present in church in small numbers, or were not addressed by the preacher even if they were there, "Preacher's Audience," 510.

[73] *Hom. in I Cor.* 7.8 (PG 61.66).   [74] *Cateches.* 3.4 (SC 366.228–30); *Hom. in Gen.* 2.1 (PG 53.27).

[75] *Hom. in Mt.* 49.6 (PG 58.503–4).   [76] *Hom. in Mt.* 17.2 (PG 57.257).

as well as men.[77] But there was another side, of course, to this apostle's opinions about women's involvement in religion. When presented with Paul's statements that women should not teach and should stay quiet, people in Antioch wondered why women should come to church at all, if they were not allowed to ask questions. Chrysostom answered that women should listen in church, but save their questions for later, when they were at home with their husbands.[78]

In his explanation of Genesis, he stopped to answer possible questions about the first women such as how did Cain have a wife when the Scriptures did not mention any women besides Eve? Eve must have had a daughter, he explained, but the biblical genealogy did not list the names of the women.[79] Although male listeners might have noticed these issues, a congregation that included women would tend to be more concerned with the failure to mention females. Likewise, a preacher facing such an audience would more likely feel compelled to explain these matters.

At other times, the preacher focused on the women in his congregation by criticizing their behavior. Like many other ancient moralists, he believed that women were more easily susceptible to vanity, which could lead them to prefer buying jewelry to giving alms.[80] Women also tended to mourn excessively for the dead, and were more easily tempted into joining the Jews in their religious worship.[81] In one of his catechetical sermons, Chrysostom devoted a special exhortation to women, in order to warn them of a sin they were especially prone to: wearing cosmetics and causing the downfall of otherwise pious men. At the very least, he told them, they should refrain from making themselves up before they came to church.[82] At other times, he specifically attacked their penchant for jewelry and nice shoes.[83]

His attention to particularly female sins did not define the preacher's general attitude toward women. Nobody was safe from sharp criticism. As we have seen, he was able to pinpoint the particular ways in which rich people, artisans, and soldiers tended to stray, and, not surprisingly, he identified what he perceived to be particularly feminine sins and condemned them. But, as with other people, he did not condemn women as a group because of

---

[77] *De Anna* 1.3 (PG 54.637).
[78] *Hom. in I Cor.* 37.1 (PG 61.316). The fact that this question was asked is itself interesting. It also implies that men, at least, spoke up in church and that asking questions was considered to be a reason to attend church.
[79] *Hom. in Gen.* 20.1 (PG 53.167).   [80] *Hom. in Gen.* 37.5 (PG 53.349).
[81] On mourning: *Hom. in I Cor.* 28.3 (PG 61.235). Chrysostom told men to prevent their wives from joining the Jews in their festivals. Interestingly, this implies that the women could and did attend religious services on their own. See *Adv. Jud.* 4.7 (PG 48.881) and 2.3 (PG 48.860–1).
[82] *Cateches.* 1.37–8 (SC 50.127–8).   [83] *Hom. in Mt.* 89.3–4 (PG 58.784–8) and 49.8 (PG 58.504).

these inclinations. Rather, at times, Chrysostom's comments about women are surprisingly sympathetic. For instance, he did not blame the women who were lusted after as much as the men who looked at them in the wrong way.[84] Chrysostom's sermons also reveal that he was conscious of particular hardships experienced by women. He was aware of their problems with abusive husbands: he advised women to stay with them, however bad they were, and told men to be kinder to their wives.[85] Even when he criticized women for their excessive mourning, he acknowledged their suffering; he knew that many had seen their young children die.[86]

Chrysostom frequently addressed women in particular or emphasized that he was speaking to both men and women. Most of his direct addresses to women were aimed at the married women. He encouraged wives to be good to their husbands and to follow biblical models.[87] When Chrysostom told husbands to discuss his lessons at home with their wives, this did not mean that the wives were absent. It merely reflected his tendency to speak in masculine terms when addressing everyone. Occasionally, he clarified that his sermons were meant for all members of his congregation: "Let the men listen, let the women listen: men, on the one hand, in order to instruct the members of their households; women, on the other hand, so that they are eager to share these accomplishments with their husbands."[88]

Another striking witness to the presence of women in the congregation is Chrysostom's use of images and stories that seem to be aimed directly at women. When he explained the story of Abraham, Sarah, and Hagar, he took special note of Sarah's strength and loyalty, unclouded by irrational emotions.[89] After describing Job's suffering in great detail, Chrysostom emphasized that it was meant to affect both male and female listeners. He included an account of Job's wife's suffering in order to appeal directly to the women.[90] Even more noteworthy in this manner is Chrysostom's series of five homilies concentrating upon the virtues of Anna, the mother of Samuel. Anna provided a model to both men and women, because of her simple and honest prayers to God. But she also gave the preacher many opportunities to speak directly to the women in his audience. Her

---

[84] *Hom. in Mt.* 17.2 (PG 57.257); *De stat.* 15.10 (PG 49.158).

[85] *Hom. in I Cor.* 26.7 (PG 61.222); *Hom. in Mt.* 67.4 (PG 58.645). His treatise *On Virginity* also displays an awareness of the abuse of wives by husbands: 40.1–3 and 52.1–7 (SC 125.232–4 and 288–98).

[86] *Hom. in I Cor.* 28.3 (PG 61.236). See B. Leyerle on Chrysostom's description of childbirth and early death of children, "Appealing to Children," *JECS* 5.2 (1997) 243–70, at 246–9.

[87] *Hom. in Gen.* 41.5 (PG 53.381), 21.4 (PG 53.180), 45.3 (PG 54.416–17).

[88] *Hom. in Gen.* 41.5 (PG 53.381).

[89] *Hom. in Gen.* 38.1 (PG 53.351).   [90] *Hom. in I Cor.* 28.5 (PG 61.238–40).

story reassured female listeners that the pains of pregnancy and childbirth were more than compensated for by their results, and that educating their children correctly was a great achievement.[91]

In retelling Anna's story, Chrysostom expressed his admiration for the heroine, and called for all of his listeners, men as well as women, to imitate her:

> Men, follow this example, women, imitate her, for Anna is a master for both sexes, so that the sterile women should not despair, and so that mothers nourish the children they have brought into the world in the same way. All should imitate the wisdom of Anna before the pregnancy, her faith during the pregnancy, and her zeal afterwards. What could be wiser than a woman who supports with patience and courage a calamity so intolerable?[92]

In connection with his praise of Anna, who suffered for years from sterility and prayed to God for a child, Chrysostom remarked that many men unjustly became angry with wives who could not have babies, even though this was not in their control, but in God's.[93] In the following sermon, he observed that everyone knew that nothing was more difficult for a woman to bear than sterility.[94]

Despite his ascetic background and occasional biting remarks against the sins of women, Chrysostom had respect and a certain amount of understanding for the ordinary women of his congregation. Many of his comments tend to single out wealthy women, such as his critiques of the female weakness for jewelry and expensive clothes. The references to women in general and also the ones concerning motherhood, however, are another matter. It would seem that all of the groups discussed above, from the wealthy to the slaves, would have perceived the church gathering to be open to women.

JEWS IN ANTIOCH

The Jewish population in Antioch attracted a number of pagans and Christians who joined them in their religious observances. The appeal

---

[91] *De Anna* 1.4 (PG 54.637–9). Elsewhere he describes his own labor pangs from having spiritual children, *De poen.* 1.1 (PG 49.278–9).

[92] *De Anna* 2.1 (PG 54.643). In this section Chrysostom also attributed the roles of both mother and father to Anna, disregarding her husband's contribution when compared to her tears and prayers. This was not the only occasion in which he asked men to imitate women. In another sermon, he told men to imitate the women who wept at Jesus' tomb, *Hom. in Mt.* 88.3 (PG 58.778).

[93] *De Anna* 1.4 (PG 54.639).   [94] *De Anna* 2.1 (PG 54.644).

of Jewish practices was particularly strong among Christians in Northern Syria. Judaizing practices ranged from celebrating Easter according to the Jewish calendar to observing food laws and attending synagogue at holidays in addition to the Christian Church.[95] The cult of the Maccabees is also related to the importance of the Jewish community in Antioch.[96] Church councils attempting to put an end to the close association between Jews and Christians provide yet another witness to their contact.[97]

Chrysostom definitely spoke to people with knowledge of Jewish practices and beliefs. His aggressive attacks against Jews and Judaizing Christians responded to the influence of these groups.[98] The presence of Jews in the congregation during his sermons is uncertain, but entirely possible. During his sermons against Judaizing, he cites an example from pagan philosophers, claiming that this reference was for the sake of the Jews.[99] At any rate, it was perhaps difficult then, and impossible now, to distinguish between Jews who might have listened to sermons, on the one hand, and the Judaizing Christians, on the other.

CHILDREN, CATECHUMENS, MONKS, DEMON-POSSESSED, HERETICS

Some parents brought their children to church. Although Chrysostom addressed them only rarely, we know that he ideally wished for people to bring children to church.[100] In his advice to parents, he suggested that children should be taught biblical stories at home so that they would be

---

[95] M. Simon, *Verus Israel: A Study of the Relations between Christians and Jews in the Roman Empire AD 135–425*, H. McKeating, trans. (London, 1996). On Syria in particular: 310; on different types of Judaizing: 306–7. For a summary of the epigraphical evidence of Jewish sympathizers or "God-fearers," see Mitchell, *Anatolia*, 8–9 for Antioch; 32–7, for Asia Minor. M. P. Bonz, however, points out that some "God-fearers" were Jews, not Jewish sympathizers, "The Jewish Donor Inscriptions from Aphrodisias: Are They Both Third-Century, and Who Are the Theosebeis?" *HSPh* 96 (1994) 281–99.

[96] On the Christianization of the cult of the Maccabees and its appeal to Judaizing Christians, see L. V. Rutgers, "The Importance of Scripture in the Conflict between Jews and Christians: The Example of Antioch" in *The Use of Sacred Books in the Ancient World*, L. V. Rutgers, P. W. van der Horst, H. W. Havelaar, and L. Teugels, eds. (Leuven, 1998) 287–303.

[97] Council of Laodicea (*c.* 360), canons 37 and 38.

[98] Chrysostom's sermons against Judaizing Christians are well analyzed in Wilken, *John Chrysostom and the Jews*. Christians were aware of some Jewish beliefs: for instance, they were aware that touching a dead body caused pollution, *Hom. in I Cor.* 20.4 (PG 61.165).

[99] *Adv. Jud.* 5.3 (PG 48.886).

[100] Mayer points to Chrysostom's references to parents *not* bringing their children to church, "Who Came to Hear?" 82–3; cf. Allen and Mayer, *John Chrysostom*, 35. Leyerle cites evidence that children did accompany their parents: "Appealing to Children," 255.

more familiar when they heard them in church.[101] Also, children could be expected to begin fasting twice a week and keep vigils.[102] In addition to his remarks about the religious education of children, Chrysostom also referred to children in the imagery of his sermons. While his discussions of children always appear to refer to the younger members of the upper-class, it has been shown that this was yet another way that Chrysostom criticized the wealthy – by comparing them to children.[103] In any case, the *Apostolic Constitutions* explicitly account for the presence of children in the church, and give instructions as to where children should be seated in the congregation.[104]

The unbaptized Christians – catechumens, candidates, or newly inter-ested – were also present, and at times prevented their preacher from speak-ing directly about the Eucharist.[105] Also, minor clergy, monks, and dedi-cated virgins attended church.[106] People possessed by demons showed up as well. At a certain point during the liturgy, the deacons ordered the possessed to stand up with their heads bowed. Everyone was expected to pray for the demoniacs, while the latter were not allowed to join in the other prayers.[107] Familiar with the sight of demon-possessed, the laity pitied them, easily distinguishing them from people who were merely drunk.[108] In two con-secutive sermons, Chrysostom referred to the presence of demoniacs – in one case "a large crowd" – and did not indicate that they had gathered there for a special occasion.[109] While the demon-possessed are not often mentioned, the fact that their presence was incorporated into the liturgy implies that this group was a fixture in the congregation.

At times, and perhaps quite often without Chrysostom even realizing it, heretics also mingled with the orthodox crowd. His sermons *On the Incom-prehensibility of God* were addressed to the challenge of the Anomoeans, who even gave him their responses to his sermons. He claimed they had been

---

[101] *De inan.* 41.569–74 (SC 188.138). When he encouraged his congregation to visit Judaizing Christians and persuade them to change their ways, he told parents to bring their children with them, *Adv. Jud.* 7.6 (PG 48.926).
[102] *De inan.* 79–80 (SC 188.182–4).   [103] Leyerle, "Appealing to Children," 243–70.
[104] *Const. apost.* 2.57.12 (SC 320.316). The role of children in the litany: *Const. apost.* 8.6.9 (SC 336.154). See F. van der Paverd, *Zur Geschichte der Messliturgie in Antiocheia und Konstantinopel gegen Ende des vierten Jahrhunderts: Analyse der Quellen bei Johannes Chrysostomos* (Rome, 1970) 198.
[105] Chrysostom, *Hom. in I Cor.* 36.5 (PG 61.313).
[106] On the rare instances of ascetics in church, see W. Mayer, "Who Came to Hear?" 84–5 and "Monasticism at Antioch and Constantinople in the Late Fourth Century: A Case of Exclusivity or Diversity?" in *Prayer and Spirituality in the Early Church*, P. Allen, R. Canning, and L. Gross, eds. (Brisbane, 1998) 275–88.
[107] *De incomp.* 3.42 (SC 28.224–5) and 4.32–41 (SC 28.254–63).   [108] *Hom. in Gen.* 29.5 (PG 53.267).
[109] *De incomp.* 4.37 (SC 28.256–7). Perhaps Chrysostom describes the prayers for the possessed because of the heretics present in the audience in this series of sermons.

stumped by his arguments in a previous sermon, but had found new biblical passages to argue with him about.[110] While these groups are not often
mentioned, it is important to keep in mind the different types of people
who could be gathered together in church on any given day. The presence
of the non-baptized and non-Christians could make the full members of
the church more aware of their privileges. The demoniacs, on the other
hand, served as tangible proof of divine powers and the dangers of sins –
immediately after his discussion of the presence of the demon-possessed,
Chrysostom assured his audience that liturgical prayers helped to ward off
demons.[111] But, with these groups, we have reached the fringes of the groups
to whom Chrysostom spoke. While non-Christians and heretics were able
to listen to sermons as well as their orthodox neighbors, small children
and the demon-possessed presumably would not have fully appreciated his
explanations of the Scriptures and morality.

CONCLUSIONS

Out of the different types of people who listened to Chrysostom's sermons, the country people are the only ones who did not make frequent
appearances in church. The other groups – the artisans, workers, slaves,
and women, among others – were not singled out in the same way as rare
visitors. Chrysostom reckoned that the majority of people in Antioch fell
somewhere in the middle between the wealthy and the poor. While it is
difficult to demonstrate without question that the congregation included
members of every social and economic level in the city, it is enough, perhaps, to establish that the audience went well beyond the confines of the
educated upper classes.

As we have seen, such a gathering of various types of people was not
unusual in late Roman cities. In Constantinople, Themistius had wished
for a law to require the entire population, including rich and poor, men,
women, and children, to listen to basic philosophical precepts in order to
improve the public's morality.[112] He wanted something systematic. In the
Christian churches, there was something new in the intensity with which
speakers attempted to convey information to their listeners and in the
regularity of the assemblies. The relationship between Christian preacher

---

[110] *De incomp.* 8.1 (PG 48.769). On Chrysostom's discussions with the Anomoeans, see Lim, *Public Disputation*, 171–81.

[111] *De incomp.* 4.41 (SC 28.258–9).   [112] *Or.* 26.321.

and layperson was more structured and more rigorous than someone like Themistius would have even hoped for. This meant that people came to listen, even when moral rules were not their favorite topic, and that preachers had to try to explain their teachings in ways that people would understand. The next chapter will examine the ways in which the preacher attempted to make his points clear to his listeners.

CHAPTER 4

Teaching to the converted: John Chrysostom's pedagogy

In the Roman Empire, as in most societies, a formal education was almost always a clear sign of privilege. Schools of grammar and rhetoric provided elite men with basic skills, not least of which was the ability to differentiate themselves from people of lower standing. But this does not mean that people outside these circles were not, in some less recognized way, educated. Some pagans and Christians in Late Antiquity had a wider conception of what counted as education and who could be considered educated. As we have seen, Themistius hoped that his speeches would disseminate philosophical learning to as many people as possible. In the tradition of the Second Sophistic, he used rhetorical skill to make the moral lessons of philosophy more appealing to his audiences in the theaters.[1] Likewise, Libanius could see how ordinary people might learn outside the classroom. He was prepared to argue that watching dance performances was an educational experience, because both rich and poor could watch historical events being acted out. The great tragic poets had once been universal teachers for all the people, but after them, when only the rich had access to education, the gods introduced forms of theatrical dance as a means of instruction for the masses. The result was that "now a goldsmith will competently discuss the houses of Priam and Laius with someone from the schools."[2]

One of Libanius' students, John Chrysostom, saw himself as a teacher and the church as his classroom where he educated large groups of people in Christian theology, ethics, and history. Standing in church, he told his

---

[1] See J. Vanderspoel, *Themistius and the Imperial Court: Oratory, Civic Duty and Paideia from Constantius to Theodosius* (Ann Arbor, MI, 1995) 44–8 and 217.

[2] Libanius answered critiques of the theater's immorality in *Or.* 64.112. Cf. Quintilian's recommendation that young students of rhetoric observe comic actors in order to master the art of delivery, *Inst.* 1.11.1–14. On spectacles and community, see J. Haubold and R. Miles, "Communality and Theatre in Libanius' Oration LXIV" in *Culture and Society in Later Roman Antioch*, I. Sandwell and J. Huskinson, eds. (Oxford, 2004) 24–34.

audience, "This is a spiritual school."[3] Sermons have not been included in traditional studies of education in the ancient world, but they are extremely important sources in this field when education is considered in a variety of contexts as the transmission of knowledge.[4] Once this source is taken into account, we can begin to see the church as a schoolhouse, the laypeople as students, and the preacher as their educator. This is, after all, how many preachers of the time viewed their work.

In their sermons, Chrysostom and his contemporaries drew upon classical traditions of psychagogy, or spiritual guidance. As we have seen, philosophers, especially those influenced by the Second Sophistic, used public speaking and charismatic appeal to get ideas across to people. They hoped to mold the minds of the young and to inculcate knowledge that would lead to a virtuous way of life. Their goals and many of their methods would have been common sense to people like Chrysostom: Christians did not hesitate to use the methods and imagery inherited from the philosophical traditions. For instance, the metaphors Christians used to talk about spiritual teaching and progress – medical care, athletic training, and child-rearing – can be traced directly to the philosophers.[5] Just as the popular appeal of preachers was not a Christian invention, many of their approaches to caring for souls were not new. These ideas, however, took on a new urgency and social context among the Christians.

Chrysostom's basic assumptions about the nature of humanity stood behind his belief that all people could be educated: everyone possessed the potential for virtue and wisdom, since both depended upon human choice.[6] Each person shared the same original nature, while all differences sprang from individual decisions. Goodness stemmed from careful attention and

---

[3] *Hom. in Mt.* 17.7 (PG 57.264). Cf. *Hom in I Cor.* 29.6 (PG 61.248) and 36.6 (PG 61.314). Clement of Alexandria made essentially the same statement in his *Paedagogus* 3.12.98 (SC 158.185).

[4] For H. I. Marrou, the sermons of Chrysostom, Basil, Ambrose, and Augustine spread Christian culture to their audiences, but did not constitute education in the proper sense, *A History of Education in Antiquity*, G. Lamb, trans. (London, 1956) 328. On churches as learning communities, see P. Rousseau, *The Early Christian Centuries* (New York, 2002) 124–52.

[5] See P. Kolbet, "The Cure of Souls: St. Augustine's Reception and Transformation of Classical Psychagogy," Ph.D. dissertation, University of Notre Dame (South Bend, IN, 2002). On the importance of balancing the continuity of the classical tradition with the transformation of ideas by Christians, see 22–3. See also D. Rylaarsdam, "The Adaptability of Divine Pedagogy: Sunkatabasis in the Theology and Rhetoric of John Chrysostom," Ph.D. dissertation, University of Notre Dame (South Bend, IN, 2000).

[6] See A. Danassis' discussion of Chrysostom's views on free will, *Johannes Chrysostomos: pädagogisch-psychologische Ideen in seinem Werk* (Bonn, 1971) 62–80. This is not so different from pagan views of virtue and learning. Cf. Plutarch, *De liberis educ.* 8: the limitations on the education of poor children were due to fortune and resources, not basic ability.

hard work, evil from laziness.[7] Virtue came easier to those who had been trained in it from childhood, but it was not out of reach for the others if they were willing to pay attention to the lessons in church and conform their actions to what they learned there.

Although the liturgy and the design of the church – its shape and decoration, as well as its fountain, courtyard, even its doorposts – served to educate the laity about Christianity, the focus here is on the preacher as an instructor to people who did not necessarily have access to traditional *paideia*. The rich, educated, or male members of the congregation were often the center of attention, but a close look at Chrysostom's homilies reveals that the preacher was clearly aware that he was speaking to people with a variety of educational backgrounds. His approach to teaching doctrine and behavior and his comments on related issues such as literacy and memory reveal that he had surprisingly high expectations of ordinary Christians. He acknowledged working people's constraints but still expected them to grapple with theological and ethical questions. Perhaps because of his hopes for a thoroughly Christianized society, Chrysostom worried more about the consequences of ignorance than the possibility that independent study would lead to heresies.

CASTING PEARLS BEFORE EVERYONE

Even though Chrysostom grew up in a relatively privileged family (his father was a town clerk) and had studied at the best schools, he did not believe that everyone had to do the same in order to learn Christian doctrine. Religious knowledge was not a matter of careers or high culture. Instead, laypeople were expected to learn basic theological concepts as well as biblical stories and their implications for correct behavior. They needed this knowledge for the sake of their immortal souls. Indeed, all Christians in this period were required to go through the crash course of catechism before they became full members who were allowed to receive the Eucharist. Although many people delayed baptism, even some part of this group turned up in church.[8] The church service was not supposed to be a passive experience. Instead, people were expected to internalize the lessons: "I do not want simply to

---

[7] *Hom. in Mt.* 59.3 (PG 58.577).

[8] On the importance of education in Christianity for Chrysostom and the Cappadocians: S. Benin, *Footprints of God: Divine Accommodation in Jewish and Christian Thought* (Albany, NY, 1993) 73. On the various forms of baptismal preparation in this period, see P. Bradshaw, *The Search for the Origins of Christian Worship: Sources and Methods for the Study of Early Liturgy*, 2nd edn. (Oxford, 2002) 144–70 and 215–20. On the increase in delayed baptism in the fourth century, see M. Dujarier, *A History of the Catechumenate*, E. Haasl, trans. (New York, 1979) 79–111.

read stories to you, but I do this so that each of the passions troubling you will be set straight."[9] Believers had to study the Scriptures carefully, because that was the only way for them to understand the depth of their meaning.[10] If, later at home, people simply forgot what they had heard in the sermon, then there was no point in going to church in the first place. Mere attendance without alert attention would not help anyone.[11] This was the preacher's point of view, at any rate. Members of his congregation, as we will see in more detail in the next chapter, often had their own spiritual priorities.

The preacher feared that if the congregation failed to pay attention to his sermons, the ordinary family might continue observing omens, practicing astrology, or swearing oaths in synagogues without even realizing that these practices conflicted with orthodox Christian belief. While the laity included the "undisciplined masses"[12] who attended the theater, it was the preacher's duty to use all of his rhetorical skill and spiritual knowledge to teach otherwise uneducated people. Chrysostom's own salvation depended on his determination at least to attempt to instruct lay Christians.[13] In addition to their accountability for their own actions, ordinary people were responsible for educating their children about the most basic religious ideas and behavioral expectations. In his treatise *On Vainglory and the Right Way of Bringing up Children*, Chrysostom discusses how children should be raised immersed in Christian stories, morals, and behavior. Although this treatise addressed the wealthier Christians of the city, one of the main points would have been applicable to everyone: children should be educated at home from a very young age about Christianity, and their behavior molded accordingly.[14] Before this could happen, however, the parents had to know what to teach their children in the first place.

The preacher crafted his homilies with his audience in mind in order to try to teach as much as possible to as many as possible. In one sermon, he made his pedagogical approach quite explicit. He had spent several days explaining a single parable so that his listeners would be able to understand

---

[9] Chrysostom, *De stat.* 14.4 (PG 49.149).

[10] *Hom. in Gen.* 45.1 (PG 54.414); Chrysostom cites John 5:39.

[11] *De stat.* 16.2 (PG 49.164). Cf. *De stat.* 5.7 (PG 49.79). For further discussion of attitudes toward church attendance, see chapter 5.

[12] *De sac.* 5.4 (SC 272.288).

[13] Chrysostom claimed that he would be rewarded for trying to instruct people, even if they did not listen, *Hom. in Gen.* 41.1 (PG 53.375).

[14] In *On Vainglory* (*De inan.*) 31–2 (SC 188.100–1) he assumes that the child would attend schools and have slaves serving him. For a study of Chrysostom's views on the education of children in particular, see Danassis, *Johannes Chrysostomos: pädagogisch-psychologische Ideen*.

it completely. His aim was for quality, not quantity, of instruction. Using a vivid metaphor of a mother feeding her baby solid food for the first time, he describes his philosophy of teaching:

So that you do not spit out what you are given, I have not tipped the cup of education for you all at once, but I have cut it up for you into many days, providing you with a break from the work of listening on some days, so that what is put down should stick securely in your thoughts, my friends, and that you should receive what I am about to say next with a relaxed and mature soul.[15]

Concerned about the combination of his audience's perceptiveness and his own clarity, he observed that a good preacher should wait until the right time, when his audience was in the right frame of mind, so that his words would have the greatest effect.[16] Outside the church, he even attempted to have informal discussions with laypeople.[17] These meetings, presumably, gave him additional opportunities to advise laypeople on how to live their lives and to learn what problems needed to be addressed in his homilies. His sense of their progress as well as which ideas and rules were particularly difficult for them must have stemmed in part from this kind of interaction.

In order to communicate clearly, Chrysostom employed a varied array of methods in his sermons. Many of these are quite obvious and were basic, widely used rhetorical devices meant to keep the attention of one's hearers. For example, in the exegetical series proceeding systematically through books of the Scriptures, many sermons begin with a short reminder or recapitulation of the contents of the previous one. Chrysostom also attempted to keep his listeners' attention by remarking on the structure of the sermon as it went along. If he found himself on a tangent and decided to return to the main topic, he told his audience what he was doing. He usually aimed to give his hearers the right amount of information, knowing that too much might confuse them.[18]

Many of Chrysostom's rhetorical strategies were meant to stamp the subject or even the exact words of the sermon onto the minds of his listeners. The story of Cain and Abel provoked twenty-seven, almost consecutive, rhetorical questions from the preacher along the lines of "Cain, what are

---

[15] *De Laz.* 3.1 (PG 48.991).
[16] *De stat.* 11.1 (PG 49.120). For more evidence that Chrysostom adjusted his sermons according to the mood of his listeners, see W. Mayer, "John Chrysostom: Extraordinary Preacher, Ordinary Audience" in *Preacher and Audience: Studies in Early Christian and Byzantine Homiletics*, P. Allen and M. B. Cunningham, eds. (Leiden, 1998) 105–37, at 132.
[17] *De stat.* 6.7 (PG 49.92); *Hom in I Cor.* 29.6 (PG 61.248); *De Laz.* 3.1 (PG 48.992).
[18] See below, n. 82. On Chrysostom's preaching style, see A. Hartney, *John Chrysostom and the Transformation of the City* (London, 2004) 53–65.

you doing? Don't you know to whom you are speaking?"[19] Chrysostom also repeated short biblical quotations as he gave his commentary, up to seven times within a few minutes of speaking, before moving on to the next verse.[20]

The style and language of Chrysostom's sermons does not appear to have been too difficult for Greek-speaking Antiochenes to understand, as opposed to the Syriac-speaking visitors from the countryside.[21] As we have seen in the first chapter, the language of rhetorically trained speakers differed from the dialect commonly spoken at the time. It leaned more toward Attic Greek and must have had an archaic ring to it, but contemporary observers and modern studies indicate that this way of speaking was still generally comprehensible. In her study of this problem, Mary Cunningham remarks that Chrysostom's sermons were less complex than most other fifth-century sermons. Also, his subjects would have been easily recognizable to his listeners, since he focused on biblical texts and moral issues.[22] Allusions to a common culture shared by elites and masses, whether it was Homer or the Gospels, could go a long way in making public speeches accessible and appealing to a large audience.[23]

Most of the Church Fathers claimed, at least, to speak to common people. Aside from any particular interest in popular beliefs and practices, a failure to attempt to teach their flocks could send them to hell.[24] In this context, the difference between the simpler Greek of the Gospels and the Greek of late antique writers is puzzling. The only likely explanations for this disparity between New Testament *koine* and fourth-century patristic writings are as follow. It is possible that traditionally educated preachers were incapable of or uninterested in communicating with humbler folk – even

---

[19] *Hom. in Gen.* 19.1 (PG 53.159).   [20] *Hom. in Gen.* 24.3 (PG 53.209).

[21] On Chrysostom's problems preaching to a non-Greek-speaking audience, see E. Dekkers, "Limites sociales et linguistiques de la pastorale liturgique de S. Jean Chrysostome," *Augustinianum* 20 (1980) 119–29; S. Brock, "Greek and Syriac in Late Antique Syria" in *Literacy and Power in the Ancient World*, A. K. Bowman and G. Woolf, eds. (Cambridge, 1996) 149–60.

[22] M. B. Cunningham, "Preaching and Community" in *Church and People in Byzantium*, R. Morris, ed. (Birmingham, 1986) 29–46, at 34. Cf. J. Barkhuizen's point that Chrysostom's language appears to have been relatively easy to follow, "Proclus of Constantinople: A Popular Preacher of Fifth-Century. Constantinople" in *Preacher and Audience: Studies in Early Christian and Byzantine Homiletics*, P. Allen and M. B. Cunningham, eds. (Leiden, 1998) 179–200. For the view that the divide between literary and spoken language was not as great in Byzantium as in the West during the Middle Ages, see R. Browning, "Literacy in the Byzantine World," *BMGS* 4 (1978) 39–54. On rhetorical devices as aids to comprehension and indications of a non-literate audience, see M. B. Cunningham, "Andreas of Crete's Homilies on Lazarus and Palm Sunday," *Studia Patristica* 31 (1997) 22–41, at 22–6.

[23] R. Van Dam, *Becoming Christian: The Conversion of Roman Cappadocia* (Philadelphia, 2003) 102–3.

[24] Chrysostom, *Hom. in Mt.* 56.5 (PG 58.556); *De sac.* 4.9 (SC 272.278–89).

though they claimed allegiance to the *sermo humilis* when pressed on the question. Or, as the first two chapters of this study indicate, their congregations could handle the rhetoric, accustomed to it from the culture of urban life that even ordinary people had access to. The latter seems to be a more likely explanation for the more elevated prose of fourth-century Christian writings, especially if we acknowledge the difference between the culture of a thoroughly Hellenized city and that of the original authors and audiences of New Testament *koine*.

WHO WAS LISTENING?

At least some Antiochenes were clearly interested in the sermons, at least some of the time. Although Chrysostom complained about the ignorance of his audience and his problems holding their attention, such comments must be examined in the context of entire sermons, and series of sermons, where his praise for members of his congregation matches his frustration and where their applause for his sermons resounded as often as he complained about their inattention. The temperament of the preacher and the congregation could shift over a period of days, or during the course of a single sermon.

The laity's mood during the church service tended to affect that of the preacher. When people showed special interest, they could inspire their preacher to continue on a certain topic, while their boredom might cause him to lose his inspiration.[25] Unwavering attention could also signal that they could handle additional subjects on that particular day.[26] Chrysostom often sympathized with their limitations and tried to preach accordingly, taking into account how long they could stand in church without tiring and how much information they could understand in one session without becoming confused. He aimed to teach them until they were exhausted, but not so much that they were unable to process the information.[27] In another instance, he told his listeners that his manner of preaching depended on their attitude: if they seemed "thoroughly awake and longing to learn," he would reveal the answers to theological problems. Otherwise, he would not bother to explain the matter to them.[28] In addition to the general level of enthusiasm, absences did not go unnoticed: Chrysostom remarked on the importance of good attendance when a conspicuous number of Christians

---

[25] *Hom. in Mt.* 1.7 (PG 57.22); *De stat.* 9.1 (PG 49.103); *Hom. in Gen.* 45.1 (PG 54.414).
[26] *Hom. in Gen.* 28.1 (PG 53.252).   [27] *Hom. in Gen.* 19.4 (PG 53.164).
[28] *Hom. in Mt.* 1.7 (PG 57.22).

had stayed home. He continued to preach, however, after asking his listeners to explain the content of the day's sermon later to the absent ones.[29]

Like other Christian teachers of this period, Chrysostom believed that people possessed the ability to learn regardless of gender or social status. While their levels of ability and interest varied and the upper classes inevitably had greater access to literary education and books, the teaching in church was not focused upon its sharpest or wealthiest members. The preacher claimed that Christian morals, ethics, and theology are easy to understand, "even to a farm worker, to a servant, to a widow, and to a child, and to a person who seems exceedingly unintelligent."[30] A humble station in life was nothing to be ashamed of, but was to be embraced. The fact that the highest knowledge available to mankind could be taught to ordinary people was presented as proof of the teacher's wisdom.[31] Chrysostom reassured the uneducated in his audience who feared they were in over their heads:

Do not, because you are an artisan, suppose that this exercise is only for other people, for indeed Paul was a tent-maker . . . Let no one, therefore, of those who have trades be ashamed but those who are raised without a purpose and are lazy, who have been supplied with many servants and enjoy having this retinue. For to support oneself by continually working is a form of *philosophia*: the souls of these men are purer and their minds are more vigorous.[32]

This comparison to Apostle Paul demonstrated that lowlier members of the congregation might even have the advantage over the others when it came to Christian learning.

Although this sentiment was on one level a rhetorical stance to humble the wealthy in his congregation, Chrysostom knew that uneducated people were capable of learning and even memorizing information. For instance, they did as much in other, worldlier, contexts. They could retain everything they heard in the theater and memorize facts about political leaders and events.[33] Chrysostom did not think he was asking too much of ordinary Christians when he told them not simply to pay attention but to memorize everything that he said.[34]

---

[29] *De stat.* 9.2 (PG 49.104–5). Cf. the exhortation to share their knowledge in public, *De incomp.* 10.1 (PG 48.785).

[30] *Hom. in Mt.* 1.5 (PG 57.20).

[31] It is likely that Chrysostom was also thinking of himself as the wise teacher when he spoke about Christ teaching the simple apostles, *Hom. in I Cor.* 5.1 (PG 61.39).

[32] *Hom. in I Cor.* 5.6 (PG 61.46–7). On Christianity inspiring a thirst for knowledge even among the barbarians: *Hom. in Gen.* 28.5 (PG 53.258).

[33] *Hom. in Mt.* 1.8 (PG 57.23).   [34] *De poen.* 8.3 (PG 49.340).

ADVANCED STUDY GROUPS

Not surprisingly, the Christian community in Antioch included people with different levels of knowledge and different rates of progress. Some had superior memories; others paid closer attention to the sermons. Some attended church more regularly, while still others were able to read the Scriptures independently outside church.[35] Chrysostom realized that he had to communicate with all of these different groups. He responded to the challenge by trying not to talk too simply lest he bore the advanced members of the congregation, while remaining comprehensible to everyone. Although everyone had to listen to the same sermon, not all of the lessons were directed at every member of the congregation: each person should be able to recognize what was appropriate for his or her own level.[36] The preacher found himself having to combine different approaches within individual sermons for this reason: "We make these frequent appeals, preparing every kind of discourse for you, since every kind of sickness is likely to exist in such a large assembly, and our task is not to heal only one wound, but many wounds of different types. Because of this, it is necessary that the medicine of the instruction be manifold."[37] We can only speculate about how Chrysostom identified certain topics as too difficult for some laypeople. His private meetings and discussions with members of his congregation after church could have given him a chance to gauge their comprehension. Most likely, though, he could tell from their expressions and noise level whether or not he held their attention as they stood face to face in the church.

One approach to a mixed congregation was to provoke rivalry among the different groups, by encouraging more advanced listeners to inspire, or even embarrass, the others into making similar progress.[38] More often, though, Chrysostom urged the more capable to remain patient while he repeated or simplified a concept for the others. Some would understand or even recognize a Bible verse just by hearing it read once, while others needed repetition and an explanation of its meaning:

[35] In her study of Chrysostom's homilies on the Epistles to the Hebrews, P. Allen found indications of a wide range of people in the audience: numerous references to literacy, illiteracy, access to books, private reading of the Scriptures, and ignorance of the Scriptures, "The Homilist and the Congregation: A Case Study of John Chrysostom's Homilies on Hebrews," *Augustinianum* 36 (1996) 397–421, esp. 410–11.

[36] *Hom. in Gen.* 6.2 (PG 53.56–7). A similar approach can be seen in instructions for monks, see W. Harmless, "'Salt for the Impure, Light for the Pure': Reflections on the Pedagogy of Evagrius Ponticus," *Studia Patristica* 37 (2001) 514–25.

[37] *De stat.* 14.4 (PG 49.149).   [38] *De stat.* 5.7 (PG 49.80).

For those able to pay close attention, what has been said is already clear, just from my reading it. But since it is fitting for us to be concerned for all people (for spiritual teaching does not recognize distinctions among people), come now, let me unveil the meaning of what I said more clearly and repeat the same words again.[39]

During one sermon, Chrysostom indicated that some of the people attending church that day already knew the story he was about to narrate, that of Lazarus and the rich man, but others did not. Some recognized the story and anticipated the interpretation immediately from the first line: "There was a rich man." Chrysostom congratulated them on their achievement, but requested them to slow down for the sake of others in the congregation. He pointed out that the Church was composed, like a physical body, from higher and lower parts, such as eyes and the heel of the foot.[40] All of these parts were connected and must be sympathetic to the others: "If you are quick, if you are prepared for listening, and you have a brother who is not closely following what has been presented, let your eye descend to the heel. Let it feel sympathy with the one who is limping along."[41] The more knowledgeable within the audience seem to have become rowdy or boastful, which is hinted at in the preacher's warning, "Do not misuse your intelligence for his destruction, but be thankful to God for your talent."[42]

Not everyone was expected to be able to understand all the details of the sermons. Occasionally, subjects too complex for the general audience, such as discussions involving physical and natural sciences, were left to the "more studious" or the "more eager" to pursue separately. For example, the relationship among the four elements and between hot and cold, and the structure and function of the different parts of the body were tangential enough to the sermon to be left to experts.[43] Also, many people did not understand the precise meaning of technical theological terms such as *logos, ousia, hypostasis,* and *anomoios*: "I know that these terms are incomprehensible to many. Therefore, I often avoid meddling with the results of this type of reasoning, because most people would not be able to follow these arguments."[44] In yet another case, the problem left for future study

---

[39] *Hom. in Gen.* 18.5 (PG 53.154).   [40] *De Laz.* 6.4 (PG 48.1032).   [41] Ibid.

[42] Ibid. On Basil of Caesarea and Caesarius of Arles' similar sentiments toward a mixed audience, see W. Klingshirn, *Caesarius of Arles: The Making of a Christian Community in Late Antique Gaul* (Cambridge, 1994) 149; P. Rousseau, *Basil of Caesarea* (Berkeley, 1994) 43.

[43] On the relationship between hot and cold as a starting point for the more ambitious: *De stat.* 10.5 (PG 49.117). On studies of anatomy and biology to be continued in private by those who wished to: *De stat.* 11.3 (PG 49.124).

[44] *In Jn* 4.2 (PG 59.48). Cf. *De Laz.* 6.9 (PG 48.1040), where he warns listeners about the difficulty of the subject he is about to turn to.

was grammatical. In this instance, Chrysostom claimed that his audience's interest would be inspired more by their own study of this problem than if the preacher himself solved it for them.[45] Presumably, the Christians who took on the more complicated points were those who had more formal training and/or free time, but we only know for certain that such people were part of the congregation. The very existence of such a group, however, reflects the preacher's success in teaching the Scriptures and encouraging discussion of it among laypeople.

The preacher's recognition of the advanced group and his requests for their patience indicate that he desired to educate all of his listeners, even with an advanced group present. In other words, his concern for the uneducated did not stem from a lack of alternatives. In most cases, Chrysostom preached with the lowest common denominator in mind. He expressed his resentment of this situation, complaining that the audience's lack of progress prevented him from examining the issues about which he wished to speak.[46] Despite this drawback, the preacher tended to err on the side of monotony because people would enjoy hearing him repeat stories and precepts that they recognized. Not only did repetition reinforce lessons they had already learned, but it also made them feel as though they were members of an exclusive community of knowledge.[47]

LITERACY AND ITS IMPACT

Some Christians clearly understood biblical stories and precepts more quickly than others, and a number of them studied more advanced and abstract topics outside church. Some of these people could read the Scriptures on their own. But how far beyond elite circles did the influence of literacy spread? How important was access to books for the ordinary Christian?

Chrysostom had high hopes for the laity's enthusiasm and capacity for studious activity. He advised them to spend an entire day reviewing the content of a sermon and to read the Scriptures in order to prepare themselves before the next sermon.[48] Such advice implies that some people were literate and had access to biblical texts, as well as the leisure to read them. In another case, the preacher told his listeners that they should go home after the sermon and discuss it together as families, with their bibles in

---

[45] *Hom. in Gen.* 26.5 (PG 53.234).   [46] *De stat.* 16.2 (PG 49.164).

[47] For example, Chrysostom advises parents that children enjoy hearing a story in church that they already knew, *De inan.* 41 (SC 188.138–9).

[48] *Hom. in Mt.* 1.6 (PG 57.21).

their hands.[49] Chrysostom even told them ahead of time what verses he would comment on so that they could read ahead and be as prepared as possible.[50] Some people had access to other books as well: when describing Christ's prediction of the Jewish wars and the destruction of the Temple, Chrysostom recommended Josephus' history to his audience as further reading.[51] This was not an isolated example of the availability of different books. The *Apostolic Constitutions* recommend that rich people with leisure should exchange their pagan books of history, poetry, and laws for the Scriptures, which encompassed and surpassed all of the literary genres.[52]

One possible interpretation of these references to literacy would be to assume that they addressed only the male, elite, classically educated segment of the congregation. The passages themselves, however, sometimes indicate that a wider range of people, including artisans, soldiers, and women, was also capable of reading the Scriptures. After ordering them to read the Scriptures in addition to paying attention in church, Chrysostom echoed some of their excuses for not reading: the Antiochenes claimed they could not leave the courthouse, their municipal responsibilities, their practice of a craft, or their families. They claimed that reading was the business of the monks in the mountain-tops.[53] These were apparently the excuses of the literate, for the illiterate would have had an even better explanation. In another sermon, Chrysostom pointed to the example of the scholarly eunuch, servant to the queen of Ethiopia, who was always reading the Scriptures despite traveling with a military party (Acts 8.2–40). The preacher held this figure up as an example to soldiers, people who lived in luxury, women, monks, and people in general who did not have occupations particularly conducive to reading and study.[54] These statements indicate that the issue at stake was, at least in some cases, the will, and not the ability, to read the Scriptures, even among women, artisans, and soldiers.[55] In this context, religious duties were a matter of enthusiasm rather than culture,

---

[49] *Hom. in Mt.* 5.1 (PG 57.55); *Hom. in Gen.* 6.6 (PG 53.61).

[50] *De Laz.* 3.1 (PG 48.991). Cf. *Hom. in Mt.* 1.6 (PG 57.21).

[51] *Hom. in Mt.* 75.3 (PG 58.690). See J. A. Munitiz, "Catechetical Teaching-Aids in Byzantium" in ΚΑΘΗΓΗΤΡΙΑ: *Essays Presented to Joan Hussey for Her 80th Birthday*, J. Chrysostomides, ed. (Camberley, Surrey, 1988) 69–83, esp. 76.

[52] *Const. apost.* 1.5.2–6.5 (SC 320.117).

[53] *De Laz.* 3.1 (PG 48.992). See chapter 5 for a discussion of the relationship between the non-ascetic laity and the monks.

[54] *Hom. in Gen.* 35.2 (PG 53.323); *Hom. in I Cor.* 36.6 (PG 61.314–15).

[55] In "Literacy in the Byzantine World," Browning distinguishes between the highly trained literacy of the few who attended rhetorical school and the more functional literacy accessible to many people, especially in administrative, ecclesiastical, and even military environments. He also points out that nearly all of the most popular saints were represented as literate. On widespread literacy, see also H. Gamble, *Books and Readers in the Early Church: A History of Early Christian Texts* (New Haven,

even when they required skills and interests that traditionally divided the elite from the rest.[56]

Inscriptions indicate that workers of various types were literate.[57] Likewise, several recent studies have argued that literacy was not confined to the upper classes to the degree that many scholars have supposed. Clearly, only the wealthiest people could afford the higher levels of training in grammar and rhetoric. As Robert Kaster remarks in his book on the subject, training in grammar was extremely important in reaffirming elite status, but it is difficult to discern the actual practical benefits of this education in instilling systematic knowledge of language, history, or philosophy.[58] The education at the grammarian's school was not vital for the acquisition of the ability to read. Other schools existed that furthered literacy, although they did little to improve one's social standing. Kaster distinguishes these schools of letters (*grammato-didaskaleia, ludi litterarii*), which were institutions of low prestige, from the schools headed by the grammarians.[59] As an indication of the relationship between the two sorts of schools, Diocletian's Edict on Prices set the grammarian's fees at four times as high as those of the teacher of letters.[60] Some rather ordinary people learned to read in schools, while others could have learned at home from family members.[61]

A comparison of the levels and distribution of literacy in other ancient Greek and Roman settings serves as a way to dispel the usual assumptions about the reach of education and literacy in society. The writing on the walls of Pompeii indicates that architects, carpenters, theater fan club members, brothel customers, and prostitutes were sometimes literate enough to write and read messages.[62] Papyri from Graeco-Roman Egypt demonstrate that

---

1995) 5. Also, Caesarius of Arles prescribed reading and claimed that the illiterate could hire people to read to them, Sermon 8 (SC 175.348–60); Klingshirn, *Caesarius*, 183–4.

[56] See P. Brown, *The Rise of Western Christendom: Triumph and Diversity AD 200–1000*, 2nd edn. (Oxford, 2002) 137.

[57] The readers in the church often had other jobs: E. Sironen collected approximately thirty epitaphs of readers with side-jobs from late antique Attica, *The Late Roman and Early Byzantine Inscriptions of Athens and Attica* (Helsinki, 1997).

[58] On the narrow and fragmented nature of this education, see R. Kaster, *Guardians of Language: The Grammarian and Society in Late Antiquity* (Berkeley, 1988) 11–14.

[59] Kaster, *Guardians of Language*, 24.

[60] Diocletian, *Edict on Prices* 7.66, cited in R. Cribiore, *Writing, Teachers, and Students in Graeco-Roman Egypt* (Atlanta, 1996) 21–2.

[61] Cribiore, *Writing, Teachers, and Students*, 3–26. On p. 6, Cribiore defines "school" and "teacher" by the activity rather than by the physical setting or the status of the person teaching. Cf. N. Horsfall, "Statistics or States of Mind?" in *Literacy in the Roman World* (*JRA* Supplement 3), M. Beard, ed. (Ann Arbor, MI, 1991) 59–76, at 60–2; Browning, "Literacy in the Byzantine World," 46.

[62] The most convincing evidence for literacy among ordinary people is the eighty-three graffiti found upon a wall that was in the midst of remodeling, apparently written by workmen, see J. L. Franklin,

literacy was an important skill even in small villages. Likewise, excavations at the fortress of Vindolanda in Roman Britain have revealed a much higher level of literacy than had been expected: the handwriting of several hundred different individuals appears in the letters and receipts found at the site.[63] Back in Antioch, Christians associated the monks in the countryside outside their city with literacy, even though the ascetics were often from humble backgrounds.[64]

The evidence at Vindolanda also includes writing and reading materials that were free of cost to anyone handy with a knife: thin leaves of wood upon which people wrote letters, folded up and mailed.[65] In Egypt, the papyri and ostraka were plentiful and inexpensive.[66] In Antioch, we know that there must have been a fair number of copyists and a good supply of writing materials available, if only from the massive number of works by Chrysostom and Libanius that were transcribed and distributed there.[67] Presumably, learning to read would involve much less expense than learning to write. The student of reading would only have needed the reading material, instead of pieces and pieces of materials upon which to practice writing.[68] A great deal of reading material did not require any expense at all: any Roman city, marked by the epigraphical habits of generations,

"Literacy and the Parietal Inscriptions of Pompeii" in *Literacy in the Roman World* (*JRA* Supplement 3), M. Beard, ed. (Ann Arbor, MI, 1991) 77–98, at 94–7. In the same volume, see K. Hopkins, "Conquest by Book," and A. K. Bowman, "Literacy in the Roman Empire: Mass and Mode"; see also *Literacy and Power in the Ancient World*, A. K. Bowman and G. Woolf, eds. (Cambridge, 1996). In contrast, W. Harris makes a low estimate of the impact of literacy in ancient society beyond elite circles in his *Ancient Literacy* (Cambridge, MA, 1989) 313–22.

[63] Hopkins demonstrates that military administrators, census workers, and tax collectors operated on the assumption that the soldiers and villagers would be able to read and write, or have easy access to a literate friend, "Conquest by Book," 133–58.

[64] On monks as literate: Chrysostom, *De Laz.* 3.1 (PG 48.992). Theodoret of Cyrhus' *Religious History* depicts two monks sitting on a rock, one reading aloud from the Gospels while the other explained the meaning of the more difficult passages, *HR* 4.6 (SC 234.302). Also, books circulated among groups of ascetics (*HR* 12.5 (SC 234.468). Several ascetics (*HR*: Asterius, 2.7; Marcianus, 3.2; Publius, 5.1; Aphrahat, 8.1; Theodosius, 10.1; Zeno, 12.1–2; Marana and Cyra, 29.2; Domina, 30.3) were from wealthy backgrounds, while others were Syriac-speaking country people.

[65] Hopkins, "Conquest by Book," 119–31, at 126–31; A. K. Bowman, *Life and Letters on the Roman Frontier: Vindolanda and Its People* (London, 1998).

[66] Cribiore, *Writing, Teachers, and Students*, 59 and 63.

[67] See A. F. Norman, "The Book Trade in Fourth-Century Antioch," *JHS* 80 (1960) 122–6, including references, mainly from Libanius, to the existence and circulation of texts, although Norman maintains the view that only the elite intelligentsia were influenced by this literary culture.

[68] Most people who have learned a foreign language know intuitively that reading and writing are different skills, and that it is quite possible to be able to read without being able to compose. See R. L. Fox, "Literacy and Power in Early Christianity" in *Literacy and Power in the Ancient World*, A. K. Bowman and G. Woolf, eds. (Cambridge, 1996) 126–48, esp. 129. On the various levels of literacy, see R. Bagnall, *Egypt in Late Antiquity* (Princeton, 1993) 246–60.

could serve as a cost-free text for aspiring readers.[69] Julian's *Misopogon* was posted in public as were other writings such as letters and edicts from the emperor. It appears that this forum might have gotten out of hand. A canon from the Council of Elvira (306) condemned the posting of documents on the doors of churches.[70] Even if only a few could read the postings themselves, the news could spread. In an unfortunate example, Basil of Caesarea reported that a nun was slandered by a placard placed upon the doors of a church.[71]

Although this evidence for literacy is scattered out from Egypt to Britain, it paints a picture of a Roman Empire in which literacy was not restricted to the classically educated. These studies provide glimpses of a range of people writing as well as reading. With this in mind, there is no reason to disregard automatically Chrysostom's references to artisans, merchants, and soldiers who were able to read. Likewise, there is no reason to assume that the women from these groups would have always been illiterate.[72]

These points are strengthened by the fact that not all of the lay Christians who could read found it to be an easy task. There were many people who complained: "'I don't understand these things, I can't understand the depth of what has been said. Simply put, why should I persist in working ineffectively on reading without having access to someone who is able to lead the way?'"[73] If this reflects accurately the congregation's complaints, then Chrysostom's congregation included semi-literate adults struggling along without teachers. Taking note of the people who did not read fluently, Chrysostom encouraged them to persist, even if it took several attempts for them to understand a particular passage: "Often what we were unable to discover today in our readings, we discover at once when we come back to it the next day, when God, who loves humanity, illuminates our minds in an

---

[69] M. Corbier, "L'écriture en quête de lecteurs" in *Literacy in the Roman World* (*JRA* Supplement 3), M. Beard, ed. (Ann Arbor, MI, 1991) 99–118, esp. 102–4. Cf. E. A. Judge, "The Rhetoric of Inscriptions" in *Handbook of Classical Rhetoric in the Hellenistic Period, 330 BC–AD 400*, S. E. Porter, ed. (Leiden, 1997) 807–28, esp. 808.

[70] M. W. Gleason, "Festive Satire: Julian's *Misopogon* and the New Year at Antioch," *JRS* 76 (1986) 106–19, at 115–17.

[71] Basil, *Ep.* 289, cited in Gleason, "Festive Satire," 116.

[72] See Cribiore, *Writing, Teachers, and Students*, 17 and 21–4, for references to female students and teachers in Egypt. The finds at Vindolanda include letters written by an officer's wife: See Bowman, "Literacy in the Roman World: Mass and Mode," 129. One hundred and twenty graffiti were found in a Pompeii brothel written by both clients and prostitutes, see Franklin, "Literacy and the Parietal Inscriptions," 97.

[73] *Hom. in Gen.* 35.1 (PG 53.322). Elsewhere, Chrysostom mentions that they skimmed through the genealogies of the Old Testament, *Hom. in Gen.* 21.1 (PG 53.175).

unseen fashion."[74] Naturally, reaching this goal was also possible for those who listened to other people read, especially the ones who could memorize information.

Chrysostom stated that it was impossible for anyone to be saved without attention to the lessons of the Scriptures. He prescribed continual reading of the Scriptures in order to avoid the temptations sent by the devil.[75] It is easy to imagine the reluctance of baptized Christians, communicants of the Eucharist, to take his warning seriously, for they would have been taught that the devil's worst attack had already been dodged. Elsewhere, the preacher recommended reading the Scriptures as a way for laypeople to supplement their knowledge. He wanted Christians to sit quietly at home and read: "When, therefore, we take an inspired book in our hand, let us concentrate, collect our thoughts, and dispel every worldly thought, and let us in this manner do our reading with great devotion."[76] Preempting possible excuses, Chrysostom assured them that even if they had no human teacher, then God would come to them through the Scriptures and act as the instructor.[77]

The tone of persuasion – that he was speaking to people who would not normally consider reading to be an appealing leisure activity – points to an audience without intellectual pretensions. Members of the congregation complained about the frustrations of not entirely understanding what they were reading, the difficulty of reading without an instructor, and being too busy to read. These objections and excuses ring true; there is little reason to count them as purely rhetorical (that is, unrelated to the reality of his listeners) as long as we remember that Chrysostom was not always speaking about the entire congregation.

The preacher understood the close connection between the written word and his religion and encouraged his people to use all their resources to learn about doctrine. He did not, however, believe that literacy was absolutely necessary for a person to become well informed in these matters. They should imitate the people in the sacred books, and could not claim illiteracy as an excuse for failing to do so: "You don't know letters and you haven't looked closely into the Scriptures so that you might learn the virtues of the ancients? This is certainly an offense: with the church continuously open, not to come in and share in those pure streams."[78] This passage implies that

[74] *Hom. in Gen.* 35.2 (PG 53.324).   [75] *De Laz.* 3.3 (PG 48.995).
[76] *Hom. in Gen.* 35.1 (PG 53.321–2).   [77] *Hom. in Gen.* 35.1 (PG 53.321).
[78] *Hom. in Mt.* 72.4 (PG 58.672).

a reader and Scriptures could usually be found in the church, accessible to everyone.

Once, while preaching on Genesis, Chrysostom revealed some of his thoughts about the role of literacy in Christianity, and also about the problem of literacy limiting access to sacred texts and knowledge. He explained to his listeners why the Scriptures were delivered so long after creation and how people understood God before this. Before Moses, God instructed man by events rather than by words: "For if God had taught through books and letters, the literate man would have learned what was written. But the illiterate man would have left without benefiting from this, unless someone else had led him to it. And the wealthy man would have bought the bible, but the poor man would not have had the means to obtain one."[79] Likewise, the people who spoke or read other languages would have also been at a disadvantage. Strangely enough, he did not explain why God ever changed His approach to revelation and education. Perhaps illiteracy was no longer a hindrance, as it would have been in the time of the Patriarchs, since the contemporary Antiochenes, even if they were unable to read or possess a bible, still had access to its contents through listening and sharing.[80] One of the most interesting points these passages make is that Chrysostom was aware of the illiterate in his congregation and tried to address their needs. Clearly, not everyone was literate, but these references in the sermons, as well as additional evidence regarding literacy in Roman society, indicate that a wider range of people could read than has been previously assumed. Also, it is clear that illiterate Christians were not overlooked in these discussions of the importance of studying the Scriptures.

MEMORY

Memory was the most accessible skill for the average Christian to use while learning the Scriptures, and the most useful for all who listened to sermons. In antiquity, there was no sharp division between oral and literate culture, since the practice of reading aloud inevitably bound the two together.[81] Each individual relied upon his or her own memory to understand the numerous homilies, whether or not it was possible to supplement listening

---

[79] *De stat.* 9.2 (PG 49.106). This is linked with the notion that true, primitive pagans had worshiped only the stars, while the decline into idolatry happened later, around the time of Abraham.

[80] Cf. Clement of Alexandria's view that illiteracy posed no problems because it was possible to hear divine wisdom, *Paedagogus* 3.11.78 (SC 158.150–2).

[81] On the historiographical debate about Christian Scriptures originating from oral tradition, see Gamble, *Books and Readers in the Early Church*, 11–41. Bibliography on orality and literacy studies at 29.

with reading the Scriptures at home. Chrysostom was aware of the limits of an ordinary person's attention span and attempted to make his sermons as understandable and memorable as possible. In many cases, he stopped himself from speaking too long because presenting too much material in one sitting would only confuse people. When explaining why he concluded the previous sermon when he did, Chrysostom clearly stated his reason for doing so:

For I was eager, not just to say a great deal, but I wanted to say as much as you were able to retain in your memory and leave here having gained some benefit. If, indeed, I intended to say more than necessary and you did not benefit from what was said, what good would that be? Therefore, knowing that I undertook this task for your benefit, I will believe that I have received sufficient compensation if I see your progress in paying attention carefully to what I say, and if you store these words in the recesses of your mind, continually turning them over and ruminating on them.[82]

Sometimes festivals or other events interrupted a series of sermons on related topics. For example, sermons against the Anomoeans were temporarily postponed because Chrysostom decided that Judaizing Christians needed immediate attention.[83] In such cases, when returning to the original topic of the series, he was careful to remind his listeners where he had left off, repeating key words and arguments before delving into new material.[84]

The preacher wanted his congregation to take home general beliefs and behaviors, such as inclinations toward almsgiving, prayer, and repentance, but he also expected them to remember the specific stories from the Bible that illustrated these concepts and proved that they were God's will. As we will see later, laypeople might expect to participate in debates with Christians from other sects as well as pagans and Jews. They were told to memorize the words of the sermons and to recall them when needed.[85] Since it was not possible to explain everything necessary at once, people would ideally make a "kind of a chain" out of the pieces of information they received each day, and would eventually be able to know the body of

---

[82] *Hom. in Gen.* 28.1 (PG 53.252). Chrysostom often claimed to end his sermons sooner than he wished for the sake of the listeners' comfort: *Hom. in Mt.* 1.7 (PG 57.22); *Hom. in Gen.* 19.4 (PG 53.164), 21.5 (PG 53.182), 20.5 (PG 53.173); *De Laz.* 3.1 (PG 48.991) and 7.5 (PG 48.1054); *De incomp.* 1.37 (SC 28.130–1).

[83] *De incomp.* 2.2 (SC 28.142–3).

[84] *De Anna* 1.2 (PG 54.634); *De incomp.* 10.1 (PG 48.783–5). On the strategies of ancient mnemotechnics, see M. Carruthers, *The Craft of Thought: Meditation, Rhetoric, and the Making of Images, 400–1200* (Cambridge, 1998).

[85] *Hom. in Gen.* 20.5 (PG 53.173). Cf. *Hom. in Gen.* 4.1 (PG 53.40) and 32.1 (PG 53.292–3).

Scriptures in its entirety.[86] At other times, Chrysostom was less ambitious about what he expected them to take home from his sermons. Like a modern political campaign ad, repetition of key phrases along with a direct statement at the end of a sermon emphasized to the audience precisely what to remember, if they could remember only one thing.[87]

In some cases, Chrysostom's pedagogy was tailored to impress the lesson of the day visually in his listeners' memories. The suffering and pain of well-developed biblical characters especially lent themselves to visualization. After one sermon, the congregation was to go home imagining the warm blood dripping from the severed head of John the Baptist.[88] On a different day, Chrysostom told both the men and the women of his congregation to sketch upon their minds "as in a picture" the story of Job and his wife's sufferings.[89] The preacher also indicated different methods that could be used by the rich and poor to have images of what they had heard in church: "Paint this parable, all of you, both rich and poor: the rich on the walls of your houses; the poor on the walls of your minds . . . it will be a school for you and the foundation of all philosophy."[90] Similarly, the walls of houses and hearts were to be inscribed with the "flying sickle" (Zach. 5:1–3), so that laypeople would see it soaring toward them whenever they stepped out of line.[91]

Everyone, even workers with neither time nor money for formal education, still had memories and imaginations that could retain many words and images. This capacity was what the preacher counted on most to aid in his instruction in Christian doctrine and behavior. We should not assume that the ability to read naturally received more respect and trust than the ability to remember. Reading was still more of an aid to memory than an improvement or replacement. The first goal for an ambitious Christian was the memorization and subsequent rumination of scriptural passages.[92] Since the poems or speeches schoolchildren used to be taught to memorize would stay with them for years, or even a lifetime, we should not be surprised at the permanence attributed to memory by the ancients. Chrysostom emphasized the permanence and convenience of a good memory: "Whenever we hear about the virtues of the righteous ones and store them away in the recesses of our minds, we are able to enjoy the fragrance

---

[86] *Hom. in Mt.* 5.1 (PG 57.56).
[87] *De Laz.* 2.6 (PG 48.991–2). In this case, the one thing to remember was the importance of almsgiving.
[88] *De stat.* 14.1 (PG 49.144).   [89] *Hom. in I Cor.* 28.5 (PG 61.239–40).
[90] *De Laz.* 4.2 (PG 48.1008).
[91] *De stat.* 9.5 (PG 49.110). He advises this as an aid to break the habit of swearing.
[92] *De poen.* 8.3 (PG 49.340).

for all time if we wish to."[93] Unlike Scripture verses read from a book, memorized thoughts repeating through one's mind could be ever-present.

For all of the members of his congregation, literate or illiterate, Chrysostom recommended ways in addition to studying the Scriptures that would reinforce the message of his sermons. The world around them was filled with potential examples that would echo the words of the Scriptures and the content of the sermons. On a starry night, all they needed was to look up at the sky in order to observe in its precision the greatness and wisdom of God.[94] Chrysostom also told his listeners to visit prisoners, miners, and the impoverished, and observe their suffering. This would convince them of the certainty of the coming judgment, since those people could not suffer as they did in the present if everyone did not eventually have to suffer such penalties.[95]

On a more positive note, he encouraged his congregation to travel out of the city, to the nearby monastic communities, where the preacher himself had spent some years. There, they could observe how the monks lived and learn from them the power of Christian simplicity. Also, these monks would say prayers for their souls. Chrysostom offered to help guide people out to the ascetics if they needed help finding them: "But there is no one to lead you? Come to me, and I will show you the dwellings of these holy men. Come and learn something useful from them."[96] Antioch and its surrounding villages and mountains attracted some of the most famous ascetics of the period. Despite the occasional shy, anti-social hermits, many of the holy men accepted visitors with hospitality, for spiritual counseling and conversation in addition to demonstrating their well-known capacity to cure sickness and expel demons.[97] Many of these monks resided upon the

---

[93] *Hom. in Gen.* 43.1 (PG 54.395).
[94] See *De stat.* 9.3 (PG 49.106–8). The bulk of this sermon describes the perfection of the stars' arrangement, the cycle of night and day, the sequence of seasons, the inscrutable fact that landmasses were supported by water, etc. These subjects often appear in hexameral literature.
[95] *Hom. in Mt.* 76.5 (PG 58.701–2).
[96] *Hom. in Mt.* 72.4 (PG 58.672); *Hom. in I Tim.* 14.3 (PG 62.574).
[97] Theodoret's *Historia religiosa* includes many accounts of monks who liked to have conversations and philosophical debates with their visitors: *HR* 4.10 (SC 234.314), 8.2–3 (SC 234.376–8), 11.3 (SC 234.456–8), 12.4 (SC 234.464), 20.3 (SC 257.66), 24.8 (SC 257.148–50), 26.25–6 (SC 257.210). Most of these monks were in or around Antioch during the late fourth and early fifth centuries. See P. Brown, "The Rise and Function of the Holy Man in Late Antiquity," *JRS* 61 (1971) 80–101; P. Escolan, *Monachisme et église. Le monachisme syrien du IVe au VIIe siècle: un monachisme charismatique* (Paris, 1999) 227–65.

slopes of Mt. Silpius, at the edge of Antioch. Although their communities were far away enough to enjoy solitude, many of their caves and huts were only a short trip from the city. Some years later, Theodoret and his mother visited ascetics there each week, apparently without any trouble with the journey.[98]

Activities outside church were accessible to all members of the preacher's audience, even to the poor and illiterate. In one sense, the poorer the Christian, the greater access he or she had to spiritual education in daily life, since poverty itself was a school and a practice field for "philosophy," which made people live a little bit more like angels.[99] Whether or not poor people perceived their situation so optimistically, this statement does indicate the preacher's view. Many people, no doubt, would have preferred to imitate angels and triumph over demons through the communion service.

CONTRADICTORY IMAGES OF THE CONGREGATION

Chrysostom often depicted his congregation as a raucous, disobedient group who used the church gathering as a chance to make business deals, for women to show off new clothing, and for men to try either to meet women or discuss politics as if they were in a barbershop.[100] At other times, though, the preacher admitted that although these troublemakers existed, the zealous and honest were also present.[101] Similarly, he might complain that his listeners were not learning anything at all from him, that he repeated the same precepts daily without anyone improving in any way, but elsewhere he complimented them on their enthusiasm, intelligence, and breadth of knowledge.[102] His respect for his audience could be so great that he would concede to their view on minor points of biblical interpretation.[103] In this case, the preacher either truly believed that their guess was as good as his, or else he was trying to spark their interest by allowing them to debate among themselves and build their own arguments. Either way, such a moment presents us with an image of a capable and alert Antiochene Christian community.

---

[98] Theodoret, *HR* 9 (SC 234.406–34).   [99] Chrysostom, *Hom. in Mt.* 90.3 (PG 58.791).
[100] *Hom. in I Cor.* 36.6 (PG 61.314).
[101] He remarked on the enthusiasm of his listeners at the beginning of sermons: *Hom. in Gen.* 45.1 (PG 54.414) and 33.1 (PG 53.305); *De stat.* 9.1 (PG 49.103).
[102] Lack of improvement: *De stat.* 5.7 (PG 49.80); *Cateches.* 6.2–4 (SC 50.216–17); *Hom. in Gen.* 41.1 (PG 53.374–5). Improvement: *De Laz.* 7.3 (PG 48.1048); *De incomp.* 8.1 (PG 48.768).
[103] *Hom. in Gen.* 19.1 (PG 53.159). Here, Chrysostom presents interpretations of a verse about Cain's sacrifice, allowing his listeners to decide which one to accept.

What, then, can we say about the level of religious knowledge and enthusiasm within the Antiochene Christian community? On the one hand, Chrysostom's alternate praise and condemnation can be interpreted as being aimed at different segments within the congregation or reflecting the daily fluctuation of the moods of both the preacher and the audience. More likely, I believe, the mixed array of attacks and compliments were pedagogical tools and did not necessarily reflect anything about the behavior of the audience. There is a good chance that the audience was never as bad as Chrysostom's sermons often imply.[104]

Especially during festivals like the Kalends of January or a big day at the races, Chrysostom attacked those who were not attending church.[105] This sort of invective was not, then, intended to excoriate the people listening to it. Rather, the listeners shared in the preacher's indignation and sense of superiority over the others. Many of these attacks on bad behavior in the church reveal at the same time the presence of "good" Christians, who were trying to listen and learn. For example, the preacher asked those who were incapable of learning at least to be quiet and not to disturb the ones paying attention. If they could not manage to be quiet, then they should leave the church.[106] This tactic could be seen as rewarding the "good" members of the congregation as much as it was meant to criticize the bad behavior of others.

The incongruity of Chrysostom's evaluation of his congregation is especially noticeable when his attitude toward them and their progress changed several times during the course of a single encounter. On one occasion, the homily began with a strong statement of the preacher's disappointment: "Today I hesitate and recoil from explaining the lesson . . ."[107] This was the prelude to his complaint that Christians who watched horse races proved that his teaching had been in vain. He lamented that he could not muster the enthusiasm to try to teach such stubborn, listless people. Nevertheless, he did not let them go without a sermon, because he revived his will to preach by remembering that he himself would be rewarded by God for

---

[104] Cf. Caesarius of Arles, whose approach is often gentler than Chrysostom's. He singled out the good and the bad elements within his congregation and clarified that he was addressing two distinct groups: Sermon 46.1 and 6 (SC 243.358 and 368), Sermon 55.1 (SC 243.466). In Sermon 42 (SC 243.294–308), he created the impression that the sinners he spoke of were not in his congregation: he denounced adulterers by telling his listeners to condemn people they know who do this. At the end of the sermon (42.6, SC 243.308), however, he indicated that his listeners probably realized that they were also guilty of some of what he condemned.

[105] *De Laz.* 7.9 (PG 48.1043–4).

[106] *Hom. in I Cor.* 36.6 (PG 61.316).   [107] *Hom. in Gen.* 41.1 (PG 53.374).

trying to teach them even if they did not listen.[108] Later in the same sermon, he suddenly developed quite a different evaluation of his listeners. After telling them to persuade others to stay away from the spectacles and come to church instead, he claimed to be convinced they would do so. He could tell by looking at them: "I see your faces and guess that you have received my instructions with pleasure."[109] But soon – in the very same sermon – the preacher again took a negative view of their level of learning and enthusiasm. After exhorting them to follow Abraham's example of hospitality, he declared that no one in the church accepted what he was saying.[110] The people, the very ones who just minutes before had received his advice with pleasure, were now completely immersed in material concerns, oblivious to their preacher's admonitions.

Clearly, it is difficult to interpret these comments in order to gain a better understanding of the people Chrysostom addressed. This strategy appears to be related to Themistius' insight about crowd psychology: that people take criticism better when they are gathered in large groups. Individuals can always assume that the attacks are made against other people.[111] In reality, the good or average Christians probably outweighed the bad ones – this makes more sense given the preacher's expectations of them, which will be discussed below.

EXPECTATIONS OF PROGRESS

The preacher articulated his hopes for his audience's progress: what he expected them to learn, how quickly, and how many of them he expected to be affected by his sermons. Despite his constant efforts, Chrysostom had no illusions that he would reach every single person in the audience. At best, his lessons might reach a good number of people. When even moderate success seemed unlikely, he consoled himself with the thought that all of his labor would be validated if just one person, even if the one person was a slave, became inspired to true faith and correct behavior.[112] In many cases, the behavior that he sought to change was so private that the preacher would never know for certain how people were conducting their lives. Speaking about temperance in food and drink, he admitted that his speaking might be futile, but he allowed for the possibility that *someone* would be listening: "I know that I say these things to no avail, but I will

---

[108] *Hom. in Gen.* 41.1 (PG 53.375).   [109] *Hom. in Gen.* 41.3 (PG 53.377–8).
[110] *Hom. in Gen.* 41.5 (PG 53.381).   [111] Themistius, *Or.* 26.321–2.
[112] Chrysostom, *De Laz.* 6.2 (PG 48.1029).

not stop saying them. For not all of you will obey, but neither will all of you disobey . . . for maybe, just maybe, I will get a hold of you through my perseverance."[113]

The preacher expressed surprisingly low expectations at times, and found some degree of satisfaction in very small steps made by laypeople on the road to exemplifying his conception of Christian knowledge and behavior. Even if people took to heart the sermon on only one day, this would improve their souls. Even if for only a single day people realized and felt sorry for their sins, this was no small achievement.[114] In another instance, the preacher stopped himself from talking in detail and pointed out that it was enough for the congregation to know which questions were important and to be interested in finding out the answers.[115] During the course of a series of exegetical homilies, they were reminded of the subject of the last sermons precisely because they were not expected to be able to remember everything. They had many other worries in their lives, mainly caring for their families and making a living, and their preacher gave them some credit for this reason: "I am troubled by these things, but I remind you about what is necessary."[116]

The restraint of Chrysostom's expectations for the congregation's progress suggests that they were based upon actual experience. He even counted in their favor the fact that they were attending church and were listening to him in the first place.[117] The ideal Christians, of course, would have been reading the Scriptures and conforming their behavior as quickly as they realized what they were supposed to do. The picture we get from Chrysostom's expectations, though, is realistic: a slow, not entirely linear path of improvement, with fast and slow learners as well as occasional troublemakers. Chrysostom did, though, expect people to make *some* progress, and indicated that people were benefiting from the lessons.[118]

Careful reading of the sermons can also reveal more direct indications of the moral, religious, and educational state of the laity. Chrysostom took some knowledge for granted, such as acquaintance with certain biblical stories or basic philosophical/religious principles. Given the fact that the preacher crafted his sermons in order to be clear and comprehensible to a wide audience, these expectations of knowledge can be interpreted as indicators of general knowledge among ordinary Christians. The sermons sometimes reveal that the laypeople *did* know biblical stories and that

---

[113] *Hom. in I Cor.* 27.5 (PG 61.232).   [114] *De Laz.* 3.3 (PG 48.996).
[115] *Hom. in Mt.* 1.7 (PG 57.22).   [116] *Hom. in Gen.* 33.1 (PG 53.306).
[117] *Hom. in Gen.* 32.1 (PG 53.293).   [118] *Hom. in Gen.* 31.1 (PG 53.283) and 32.1 (PG 53.293).

theological questions *were* being tossed around in Antioch's agora. For instance, Chrysostom could assume that his listeners knew that human beings were composed of two elements, a body and a soul.[119] The congregation also seemed to have grasped the idea, found in several sermons, that the sins or virtues of one's relatives did not affect one's own soul. Having a martyred grandmother or ascetic uncle did not help a person get to heaven. Because they were familiar with this concept, they became perplexed when they heard, during a sermon on Genesis, that Ham's descendants were cursed on account of his sin. Chrysostom called this problem a "well-known one, which is tossed about everywhere."[120] The confusion caused by this story indicates some degree of knowledge among the listeners. In other cases, what the audience did understand was mentioned in the context of what they did not yet understand. Chrysostom used their belief in the account of creation in Genesis as an argument in support of the truth of the resurrection. If they believed that God created the world *ex nihilo*, which apparently they did, then belief in the resurrection should automatically follow. Re-forming bodies out of dust would not be any problem for a God who created them out of nothing in the first place.[121] Such an argument would not have been at all convincing to people who did not already understand and believe in the Judaeo-Christian creation story.

Chrysostom sometimes claimed to require a certain level of knowledge from laypeople before he would allow them to stay in the church. In one instance, he threatened to forbid those who continued the practice of oath-swearing to participate in communion.[122] He was disturbed that it was possible for pagans and Jews to understand basic ideas, such as the perishable nature of the physical world or the importance of almsgiving, while some Christians could not. He told his audience, if they could not understand this point: "Stand outside the sanctuary for now: stay in the doorway because you have not become worthy of the entrance to the kingdom of heaven."[123]

As to the preacher's progress in changing behavior, more will be discussed in a later chapter. For now, we can point out that Chrysostom occasionally remarked upon his congregation's improvement. Even though they were not doing enough of it, they were giving alms.[124] In a more satisfying case, after many consecutive sermons dealing with the issue of oath-swearing and why it was a sin, many reported to the preacher: "'We have done what was commanded, by making laws for each other, determining penalties for

---

[119] *Hom. in Gen.* 21.6 (PG 53.183). This, of course, was not an exclusively Christian belief.
[120] *Hom. in Gen.* 28.4 (PG 53.257).   [121] *Hom. in I Cor.* 17.2 (PG 61.141).
[122] *Hom. in Mt.* 17.7 (PG 57.264).   [123] *Hom. in I Cor.* 29.6 (PG 61.248).
[124] *Hom. in Mt.* 66.3 (PG 58.630).

those who swear and bringing retribution against those who transgress the law.'"[125] Apparently, some people, outside church, had discussions about and evaluated each other according to precepts they had learned from his sermons.

FROM STUDENTS TO TEACHERS

Chrysostom ultimately wished for laypeople to learn enough to instruct others. The first step in educating Christians was to teach them enough to make judgments about their own behavior and beliefs. The next step was to encourage the ones who were competent in this knowledge to convey it to others during conversations at home or in the agora. In the *Address on Vainglory*, Chrysostom suggested that parents tell their children stories from the Bible repeatedly, until they were able to narrate them back.[126] Likewise, he urged each member of his congregation to learn biblical stories, with the goal of being able to repeat them to each other outside church.[127]

Despite Chrysostom's frequent complaints about his audience's low level of knowledge or enthusiasm, he believed in the possibility of laypeople taking on the role of teachers. The words spoken in church, if remembered later, would prepare the listeners to become instructors of others. He encouraged husbands and wives to "philosophize" about Christian matters at home, instructing their children all the while.[128] He also envisioned a wider network of teachers and followers: "You must be teachers and lead the way. Friends should take their neighbors in hand and instruct and lead them, and household slaves should do the same for fellow slaves, and youths for their peers."[129] Each individual should share his or her knowledge with others, forming a "spiritual commerce" that would ultimately pay off in the salvation of their souls. If people repeated stories and doctrinal arguments outside church, not only would they reinforce their own knowledge but they would also have the chance of reaching the ears of people who did not attend church.[130] Surprisingly trusting in an age of theological controversies, the preacher gave those who understood Christian precepts the full authority of teachers over their students. In one of his best-known statements, he told them: "Bring the blasphemers of the city to their senses for me. If you hear anyone in the street or in the middle of the forum

---

[125] *De stat.* 9.1 (PG 49.103).   [126] *De inan.* 39–46 (SC 188.131–45)

[127] *De stat.* 14.6 (PG 49.151–2).

[128] Listeners as instructors: *Hom. in Gen.* 28.1 (PG 53.252); husbands and wives: *De stat.* 5.7 (PG 49.80), *Hom. in Gen.* 29.2 (PG 53.262–3).

[129] *De stat.* 16.6 (PG 49.170–2).   [130] *Hom. in I Cor.* 5.5 (PG 61.46).

blaspheming God, go up to him, rebuke him, and if it is necessary to inflict blows, do not refuse to do so. Strike him on the face."[131]

Chrysostom envisioned ideal Christians acting exactly like himself when they were outside the church, only these people would possess the advantage of having even more frequent contact with their fellows. Everyone, of course, was able to admonish his or her neighbors' behavior.[132] Presumably, this would have been a common practice for Christians and non-Christians alike, even if their standards of behavior differed in some details. The preacher instructed his listeners to lead people away from the games and the theater and into the church, reasoning with them about the risks and benefits of these activities. They should do this continuously, never giving up, even if they received no response, because one day their persistence itself, if not the reasoning behind it, would persuade at least some of the sinners.[133] The similarity between what Chrysostom wished his congregation to do and what he saw himself as doing is clear: earlier in the same sermon, he had said the same thing about his own attempt to convince his listeners through sheer determination. After this declaration, he stopped to imagine how full his church would be if everyone went out and brought another person to church.[134] Evidently, the preacher believed that at least some element within his audience would understand his arguments and remember them well enough to explain them to people who had not attended church, or to review the contents of the sermon with those who had had trouble following it. He knew this was possible because it actually happened sometimes.[135]

Another example of lay teaching outside church appears in the church historian Sozomen's account of the success of Chrysostom's preaching. A certain heretic "happened to hear him teaching how one should think about God. He admired this explanation and encouraged his wife to agree with him." Because she was accustomed to what she already believed, which her female friends also adhered to, she resisted switching over to her husband's beliefs. After his arguments had failed to persuade her, he threatened to abandon her, which prompted her to pretend to join him. Sozomen goes on to report that, ultimately, the wife was converted by a miracle when she tried to substitute the Eucharist with her own bread and this bread turned to stone in her mouth. After that, she was convinced to adopt the same beliefs as her husband.[136] This story shows the success of a sermon upon

---

[131] *De stat.* 1.12 (PG 49.32).   [132] *Hom. in Gen.* 32.1 (PG 53.293).
[133] *Hom. in Gen.* 41.2 (PG 53.377).   [134] *Hom. in Gen.* 41.1–2 (PG 53.375–7).
[135] *De stat.* 9.1 (PG 49.103).   [136] Sozomen, *HE* 8.5.3–4.

one person in a household, who in turn attempted to use his influence to teach someone more difficult to convince. Although the lay teacher's point was driven home to his wife by divine intervention, presumably his future lessons were easier to swallow.

GOOD EXAMPLES FOR OUTSIDERS

Aside from orthodox Christians who needed extra guidance, many pagans, Jews, and heretics lived in Antioch. Chrysostom viewed these groups as people the Christians needed to impress with their virtuous lives.[137] The orthodox laity needed to know how to live correctly in order to demonstrate their superiority, or, at the very least, to avoid being worse than these others. Ideally, Christians would learn enough Scriptures and theological arguments to dispute with non-Christians. Despite being the author of harsh anti-Judaizing sermons, Chrysostom did not forbid laypeople from having contact with Jews, but encouraged them to engage their Jewish neighbors in theological debates.[138]

Laypeople participated in public discussions in Late Antiquity. Richard Lim has pointed out that this practice was common at least for a short time, while bishops still trusted laypeople to accomplish more good than harm in disputations. Eventually, however, the increasingly precise definitions of orthodoxy as well as the establishment of an educated Christian elite brought an end to these debates, or at least the officially sanctioned ones. Bishops began to perceive a threat of heresy in unsupervised theological discussions and condemned them.[139] For a time, though, some authorities attempted to prevent heresy through education, leaving open the possibility of discussion. The writers of the *Apostolic Constitutions*, for example, were concerned with the possibility that old women retelling Christian stories would accidentally blaspheme. Their ignorance, not the discussions per se, cried out for correction.[140]

As late as Chrysostom's time, however, the situation was still fluid. He had no qualms about encouraging his congregation to read and discuss the Scriptures independently. He welcomed such infringements upon his role as teacher, seeing such initiatives as signs of his own success. To prepare

---

[137] Chrysostom, *De Laz.* 7.1 (PG 48.1045–6).
[138] *Hom. in Gen.* 40.4 (PG 53.374) and 8.4 (PG 53.73).
[139] See R. Lim's examination of this issue in *Public Disputation, Power and Social Order in Late Antiquity* (Berkeley, 1995) 219–29.
[140] *Const. apost.* 3.5.6 (SC 329.131). See also 1.10 (SC 320.133): laypeople are called on to be good representatives of Christianity when among pagans, and thus encourage them to convert.

them for discussions in the agora, he taught rhetorical methods as well as a body of information in his sermons: "Pay attention to me very carefully here, and see that nothing of what I am saying escapes you. For truly the battle is with our enemies, therefore we must practice in advance the *reductio ad absurdum*, which Paul also frequently uses."[141] After hearing sermons on Genesis, people could try to convince the pagans of their error in worshiping creation rather than the Creator.[142] In another instance Chrysostom told them to make plans to dispute with pagans and to work out their arguments in advance. They should not be intimidated by pagan-philosopher types – they had their own wisdom tradition that was more accessible. The preacher encouraged them to embrace the simplicity of the apostles in comparison to pagan heroes such as Plato, the point being that the apostles had prevailed by the grace of God.[143] When dealing with Judaizing Christians, people were to begin the conversation with other topics, so that their true purpose would not be immediately obvious.[144] Perhaps some people had achieved success with these discussions: Chrysostom refers to how educated Greeks "hide their faces when they see the artisan or the man in the marketplace philosophizing more than themselves."[145] In addition to the triumph of Christian over pagan, Chrysostom seemed particularly proud of the victory of the "uneducated" over the "educated."

CONCLUSIONS

Although most people did not consider church services to be a replacement for classical education, both types of education focused upon central texts that illustrated philosophical and ethical precepts. In the case of Christian learning, however, literacy was not required because the necessary texts were supposed to be accessible to whoever was interested. The church, at least during this great age of preaching in the fourth and fifth centuries, was an educational institution that attempted to spread knowledge to people regardless of their social status.[146]

When the nature of the audience is taken into account, with regard to gender and social status, sermons can be considered encounters between elite and non-elite segments of society during the process of

---

[141] *Hom. in I Cor.* 39.4 (PG 61.337).   [142] *Hom. in Gen.* 6.6 (PG 53.60).
[143] *Hom. in I Cor.* 3.4 (PG 61.28).   [144] *Adv. Jud.* 8.5 (PG 48.934)
[145] *Hom. in I Cor.* 5.2 (PG 61.40).
[146] On the quality, quantity, and function of preaching in Late Antiquity in contrast to that of the Early Middle Ages, see E. McLaughlin, "The Word Eclipsed? Preaching in the Early Middle Ages," *Traditio* 46 (1991) 77–122.

Christianization. From various references in the sermons surviving from Chrysostom's years in Antioch, it is clear that the preacher planned his sermons carefully with his listeners in mind and that they led him to concentrate upon what they wanted or needed to know. The sermons do not create a picture of the preacher's audience as a small, highly educated group or, conversely, as a throng of people with little knowledge of their religion. Instead, the congregation seems to have been somewhere in between, with ordinary people who knew enough about their religion to debate doctrine among themselves and evangelize others. Moreover, some laypeople disagreed with their preacher's instructions, preferring their own interpretations and practices in some cases. In the next two chapters, the focus will turn to what Chrysostom's sermons can tell us about the beliefs and practices of lay Christians in Antioch: their views that diverged from those of their preacher, their reasoning for this, and the ways in which they responded to their preacher's attempts to influence them.

CHAPTER 5

Practical knowledge and religious life

By the late fourth century, many Christian beliefs and practices were already well established among the laity. But the increasingly precise definition of orthodoxy called some of them into question and created conflicts that varied from region to region. The distinction between correct practice and so-called pagan survivals, heresy, and Judaizing depended on one's point of view. This matter was at the heart of the differences between the world-views of church authorities and the laity. Those who encouraged unity and orthodoxy faced a problem larger than an issue of cleaning up a few inconsistent rituals. Instead, they were faced with disparate perceptions of the religious importance attributed to one's actions and thoughts and to particular times and places. For example, after the conversion of Constantine, widespread reverence for martyrs' tombs and the sites of Jesus' life in Palestine led to the proliferation of new Christian holy places and more holidays in the liturgical year.[1] Eusebius considered holy places to be important for pagans and Jews, but not for Christians. Although Gregory of Nyssa and Jerome agreed with this view, Cyril, bishop of Jerusalem in the mid-fourth century, prized the holy places in his see, while Augustine changed his mind on these matters over time.[2]

Chrysostom agreed with the view that did not distinguish certain times and places as more holy than others. He respected the feast days of the martyrs and gave appropriate sermons in their honor, but he did not consider those days as particularly holy times or the Christian buildings as particularly holy places, independent of the worship performed there. Likewise, he did not understand the laity's practice of washing their hands before they

---

[1] R. A. Markus, "How on Earth could Places become Holy? Origins of the Christian Idea of Holy Places," *JECS* 2.3 (1994) 257–71; B. Caseau, "Sacred Landscapes" in *Late Antiquity: A Guide to the Postclassical World*, G. W. Bowersock, P. Brown, and O. Grabar, eds. (Cambridge, MA, 1999) 21–59; P. Brown, *The Cult of the Saints: Its Rise and Function in Latin Christianity* (Chicago, 1981); R. A. Markus, *The End of Ancient Christianity* (Cambridge, 1990), esp. 139–56.
[2] Markus, "How on Earth," 259–60.

entered the church and objected to the fact that they acted differently, with increased levels of piety, within the church than they did after they had left its confines.[3] His view of the all-encompassing, continuous observance of Christian life, which will be discussed in more detail in the next chapter, opposed the concentration of holiness in distinct times, places, and people. The preacher's position on this matter had much to do with his uncompromising stance against the Judaizing tendencies of his congregation.[4]

For Chrysostom, the key function of his sermons was to enhance the laity's education in living a proper, moral Christian life.[5] Most of his work as a preacher was not in fact Christianization (much less conversion) but rather the reorienting of his followers' practices and beliefs to align better with his own conception of orthodoxy. His emphasis on the importance of the laity's attention to his sermons was perhaps in part egotistic, but he also believed that his lessons would increase their knowledge about Christianity, which in his view was the only way to salvation. Knowledge, not merely belief, was necessary in order to become a full member of the community, and after that, to distinguish incorrect from correct behavior and heresies from orthodoxy.

This chapter will examine how this knowledge of proper belief and practice, which defined orthodox Christians in opposition to others, was contested in the interaction between the preacher and the laity. Often, Chrysostom's critiques of his congregation reveal aspects of lay spirituality that were not necessarily founded on ignorance or a lack of interest, but rather on a difference of perspective. For example, the preacher and the congregation differed in their judgments of the importance of certain religious observances and the danger of various sins. In many cases, indications of a widespread belief among the laity in a strong divide between the holy and the ordinary as well as a concern for physical purity emerge from

---

[3] Washing hands: *De poen.* 3.2 (PG 49.294). For Augustine's reactions to a similar issue, see P. Brown, "Augustine and a Practice of the *Imperiti: Qui adorant columnas in ecclesia*" in *Augustin prédicateur*, G. Madec, ed. (Paris, 1998) 367–75. Chrysostom had additional complaints about different behavior inside and outside the church, *Hom. in Mt.* 68.4 (PG 58.646); *Hom. in I Cor.* 27.5 (PG 61.231).

[4] On the appeal of Jewish practices among Eastern Christians (and pagans), to which many church leaders responded as to a grave threat, see M. Simon, *Verus Israel: A Study of the Relations between Christians and Jews in the Roman Empire AD 135–425*, H. McKeating, trans. (London, 1996) 306–38; R. Wilken, *John Chrysostom and the Jews: Rhetoric and Reality in the Late 4th Century* (Berkeley, 1983) 66–94.

[5] Not all preachers of this period concentrated upon the Christian life. See K.-H. Uthemann's study of one of Chrysostom's contemporaries, "Forms of Communication in the Homilies of Severian of Gabala: A Contribution to the Reception of the Diatribe as a Method of Exposition" in *Preacher and Audience: Studies in Early Christian and Byzantine Homiletics*, P. Allen and M. B. Cunningham, eds. (Leiden, 1998) 139–77.

Chrysostom's sermons. The purpose here is to examine how the sermons reflect a dialogue between the preacher and his audience, in order to observe how the concerns of the laity affected the preacher's choice of subjects and also how lay Christians opposed their preacher in favor of their own beliefs.

A COMMUNITY OF KNOWLEDGE

Infant baptism was not yet widespread in this period and so the mysteries of the church were not open simply to anyone interested in them.[6] Attendance at communion was guarded from outsiders to the extent that baptized Christians who traveled away from home were required to carry signed letters from their bishops certifying their eligibility to participate in the entire church service.[7] The Church encouraged converts, of course, but newcomers had to gain a certain amount of knowledge of the doctrine, rituals, and proper conduct before they underwent baptism and were accepted as full members. Once people decided to be baptized, their Christian sponsors brought them to clergy who then interviewed the candidates to confirm their serious intent. If approved, they became catechumens, participating in Christian life in every way, short of attending communion. During Lent, they met for sermons instructing them on the elements of doctrine.[8] Right before they were to be baptized, a member of the clergy carefully explained to them the meaning of the different stages of the transformation they were about to undergo.[9]

Eleven catechetical sermons by Chrysostom survive, revealing what he chose (or what the bishop instructed him to choose) as the most fundamental concepts of Christianity for new members. In five of these homilies, he addressed the catechumens before their baptism. In the first sermon of this series, he recited the creed, and told them that they must remember it and

---

[6] E. Ferguson, "Inscriptions and the Origin of Infant Baptism," *JThS* 30.1 (1979) 37–46. For a chart comparing Chrysostom's baptismal sermons to middle Byzantine and modern Orthodox rites, see K. W. Stevenson, "The Byzantine Liturgy of Baptism," *Studia Liturgica* 17 (1987) 176–90, at 190.

[7] *Const. apost.* 2.58.1 (SC 320.320). The doors were guarded in order to keep out the uninitiated: 2.57.21 (SC 320.320). On the exit of catechumens and the closing of the church doors, see F. van der Paverd, *Zur Geschichte der Messliturgie in Antiocheia und Konstantinopel gegen Ende des vierten Jahrhunderts: Analyse der Quellen bei Johannes Chrysostomos* (Rome, 1970) 165–75.

[8] The length of prebaptismal instruction varied. For an overview of the diversity of initiation preparation and rituals, see P. Bradshaw, *The Search for the Origins of Christian Worship: Sources and Methods for the Study of Early Liturgy*, 2nd edn. (Oxford, 2002) 144–70 and 211–30; F. van der Paverd, *St. John Chrysostom, the Homilies on the Statues: An Introduction* (Rome, 1991) 196–201.

[9] On the stages of the catechumenate in this period, see *Const. apost.* 7.1–49 (SC 336.24–114) and Egeria, *Itinerarium* 46. On the catechetical homilies from this period, see *The Study of Liturgy*, C. Jones, G. Wainwright, and E. Yarnold, eds. (Oxford, 1992) 91–3 and 130–42.

be able to defend their faith with it because of the possible confrontation with an Arian or Sabellian.[10] This was sufficient doctrine for beginners, as long as they did not allow themselves or others to question its logic or veracity: "Let no one confuse you again, by bringing the inquiries based on his own reasoning into the doctrines of the church, hoping to muddy the correct, sound doctrines."[11]

Immediately before the ceremony of baptism, Chrysostom explained the details of the process: exorcism, the rejection of the devil, anointing with oil, and immersion in water.[12] The primary purpose of these explanations was to prevent the new Christians from becoming frightened or confused during their initiation. Aside from this, the main emphasis of the prebaptismal instruction fell upon behavior, including a list of forbidden activities such as wearing cosmetics, attending horse races, swearing oaths, and observing omens.[13]

The remaining six baptismal homilies focused on the neophytes, those who had just been baptized. They were encouraged to take full advantage of their purity by maintaining it, since this was easier than regaining it once it was lost.[14] These sermons to new Christians included explanations of the creed, but, like the prebaptismal sermons, concentrated upon the importance of a religious life and the clarification of exactly what good behavior entailed. It is unclear whether this series was a full set of catechetical sermons. It is possible that catechumens learned doctrine in greater detail than the recitation of the creed in these sessions, and perhaps they studied the Scriptures. Many catechumens would have attended church for years before signing up for baptism.[15] Chrysostom's baptismal sermons indicate that the catechumens had some knowledge of stories from the Scriptures. For example, when Chrysostom referred several times to Herod's oath to Salome, he did not explain the story in detail, assuming that his listeners knew how it ended.[16] Gaining knowledge, especially about the rules of Christian behavior and the reasons for them, was fundamental from the first steps of initiation.

In addition to this minimal amount of knowledge required in catechism, people learned the details of faith and behavior by attending church and

---

[10] Chrysostom, *Cateches.* 1.22 (SC 50.119).
[11] *Cateches.* 1.24 (SC 50.120).   [12] *Cateches.* 2.11–27 (SC 50.139–49).
[13] *Cateches.* 1.39–43 (SC 50.128–30).   [14] *Cateches.* 5.26 (SC 50.213).
[15] For an example of a catechumen who had never entered the church, see R. Lim, "Converting the Un-Christianizable: The Baptism of Stage Performers in Late Antiquity" in *Conversion in Late Antiquity and the Early Middle Ages: Seeing and Believing*, K. Mills and A. Grafton, eds. (Rochester, NY, 2003) 84–126, at 95.
[16] *Cateches.* 10.21–30 (SC 366.198–294).

listening to sermons before and after baptism. Laypeople needed to know exactly what actions were sins, and the ability to respond to all situations with confidence required extensive learning. Chrysostom insisted that the church was the only reliable place for people to learn how to respond to the conflicts stemming from families, neighbors, lawsuits, poverty, and the temptations of life in the city.[17] He suspected that parents did not know the rules of conduct well enough to teach their children the basics on their own. After listing a variety of mortal sins that children needed to be aware of, he asked parents: "You do not know that these laws even exist? How then will your son be able to carry out these commands, when his father, the one who should teach him, does not know the laws?"[18]

Knowledge of the Scriptures offered Christians their only hope of salvation – ignorance of their contents was a "an abyss."[19] Chrysostom warned the laity that they could not depend on their own judgments of right and wrong: they had to *learn* precisely which actions and thoughts were sins. If they tried to live a good life without his instructions, they would perish. If they did not know what actions were sinful, they would not know how to pray for forgiveness.[20] In contrast to the simpler times described in the Old Testament, when people only needed to fear God and follow certain clearly stated rules, Christians accepted the responsibility to gain greater knowledge.[21] Meanwhile, many people did not yet agree that attending the theater, swearing oaths, dancing or singing, overeating, wearing make-up, foul language, and playing dice could cause serious damage to their souls.

In addition to the knowledge necessary to get through the day without sinning, Christians were also expected to be able to distinguish orthodoxy from heresy. In a discussion of cosmology, Chrysostom made the unusual request that the laity learn both the right and the wrong interpretations of a passage from Genesis. He explained a problem in the translation of the word "Heaven" by referring back to Hebrew grammar and how this word was rendered into Greek as a plural. The preacher wanted everyone to know that there was only one heaven and to be prepared to argue against other interpretations. He explained that this was one of the primary functions

---

[17] *De Laz.* 3.1 (PG 48.992–3).

[18] *Adv. opp.* 3.5 (PG 47.357). Cf. *De inan.*, *passim* (SC 188), and *De Anna* 1.3 (PG 54.636). Both mothers and fathers were exhorted to teach their children moral values.

[19] *De Laz.* 3.3 (PG 48.995). For the same idea in more positive terms, see *Hom. in Gen.* 35.1 (PG 53.321–2).

[20] *Hom. in Mt.* 14.4 (PG 57.221). Consequently, such knowledge was the first move toward a good life: "It is no small step on the way back to virtue to know the magnitude of your sins," *Hom. in Gen.* 6.2 (PG 53.56).

[21] *Hom. in Mt.* 36.3 (PG 57.417).

of church gatherings and sermons: so that they would be able to ward off anyone else who might try to convince them to believe something that was false.[22] Because of this possibility, theological knowledge was necessary for everyone.

Without the carefully presented instruction in church, misconceptions could arise from partial knowledge of the religion. Some Christians in Antioch did not share their preacher's view of a hard line distinguishing their religion from Judaism.[23] Chrysostom was disturbed by the laity's ambiguity regarding this matter and hoped that it was only due to their ignorance. He claimed that if one were to ask the Judaizing Christians the difference between, for example, Easter and Passover, they simply would not know.[24] In response to the possibility that people might think that the two religions were similar or even interchangeable, he tried vehemently to demonstrate that this was wrong. He presented as proof observable facts. For instance, Jews did not fast on Good Friday and did not celebrate the feasts of the martyrs.[25] If people knew essential facts then they would not continue making such mistakes. Basic knowledge of rituals and their meanings would (ideally) keep ordinary Christians consistently orthodox in their understanding of their religion.

Unfortunately for both Chrysostom and his listeners, he had to balance two conflicting inclinations. On the one hand, as we have seen, he endeavored to educate lay Christians, training them with precise rules and doctrine. On the other hand, the image of the simple, unlearned believer – like the fishermen and tent-makers of the Gospels and Acts – was fundamental to Christian self-conception in this period vis-à-vis the classical culture of the pagans. If lay Christians, or even the monks, became too sophisticated or knowledgeable, they would lose the claim to the simple person who was wiser than a philosopher. Similarly, if ordinary people inquired too deeply into theological matters, they could easily come up with their own ideas. So, Chrysostom had to teach his listeners to know the limits of what they should try to understand. They should accept that they could not know everything and they should know when to stop asking questions and using logic.

These are the basic themes of the series of sermons entitled *On the Incomprehensibility of God*, which were addressed against the Anomoeans. Further complicating the tension between knowledge and simplicity, the

---

[22] *Hom. in Gen.* 4.4 (PG 53.43).
[23] Simon, *Verus Israel*, 306–38 and Wilken, *John Chrysostom and the Jews*, 66–94.
[24] *Adv. Jud.* 3.2 (PG 48.864).   [25] *Adv. Jud.* 4.3 (PG 48.876).

Anomoeans claimed to offer a simpler version of theology. Arguing against simplicity was an awkward thing for late antique Christian preachers. Although knowledge was necessary for understanding piety, human intellectual abilities were limited. Offering himself as an example, Chrysostom claimed that he knew God existed and had a Son, but did not understand precisely *how* this worked. But this did not distress him: he did not know exactly how the digestion of food worked, but he knew that it happened.[26] Instead of trying to explain the differences between orthodox and Anomoean theology, Chrysostom told his listeners that their attempt to analyze God's essence was to be condemned, that they only needed to know that God exists. With this argument, he could reclaim the advantage of simplicity for orthodoxy.[27]

CONTESTED SINS AND VIRTUES

The relative moral value of different sins and virtues provoked disagreements between the preacher and the laity. In numerous cases, all agreed that certain actions were sins, but some did not share the preacher's views of how these different faults related to one another in importance. The laity did not always share the church leaders' assumptions that informed their views about whether traditional crimes, such as adultery or physical assault, were more or less offensive than intangible sins such as anger and envy. Similarly, not everyone instinctively agreed on which virtues deserved the highest esteem. Chrysostom's responses to what he perceived as the laity's misconceptions allow us to discern the preacher's conception of the relative good and evil of different activities, as well as the ways in which ordinary people viewed them.

Chrysostom taught that no person, not even himself, was completely righteous. No clear divide existed between sinners and the virtuous: everyone was part of a continuum.[28] The preacher never explained this continuum systematically, but in several sermons he compared different sins and virtues and explained how they related to each other on this scale. As a general principle, the easier the sin was to avoid, the worse the punishment was for engaging in it.[29] He also emphasized the sinful nature

---

[26] On knowledge and piety, see *De incomp.* 1.9 (SC 28.102–3); on digestion: 1.19 (SC 28.110–13). They should not trust people who claimed to know everything and should not be "curious" about the nature of God, *De incomp.* 1.23 (SC 28.116–17) and 5.27–9 (SC 28.292–7). Cf. P. Rousseau, *Basil of Caesarea* (Berkeley, 1994) 124–6.

[27] *De incomp.* 5.40 (SC 28.304–5).   [28] *De Laz.* 6.9 (PG 48.1040–2).

[29] *De stat.* 10.6 (PG 49.118).

of deeds involving internal feelings more so than physical sexual or violent transgressions. Chrysostom believed that the sex drive shared by all humans was stronger than the love of money, and so succumbing to the lesser temptation of greed was more sinful.[30] Likewise, envy was worse than fornication, even though most people clearly believed otherwise. The congregation knew that those guilty of fornication were not allowed to enter the church, but many probably began to worry when they heard their preacher say that fornicators were more worthy of being there than people who felt envy.[31]

The laity understood quite well that adultery was a sin: there seems to have been no confusion about that. On the other hand, when their preacher explained that dancing was a sin, because it could lead to adulterous thoughts and actions, he faced an incredulous audience. Chrysostom juxtaposed long-established sins, such as illicit sex, to the less obvious types of sins that were not prevented by traditional communal and family vigilance. The preacher did not downplay the danger of sexual sins, but he emphasized the corrupt nature of other actions, by comparing them with sex, in order to make his listeners take these other actions seriously as offenses to God.[32] As we shall see in the next chapter, Chrysostom counted on the force of habit to improve the life of Christians, if they would only take the time to pick up better habits. He wanted their habits of thinking about sin to change, and he wanted them eventually to stigmatize and ridicule whoever ignored beggars as much as or more so than the loose woman or gluttonous man.[33] The love of money and the accumulation of possessions were at the top of his list as the peak of evil.[34] At the opposite end of the scale, sins motivated by poverty were more easily overlooked than sexual misbehavior.[35] Accumulation and protection of wealth were premeditated, long-term sins in comparison to the momentary weakness of fornication or theft. Chrysostom was well aware of the time and energy that becoming or staying wealthy required – nobody could claim that their corrupt business practices had been an accident on one drunken night. Also, attachment to

---

[30] *Hom. in Mt.* 77.1 (PG 58.701–2).   [31] *Hom. in Mt.* 40.3–5 (PG 57.442–6).

[32] Some "sins" had already been banned by Roman law, while new prohibitions of activities were controversial. See W. Klingshirn, *Caesarius of Arles: The Making of a Christian Community in Late Antique Gaul* (Cambridge, 1994) 188.

[33] *Hom. in Mt.* 77.6 (PG 58.710). On the relationship between the beggar and almsgiver as parallel to that between the believer and God, see P. Brown, *Poverty and Leadership in the Late Roman Empire* (Hannover, NH, 2002) 86.

[34] *Hom. in Gen.* 20.5 (PG 53.173).

[35] *De stat.* 10.6 (PG 49.118). For Chrysostom's comments blaming the wealthy for creating thieves, see *Hom. in I Cor.* 21.5 (PG 61.176).

wealth worked against the highest virtue, almsgiving, while illicit sex only violated the lesser virtue of celibacy.

Regarding virtues, Chrysostom presented prayer as more important than fasting, although he reassured his audience that fasting, especially abstinence from wine, was admirable.[36] The most impressive virtues were those that helped other people, which meant that spiritual instruction and alms were superior to other types of righteousness, including asceticism: "Fasting, therefore, and sleeping on the ground, and practicing virginity and self-control, these things profit the ones who do them. But the things that pass from ourselves to our neighbors are almsgiving, teaching, and love."[37] With great shock value, most likely, the preacher announced to his congregation that it would be better for a virgin to desire a man than to fail in almsgiving.[38] Apparently, he did not fear that such statements would encourage sexual antics among the dedicated virgins. In this case, while encouraging his listeners to concentrate more upon charity, Chrysostom reveals the solidity of their respect for the Christian sexual code.

Ascetic practices were ineffective unless they were coupled with helping the poor. For instance, a person who fasted without giving alms was worse than a glutton.[39] Treating virginity in the same manner, he stressed its limitations as a virtue and promoted almsgiving as the key virtue. The biblical parable of the virgins who lacked oil in their oil lamps demonstrated the limits of self-denial in one's pursuit of salvation.[40] At one point, he told his listeners explicitly that God's expectations of them were not as difficult to achieve as they might imagine: they did not need to be virgins who had relinquished all of their property, but married couples could fulfill His demands by dedicating a half, or even as little as one third, of their property to almsgiving.[41] Chrysostom's approach to teaching about the morality of various activities indicates that he knew that the laity had different views. It is clear that he reacted to his congregation's tendency to emphasize the virtue of self-denial and sins related to sex and violence by promoting a more subtle admiration for asceticism and a greater awareness of less tangible sins.

Valuing the community over the individual led Chrysostom to argue that, however praiseworthy and selfless the martyrs were, whoever had

---

[36] *Hom. in Mt.* 57.4–5 (PG 58.563–4).   [37] *Hom. in Mt.* 77.5 (PG 58.709).

[38] *De poen.* 3.3 (PG 49.296).   [39] *Hom. in Mt.* 77.6 (PG 58.710).

[40] On almsgiving superior to virginity: *De poen.* 4.3 (PG 49.303); *Hom. in Mt.* 43.5 (PG 57.464), 46.4 (PG 58.480), 47.4 (PG 58.486), 77.6 (PG 58.710); *Adv. opp.* 3.2 (PG 47.351); *Hom. in Gen.* 8.6 (PG 53.74–5). References to the parable of the virgins and the lamps: *Hom. in Mt.* 78.1–2 (PG 58.711–14); *De poen.* 3.2–3 (PG 49.293–6); *De virginitate* 77 (SC 125.368).

[41] *Hom. in Mt.* 45.3 (PG 58.474).

the choice between martyrdom and teaching others about Christianity should choose the latter. No amount of self-sacrifice could equal the virtue of the person who took time to instruct his or her neighbor on how to live well.[42] Likewise, it was better to die in Christ's name than to raise the dead, and better to live in poverty than to work miracles, because of the impression that the actions made upon observers.[43] Miracles could always be faked, while positive changes in public behavior could not. Also, living a virtuous life was a more advanced state of Christian faith: the ultimate goal of miracle-working had been to lead people in that direction.[44] These statements must have also sounded strange or even shocking to lay Christians. Ultimately, literary and archaeological sources from this period all attest to the veneration of martyrs, while Chrysostom's own sermons indicate the importance of miracles to laypeople.

In addition to the varying levels of moral value of different actions, Chrysostom taught that certain sins and virtues counted differently for people depending on individual situations. For example, destitute Christians were not required so much to serve others with almsgiving: poverty itself was enough of a trial. The ones who lived in luxury and ignored the poor were the ones who would face punishment for neglecting their duty. Likewise, those who passed by beggars once or twice without helping them would not be liable to the same punishment as the person who managed to ignore the poor on a regular basis.[45] Also, as mentioned earlier, Chrysostom did not consider stealing motivated by poverty to be a serious sin, since the wealthy drove thieves to lives of crime.[46]

Possession of wealth also increased one's responsibility to be virtuous in contexts other than almsgiving. Chrysostom requested his congregation to imagine two fornicators, one rich and one poor. He asked his listeners to tell him which sinner had more hope of salvation and they gave the correct answer: "Clearly, we agree that it is the poor man."[47] In another case, Chrysostom mentioned that rich and poor "harlots" would be judged differently for the same sinful actions, because God would take their backgrounds into account during the judgment and demand more virtue from

---

[42] *Adv. Jud.* 8.4 (PG 48.933); *Hom. in Mt.* 77.6 (PG 58.709–10). Chrysostom's own choice to leave the ascetic life for the pastoral duties of an urban priest most likely played a part in his interpretation of the relative value of the different types of virtue.

[43] *Hom. in Mt.* 46.3 (PG 58.474–5).

[44] On fraudulent miracles: *Hom. in Mt.* 32.8 (PG 57.387–8). On virtue as the aim of miracles: *Hom. in Mt.* 66.3 (PG 58.629–30). Cf. *Hom. in Mt.* 48.1 (PG 58.487) and *De incomp.* 1.6 (SC 28.96–9), where Chrysostom also downplays miracles.

[45] *De Laz.* 1.7 (PG 48.971).   [46] *Hom. in I Cor.* 21.5 (PG 61.176).

[47] *De Laz.* 6.3 (PG 48.1031).

the wealthy.[48] The reason for this was that poverty tended to be an effective and inescapable teacher of wisdom for those who were struck by it. The suffering that poverty brought was compensated for by a more lenient judgment of one's actions. On the other hand, the possession of wealth brought with it a greater burden in this regard, especially if it was gained in questionable ways.[49] The easy life afforded the wealthy no excuse when they committed sins of passion or desperation. Chrysostom indicated that most people already knew that the rich sinner would face harsher punishments than the poor one. In this case, the relationship between the preacher's version of the sin, the situation, and the punishment seems to have matched the common sense of the laypeople. The congregation immediately agreed with their preacher that the wealthy were subject to higher expectations when it came to sin and virtue.

Economic considerations were not the only factor that went into calculating liability for sins. Wealth or poverty of knowledge also affected how much their sins counted against them in the final reckoning. Priests would be punished more harshly for their sins, because they could not claim ignorance as an excuse.[50] The friends and relatives of martyrs also faced elevated expectations of virtue for the same reason.[51] The same sinful action could result from many situations, and so each case would be punished appropriately: fornication is punished differently, depending on whether a person is a priest or layman, a rich woman or a poor woman, a catechumen or baptized believer, the daughter of a priest or of a layman.[52] Here, he encouraged his congregation to consider the individual's level of knowledge about his or her responsibilities as just as relevant in the end as the act itself.

The religious status and special responsibilities of monks were a point of disagreement between the preacher and his congregation. The laity believed that many actions considered sins for monks were permissible for themselves, because they lived in the city and had not taken on the obligation to lead an ascetic life. If they made no claim to be especially holy, as the monks had, then they believed that they did not need to act as if they had done so. For example, they agreed with their preacher that oath-swearing was a punishable sin for the monks in the hills outside town, but not for themselves, because they lived in the city and needed to swear oaths to get on with their daily business transactions.[53] Chrysostom argued against this

---

[48] *Hom. in Mt.* 75.5 (PG 58.693).   [49] *Hom. in Mt.* 75.5 (PG 58.692–3).
[50] *Hom. in Mt.* 75.5 (PG 58.693).   [51] *De Laz.* 3.9 (PG 48.1006).
[52] *Hom. in Mt.* 75.5 (PG 58.693).   [53] *De stat.* 15.5 (PG 49.161).

view, downplaying the differences between the monks and the Christians in the city. In contrast to the laity's opinion that monks were held to higher standards, he maintained that the same sins incurred the same penalty, regardless of whether one chose asceticism in the hills or a family life in the city.[54] As we have seen, he acknowledged that the clergy took on more of a burden and would face a more rigorous judgment. The laity, on the other hand, placed the monks and the clergy in the same category, and attributed greater moral obligations to both of them than to themselves.

MONKS AND LAYPEOPLE

When Chrysostom and his congregation diverged at points in their inter-pretations of the Christian life, their differences followed a general pattern, in which the laity tended to perceive more distinctions between the sacred and the ordinary. In many cases, what the laypeople considered particularly sacred – a monk's ascetic practice, or specific times such as martyrs' festi-vals, Lent, and Easter – Chrysostom saw as signposts that drew attention to basic Christian practices that should be undertaken by all people at all times.

Many laypeople revered the monks as people who had attained a higher level of spirituality than they had. They did not think it was necessary, or even possible, for city people such as themselves to live like monks. Chastity and rigorous, continual self-denial led to a different kind of purity, superior to their own, which also brought added responsibilities. Since they were not ascetics, they were not required to fulfill acts of devotion such as frequent reading of the Scriptures or abstaining from public spectacles. Such continual and intense devotion, in their view, was the work of the specialist, not of the layperson.[55]

The divide between the monks and the ordinary laypeople was also obvious to non-Christians. Pagan observers noticed the difference between the monks – unsavory fanatics – and the more likable ordinary Christians. Libanius, as we have seen, counted several Christians among his colleagues and students and gave no indication that the difference of religion caused any conflict. Reasonable Christians apparently did not offend him, but the

[54] *Adv. opp.* 3.14 (PG 47.572–7).
[55] On the fluidity of what "monasticism" meant, see W. Mayer, "Monasticism at Antioch and Con-stantinople in the Late Fourth Century: A Case of Exclusivity or Diversity?" in *Prayer and Spirituality in the Early Church*, P. Allen and L. Gross, eds. (Brisbane, 1998) 275–88, esp. 285–8 regarding the viewpoint of the laity. On the laity's distinction between monastic life and ordinary Christian life, see P. Brown, *The Body and Society: Men, Women and Sexual Renunciation in Early Christianity* (New York, 1988) 311; Klingshirn, *Caesarius*, 189–201.

monks did. In a famous passage, the rhetor compared the monks, who had been tearing down the temples in the countryside, to a herd of elephants.[56] Similarly, the pagan writer Eunapius had studied under Prohaeresius, who was a Christian and the leading sophist in Athens in the mid-fourth century. Eunapius' admiration for a Christian sophist did not prevent him from describing the monks as impious criminals who lived like pigs.[57] Even the most enthusiastic supporters of classical civilization and traditional religion could be friends and colleagues of Christians, content to blame the ascetics for the practices that most offended them, from the heartless destruction of the peasants' holy places to the practice of revering the relics of martyrs.[58] In contrast, Chrysostom believed that the distinctions between the laity and the monks should be few, and instead, the differences between Christians and non-Christians should multiply until *that* distinction was obvious at any given moment.[59]

When Chrysostom tried to convince his listeners that Christians with families and occupations needed to pay special attention to the Scriptures, the laypeople maintained their view that this type of devotion was for monks.[60] Supporting a family, they claimed, excluded them from the more rigorous practices found among the holy men outside the city. Chrysostom articulated their views in several sermons: "This is what many people tend to say when I encourage them to take pains over the hard work of being virtuous or reading the Scriptures: 'This is not for me,' he says, 'have I renounced the world? I am not a monk, am I?'"[61] Elsewhere, he voiced a similar concern: "'I am a worldly man, I have a wife and children. These matters are for priests, these matters are for monks.'"[62] The preacher countered that the way to salvation was the same for everyone. When people claimed that they could not attain the same level of piety as the monks because they were living in the city, concerned with their work and families, he reminded them of the example of Lot, who remained virtuous

---

[56] Libanius, *Or* 30.8. Libanius on monks as drunken cave-dwellers: *Or*. 2.32.

[57] Eunapius, *VP* 472.

[58] Eunapius, *VP* 423–5. For monks as devotees to relics: Eunapius, *VP* 473–4. Liebeschuetz points out that Libanius' invectives against the monks are similar to those against government agents, theater claques, and his personal enemies: *Antioch: City and Imperial Administration in the Later Roman Empire* (Berkeley, 2001) 33–4.

[59] On Chrysostom's use of the ascetics as both an idyllic literary topos, similar to Roman nostalgia for the countryside, and as a concrete model of the virtues he wanted his urban listeners to emulate, see A. J. Festugière, *Antioche païenne et chrétienne: Libanius, Chrysostome et les moines de Syrie* (Paris, 1959) 330 and 344–6. On visible distinction between religious groups: Chrysostom, *Hom. in Mt.* 4.7 (PG 57.47–8).

[60] *De Laz.* 3.1 (PG 48.992).   [61] *Hom. in Gen.* 21.6 (PG 53.183).

[62] *Adv. Jud.* 8.4 (PG 48.932). Cf. *Hom. in Mt.* 2.5 (PG 57.30) and 43.5 (PG 57.464).

in the most sinful of cities.[63] The first Christians also served as good models in this context. Chrysostom reminded his audience that the earliest Christians, converted by apostles, had been married, lived in cities, and several of them were known to have run workshops.[64] Furthermore, he continued, prophets including Isaiah, Ezekiel, and Moses were married and had property and this did not detract from their virtue.

Chrysostom emphasized the similarities between the monastic life and how he wished urban Christians would live. Except for the issue of celibacy or marriage, all of the rules were the same.[65] But leaving the city did not in and of itself increase one's virtue. In contrast to popular perception, he claimed, it was only a path that some people chose. Ideally, he preferred that virtuous people stay in the city, so that they could be good examples to other Christians and attract new converts to the church.[66] They would impress the pagans, for whom, the preacher claimed, living a life of self-denial was more extraordinary than raising the dead.[67]

Although Chrysostom downplayed the differences between the expectations of the monk and the layperson's behavior, there were obvious differences between the average working mother and father in the city and the monks who lived in the hills, starving themselves and spending long periods of time isolated in cisterns or, a generation later, perched on pillars. Chrysostom conceded one major difference between the monks and laypeople: the ascetic life provided an easier way to achieve a high level of piety. The monks were carefree, compared to the city people; they lived like Adam before the fall, without any sorrow, political concerns, envy, or lust.[68] Hoping to make the monks appear more similar to ordinary Christians, Chrysostom claimed that the ascetics' achievements owed more to their isolated environment than to any special spiritual ability.

In several sermons, Chrysostom made a concerted effort to explain how the monks had developed preferable alternatives to ordinary life. It is clear that he addressed these comments to people who assumed that the ascetic life was arduous and generally unpleasant. In an interesting passage, Chrysostom encouraged the laity to visit the monks as a form of entertainment, a spectacle better than the theater. Watching the monks would bring all sorts of advantages to the ordinary layperson, especially compared

---

[63] *Hom. in Gen.* 43.1 (PG 54.396).   [64] *Hom. in Mt.* 55.6 (PG 58.548).
[65] *Hom. in Mt.* 7.7 (PG 57.81).   [66] *Hom. in Gen.* 43.1 (PG 54.396).
[67] *Hom. in Mt.* 43.5 (PG 57.464).
[68] *Hom. in Mt.* 68.3 (PG 58.643–4). On Chrysostom's vision of an ideal Christian city, see Brown, *Body and Society*, 305–22; A. Hartney, *John Chrysostom and the Transformation of the City* (London, 2004) 23–32, 117–32.

to more traditional leisure activities. Theater actresses could imprint themselves on men's minds, making them reluctant to return home to their less glamorous wives. But, if a man had been watching the monks instead, his wife "will receive her husband gentle and mild, freed from all unnatural lust, and she will be subject to him more calmly than before."[69] The singing of monks offered an enjoyable spectacle, which could serve as an alternative to the sinful music of the theaters. What was more, wonderful food was to be found among the ascetics: the honey of the oracles of God, produced by God's honeybees, the monks![70] We can only guess at the incredulous response of Chrysostom's congregation at this point: at other times, they had made it clear that they had no intention of giving up the theater despite his frequent condemnations of it.[71]

Chrysostom continued with this theme later in this same series of sermons. Telling his congregation to exchange their elaborate clothes for plainer attire, he again pointed toward the monks. These admirable people wore goat- and camel-hair clothing, not anything shiny, soft, or bright. He presented the monastic lifestyle to his listeners as easier and more pleasant than their complicated lives. The monks' tables were uncluttered with meat and its unpleasant smells, holding only bread and water, and maybe some fruit.[72] Appealing, perhaps, to lower-status Christians, he pointed out that monastic society was not divided into a hierarchy: "In that place, there is no master and slave; all are slaves, all free men . . . for they are slaves of one another and masters of one another."[73]

Other aspects of the ascetic life offered calming alternatives to the anxieties of the wealthy. Since the monks knew no hierarchy, they did not have to worry about improving or even maintaining their status and reputation. Because the monks had no houses, they did not fear robbers. No houses, no candles: the very last thing they had to worry about was a house fire.[74] During his description of the monks' poverty, Chrysostom reversed his opinion expressed elsewhere, about the similarity of the monks and laity: "Everything with them has been made different from what we have:

---

[69] *Hom. in Mt.* 68.4 (PG 58.645). For an examination of Chrysostom's use of theatrical imagery, see B. Leyerle, *Theatrical Shows and Ascetic Lives: John Chrysostom's Attack on Spiritual Marriage* (Berkeley, 2001).

[70] *Hom. in Mt.* 68.5 (PG 58.646).

[71] The congregation was aware that the theater was still legal, *Hom. in Mt.* 37.6 (PG 57.427). Chrysostom cites the legality of spectacles in an argument that humans do not make good laws, *Hom. in I Cor.* 12.5 (PG 61.102).

[72] *Hom. in Mt.* 69.2–3 (PG 58.650–3). This aspect of the simple life might have been of special interest to the wives and servants in the congregation who were in charge of preparing meals for the others.

[73] *Hom. in Mt.* 69.4 (PG 58.653).   [74] *Hom. in Mt.* 69.3 (PG 58.651–2).

clothing and food, and houses and shoes, and the way they speak."[75] But he emphasized the differences between the world of the monks and that of the wealthy laity in order to stress how far most people were from the true Christian life. Ideally, however, there would be no difference. Ideally, the Christians in the city would realize that this monastic life was the same life they were expected to strive for, despite the urban environment, their families, and their work. If people visited the monks, they would see what was truly necessary in life.[76] In general, it is clear that the preacher was not trying to convince his listeners to become hermits, but rather to accept certain ascetic practices as the core of mainstream Christian life.

The congregation might have found this instruction to act like the monks as troubling as if their preacher had asked them to act like priests without having been consecrated. In addition to their difficulty, these suggestions probably seemed improper to ordinary laypeople. Before the institution of monastic rules setting clear boundaries between the pious laity and the monks, there were different ways of defining the relationship between the two groups. Chrysostom saw them all as members of the laity, with the monks taking a particular approach to the Christian life. Most Christians, however, saw the monks as different – more akin to the clergy than to themselves – with different responsibilities and different honors.

ATTITUDES ABOUT CHURCH ATTENDANCE: WHEN AND WHY?

Despite all of the preacher's complaints about his listeners and suggestions for improvement, his sermons indicate that they took their religion quite seriously. For one thing, they attended church, and the regulars were not always the ones considered to be the most orthodox or even the most virtuous. When special events attracted Christians to the theater or hippodrome, the change in the size of the audience was noticeable, and the reason for the decline was not difficult for the preacher to guess. He began several sermons with minor variations on the same refrain: "Again there are horse races and satanic spectacles, and our congregation has become smaller."[77] The people at the races must have attended church on less eventful days, or

---

[75] *Hom. in Mt.* 69.4 (PG 58.654).

[76] *Hom. in Mt.* 70.4–5 (PG 58.659–62) and 72.4 (PG 58.671–4).

[77] *Cateches.* 6.1 (SC 50.215). Cf. *De incomp.* 7.1 (PG 48.755–6); *Hom. in Gen.* 41.1 (PG 53.374–5). Noisy people: *Hom. in Mt.* 32.7 (PG 57.385–6). On the frequency of church services and the difficulties of determining this, see W. Mayer, "At Constantinople, How Often Did John Chrysostom Preach? Addressing Assumptions about the Workload of a Bishop," *Sacris Erudiri* 40 (2001) 83–105.

else they would not have been missed. As much as Chrysostom considered the attraction of the two venues to be antithetical, enthusiasm for spectacles did not diminish enthusiasm for church: "Some of the people who are listening to this (for I am not convicting all of you, God forbid) have forgotten everything and have surrendered themselves again to the satanic spectacle of the horse races." The preacher noted his congregation's inability to focus their enthusiasm exclusively on his sermons: "Simply obeying some habit, they applaud what I say and show me that they receive my words with pleasure, and after this, they run back to the hippodrome and the applause for the charioteers is greater and their frenzy is uncontrollable."[78] On another occasion, some people showed up who had also joined the Jews at their synagogues to celebrate fasts and festivals with them. Chrysostom asked how they could worship Christ and then celebrate festivals with "His foes," the Jews.[79] Such complaints, though, indicate that people with different views about acceptable activities attended church.

Attending church, in Chrysostom's view, was not intrinsically valuable: it alone, however frequent, would not benefit anyone's soul. He reminded his listeners that they were to use their time in church studying the Scriptures or else they would be wasting their time.[80] He feared that the social attraction of belonging to the body of the church would become dominant at the religious services. He warned them to focus on spiritual learning rather than the latest news from their neighbors.[81] Chrysostom invoked the image of parents who sent their children to school, expecting them to improve themselves by paying attention to their teachers. He told them to apply these expectations to themselves and realize that "we at our mature age attend this spiritual school."[82] Like the schoolchildren, they should take note of what they learned each day and connect it to their previous lessons.

If people were not paying attention and learning, though, standing in church at least would keep them away from trouble. The preacher also believed in the chance that, over time, just by virtue of repetition, useful knowledge would sink into even the most passive mind. Although some people dismissed his sermons as nonsense, he felt certain that he would win these over sooner or later.[83] Attending church was the first step in

---

[78] *De Laz.* 7.1 (PG 48.1045).   [79] *Adv. Jud.* 4.4 (PG 48.876).

[80] *Hom. in Gen.* 18.7 (PG 53.158) and 32.1 (PG 53.292); *De stat.* 5.7 (PG 49.79).

[81] *Hom. in Gen.* 32.1 (PG 53.293). Cf. *Hom. in Acts* 29.3 (PG 60.218), where he emphasizes that their forefathers had built the churches because gatherings of religious teachers and learners were different from the socializing that took place in other public places.

[82] *Hom. in Gen.* 32.1 (PG 53.293).   [83] *Hom. in Gen.* 35.8 (PG 53.331).

one's progress to more advanced levels of religious observation.[84] However critical he was, Chrysostom was realistic enough to appreciate the fact that people showed up in church at all. Even if they did not always listen to him or agree with what he said, church attendance demonstrated some level of commitment to the Christian life. He acknowledged that he and his congregation had different duties, with himself devoting all of his attention to pastoral, liturgical, and theological matters, while they had to work and care for their families.[85]

Regular church attendance was a sign of piety among Christians. It was not completely necessary, though, since people who did not attend church were still considered part of the religious community. Some of the Judaizing Christians did not attend church: Chrysostom had to send laypeople out to find them, instruct them, and convince them to come to church.[86] The preacher also observed that some people received communion only a few times a year, while others did so more often. Hermits, as an extreme example, only participated in communion once every few years. The frequency did not matter, Chrysostom claimed, but only the way one lived one's life.[87] Also, for Chrysostom, no single day at church held any more importance than another. In contrast to earlier Christian practice of observing the Sabbath, Chrysostom taught that this should be stopped because all days were holy and so the faithful were expected to worship continually.[88] But still, many ordinary Christians believed that the imperative to attend services varied according to the significance of the commemoration, due to particular respect for the martyrs and holy days.

Not surprisingly, times of crisis attracted larger numbers of people to the church. The preacher was pleased to see the numbers grow during disasters, but he did not approve of the motivations behind the sudden interest in church attendance. He noticed a pattern: the church overflowed with people during times of crisis, such as famines, natural disasters, and enemy invasions.[89] After an earthquake, many people came to church who did not usually show up: when the city started to fall apart, crowds of people

---

[84] *De poen.* 3.1 (PG 49.291).   [85] *De poen.* 3.1 (PG 49.291).

[86] *Adv. Jud.* 2.1 (PG 48.857). Chrysostom uses hunting and fishing imagery when encouraging his listeners to "track down" Judaizers, circle them like a pack of hunting dogs, and then sweep them up in their "nets of instruction."

[87] *Hom. on Hebrews* 17.4 (PG 63.131–2). See P. Allen, "The Homilist and the Congregation: A Case Study of John Chrysostom's Homilies on Hebrews," *Augustinianum* 36 (1996) 397–421, at 416–18. Theodoret indicates that monks rarely received communion, *HR* 20.4 (SC 257.66–8). But elsewhere the monk Zeno goes to church, 12.5 (SC 234.466–8).

[88] *Hom. in Mt.* 39.3 (PG 57.436–7).   [89] *De poen.* 4.2 (PG 49.301–2).

ran screaming into the church.[90] The preacher encouraged this reaction to natural disasters, pointing to them as demonstrations of God's anger at their sins. Not wanting to criticize and scare off the people who had come because of the crisis, he still attempted to explain that being pious without fear of sudden earthly danger would bring them more honor in the eyes of God.[91] In this sermon, he revealed that he had originally planned to criticize the Jews for their tendency toward intermittent, emergency worship and their utilitarian *do ut des* attitude to religion, but looking out at his own audience he realized that they also acted in this way. Nonetheless, even if listeners had come to church inspired by the wrong reasons, the preacher was happy to have the opportunity to explain to them what they were doing wrong.

The fear of imperial wrath after the Riot of the Statues had a similar effect on church attendance. Again, Chrysostom welcomed this opportunity to have increased contact with the Christians of the city and encouraged them to cultivate their piety to outlast the crisis.[92] Unlike most of the Antiochenes, Chrysostom welcomed the emperor's response to the riot. By shutting down the city's baths and theaters, the imperial punishments attracted to church people who would have otherwise been distracted by other options.

In addition to times of crisis, Christians attended church in greater numbers and more frequently during Lent.[93] The preacher naturally noticed the increased size of the Lenten congregation but was unimpressed by their fasting. He explained that if their hearts were not in their religion, then they should not feel compelled to come to communion because of a particular festival. On the other hand, those who were pure at heart should not be discouraged from coming to church by the lack of a festival.[94] In short, he did not want the liturgical calendar to have any effect upon anyone's habits of church attendance. What his complaints also make clear, however, is the fact that the calendar *did* affect the ordinary Christian's interpretation of religious duties.

FASTING

Not only did people attend church more often during Lent, they also willingly observed the fast. Even catechumens kept the Lenten fast each

---

[90] *De Laz.* 6 (*PG* 48.1027).   [91] *De poen.* 4.2 (PG 49.301–2).
[92] *De stat.* 17.1 (PG 49.171–12); cf. *De stat.* 3.7 (PG 49.57–8).
[93] On Easter crowds, see *Hom. in Acts* 29.3 (PG 60.218). On liturgical services during Lent in Antioch and their frequency, see Paverd, *Homilies on the Statues*, 161–201.
[94] *Hom. in I Cor.* 28.1 (PG 61.233).

year, although they were not permitted to receive communion until they had been baptized.[95] Chrysostom was aware of his congregation's rigorous adherence to the fast. He noticed mid-Lent discussion among the laity: "I have seen many people rejoicing and saying to each other, 'we have conquered, we have held on, half the fast is spent.'"[96] He went on to remark that he saw "many who are so small-minded that at the present time, they worry about the following Lent."[97] Whether this observation was meant as a joke or a criticism – or both – it reveals serious and widespread adherence to the Lenten fast among people who found it to be a challenging but necessary demonstration of their faith.

Even the less rigorous Christians observed the fast: Chrysostom warned such people that their fasting did not help them when they spent the entire day playing dice.[98] After noticing that many had abandoned the church for the races, even during Lent, he acknowledged that many of those people observed the fast.[99] Indeed, the least enthusiastic members of the congregation observed this practice: during Lent, "the laziest fast, even without prodding."[100] The fact that Chrysostom did not have to remind them to do this is in itself striking. Although good arguments usually do not stem from a lack of information, the preacher's silence reveals much in this case. As we have seen, Chrysostom did not hesitate to point out the religious shortcomings of the members of his congregation. As it was, he discussed Lent and the issue of fasting quite often, and all of his observations about the laity's practice indicate that they erred solely on the side of too much enthusiasm. For instance, referring to Paul's problems with the Corinthians, Chrysostom pointed out that there was danger in too much attention to fasting: if one began to hate the proscribed food, then fasting no longer brought any benefit and instead became a sin.[101]

The practice seems to have been so entrenched in the religious lives of the laity that the preacher could take it for granted and also use it as an example to encourage additional religious practices. He suggested that people should use fasting as a way to inspire themselves to pray more often and to give alms.[102] In another instance, Chrysostom applauded his congregation for

---

[95] *Adv. Jud.* 3.5 (PG 48.868). [96] *De stat.* 18.1 (PG 49.179).
[97] *De stat.* 18.1 (PG 49.181); *De Anna* 1.1 (PG 54.633).
[98] *Hom. in Gen.* 6.6 (PG 53.61). [99] *Hom. in Gen.* 6.1 (PG 53.55).
[100] *De poen.* 5.1 (PG 49.305–6); *Adv. Jud.* 3.4 (PG 48.867). Chrysostom notes that even the most sluggish (ῥᾳθυμοτέρους) and the laziest (νωθρότατος) had come to church in anticipation of the fast. Cf. *Hom. in Gen.* 2.1 (PG 53.26). On the early development of Lent, see Bradshaw, *The Search for the Origins of Christian Worship*, 183–5. For a general overview of late antique views of fasting, see V. E. Grimm, *From Feasting to Fasting, the Evolution of a Sin: Attitudes to Food in Late Antiquity* (New York, 1996).
[101] *Hom. in Mt.* 86.3 (PG 58.768). [102] *Hom. in Gen.* 30.5 (PG 53.279).

fasting from meat, but prodded them to fast from sins as well.[103] Only these additional practices, rather than fasting alone, would distinguish the truly pious. The preacher made this quite explicit when he called those who had improved themselves during Lent to come closer to him, and told the others who had merely fasted from food to leave without taking part in communion.[104]

Chrysostom also hoped that the Lenten fast would inspire deeper spirituality and moderate habits throughout the year: "When, after a meal and sleeping, you come to the public square and already you see the day hurrying toward the evening, come into this church, approach this bema, and remember the time of the fast when the church was full with the crowds around us, who were also zealous to listen."[105] For Chrysostom, the best direct result of the laity's fasting was greater attention to his sermons. Self-denial made them more alert. Comparing the fast to the season of sowing seeds, he called Lent the season for Christian learning, when his sermons would become firmly planted in his listeners' minds.[106] Their increased alertness was a "positive result from fasting,"[107] and he took advantage of the increased mental energy to accelerate the level of instruction. He explained that if they were ever to understand the more complex issues, such instruction should be done during the fast when "our limbs are nimble for swimming and our mind's eye is sharper, without being troubled by the evil stream of luxury."[108] The congregation's enhanced awareness was due both to the mind focusing powers of self-denial and to the fact that they attended church much more often during Lent.[109]

Observing Lent could also bring the Christian community closer together through simple eating habits. On one day during the fast, Chrysostom remarked with wonder that everyone was eating the same food, despite divisions of gender, class, culture, and status.[110] There were also earthly benefits of an abstemious diet: the doctors promoted fasting for health reasons, and everyone knew that its opposite, gluttony, caused illness.[111]

Despite the advantages of fasting, it could also lead to conflicts. During Lent one year, some people who had broken the fast began to avoid the church because they did not believe that they were allowed to enter

---

[103] *De stat.* 3.3 (PG 49.51–2).
[104] *De stat.* 20.1 (PG 49.197). On the ineffectiveness of fasting without alms, cf. *De stat.* 16.6 (PG 49.169–70).
[105] *De Anna* 1.1 (PG 54.633).   [106] *Hom. in Gen.* 2.1 (PG 53.27).
[107] *Hom. in Gen.* 4.1 (PG 53.40).   [108] *Hom. in Gen.* 9.1 (PG 53.76).
[109] *Hom. in Gen.* 25.1 (PG 53.218). Cf. *Hom. in Mt.* 57.4 (PG 58.563).
[110] *Hom. in Gen.* 2.2 (PG 53.27–8).
[111] *Hom. in Gen.* 10.2 (PG 53.83–4); *De poen.* 5.4 (PG 49.312).

it. In response, Chrysostom explained that abstinence from food did not necessarily make one a good or effective Christian: an alert listener who broke the fast was better than a fasting, daydreaming, yawning person.[112] His listeners were expected to explain to people who were absent that they could come to church if they had broken the fast, as long as they were sober.[113] People concentrated too much on the lack of food, he claimed, at the expense of paying attention to spiritual duties. The preacher clarified that he did not discourage fasting, but just wanted people to engage actively with the sermons instead of passively listening out of habit.[114] He went on to explain that if some people found the fast too difficult, then they should eat and not feel guilty about it. Fasting was not to be done for its own sake, but as a means to an end:

> He [God] does not simply demand abstinence from food, for us to perform the fast in order to persevere without food as an end in itself, but for us to withdraw ourselves from affairs of this life and spend all our spare time on spiritual matters. If we regulate our lives with sober minds, dedicate all of our spare time to spiritual matters, eat food only for necessary nourishment, and spend all our lives with good practices, we would have no need of the help from fasting.[115]

If people broke the fast, they could compensate for it with almsgiving and prayers. According to Chrysostom, fasting did not do their souls any good in the absence of these other actions.[116] For the laity, however, the strict observance of the fast was a distinct, valuable act of religious devotion, even when not accompanied by prayer and good deeds.

The preacher was also concerned about how the practice affected their behavior before and after Lent. He disapproved mildly when they seemed gloomy about the approach of Lent and attempted to cheer them up. Likewise, people tended to be too happy for his tastes at the end of the fasting period.[117] The Antiochenes readied themselves for Lent by gathering at the public baths and drinking wine before they had to give it up. While these preparations seemed sensible to the laity, Chrysostom could not understand their logic: "Certainly it is strange to receive this most beautiful feast with a pure body but an impure, drunken soul."[118] He also worried, probably with

---

[112] *De stat.* 9.1 (PG 49.104). Cf. *Hom. in Gen.* 10.1 (PG 53.81–2).
[113] *De stat.* 9.1 (PG 49.103–4).
[114] *Hom. in Gen.* 10.1 (PG 53.82). Cf. *Hom. in Gen.* 8.6 (PG 53.74–5).
[115] *Hom. in Gen.* 10.1 (PG 53.82).
[116] *Hom. in Gen.* 10.1 (PG 53.82–3). People assumed that fasting was enough for their salvation, but they needed to give alms also: *Hom. in Mt.* 46.4 (PG 58.480–1).
[117] For dread at beginning of Lent: *Hom. in Gen.* 1.1 (PG 53.21); rejoicing at end of Lent: *De Anna* 1.1 (PG 54.633).
[118] *De poen.* 5.5 (PG 49.314).

good reason, that the end of Lent would be used as an additional excuse for excess.[119]

Chrysostom perceived that non-Christians dreaded their fast days, and encouraged his congregation to act in the opposite way. The pagans and Jews would be impressed, he hoped, by Christian cheerfulness about fasting.[120] In order to make the correct impression on non-Christians, laypeople were instructed to explain their reasons for fasting carefully: "If a Jew or a pagan asks you why you are fasting, do not say that it is because of Pasch or because of the cross . . . but it is because of our sins when we are about to approach the mysteries."[121] He wanted everyone, including non-Christians, to understand that their fast was not out of grief for the death of Jesus.

JUDAIZERS

Some groups within the Christian community also observed Jewish fasts.[122] The appeal of the Jewish community in Antioch is evident, mirrored as it is in Chrysostom's fervent arguments against Judaizing Christians. He resorted to intense attacks in a series of sermons inspired by Christians who fasted with the Jews on the Day of Atonement. Participation in Jewish life by non-Jews was a widespread phenomenon in the Greek East during the Roman period, attested to by inscriptions as well as stories in the Acts of the Apostles. As we have seen, the frequency of "Judaizing" among Eastern Christians is evident because of the anxiety it caused orthodox leaders. Their attempts to stamp it out through canon law and heated sermons left a paper trail that details this religious tendency, which ranged from beliefs in the powers of Jews in exorcism and healing to the observance of the Sabbath and other holy days.[123]

Chrysostom's sermons against Judaizing Christians are the best-known texts from Late Antiquity that dealt with this issue. In this series of sermons, he focused his anger as well as his rhetoric on the likelihood that some members of his congregation would join the Jews in celebrating their High Holy Days. The eagerness of the Antiochenes to observe the fast of the Day of Atonement is not very surprising, given their attitude toward Lent. Clearly, solemnity and self-denial were not off-putting to the religious people of Antioch, despite their reputation for lightheartedness.

---

[119] *Cateches.* 5.15 (SC 50.208).   [120] *Hom. in Gen.* 1.1 (PG 53.21).
[121] *Adv. Jud.* 3.4 (PG 48.867).   [122] *Adv. Jud.* 4.3 (PG 48.875).
[123] On Jewish sympathizers or "God-fearers," see above, chapter 3, n. 95. On Jewish influence on Christian prayers and grave inscription formulae: Simon, *Verus Israel*, 307–8.

Chrysostom tried to undermine the appeal of the Jewish fast by arguing that something that was usually seen as holy could be evil if done for the wrong reasons.[124] Comparing the issue of fasting to that of circumcision, he argued that the problem was not the physical act itself, which was neutral, but the way it symbolized obstinacy.[125] Elsewhere, he claimed that the Jewish fast was worse than drunkenness because of the motivations for it.[126] Many Christians, however, held a firm idea about the virtue of fasting. Chrysostom continued to try to convince them that the motivation for and context of the act held more weight. He pointed out that both criminals and the Christian martyrs suffered from torture, but the reason for their suffering was what distinguished the two. In the same way, he argued, Christian and Jewish fasting were completely different activities.[127]

In his third sermon against Judaizers, Chrysostom faced a congregation that was less than certain about what distinguished their own springtime religious holiday from that of the Jews. Since the Council of Nicaea in 325, the official method of reckoning the date of Easter guaranteed that the two religions' holidays would not coincide. However, many Antiochenes in Chrysostom's time observed the previous tradition, refusing to respect the changes because they believed that it was crucial to fast on the correct days.[128] The laity's view was also current among the monks in the nearby countryside, even later than Chrysostom's period.[129] Chrysostom attempted to convince them that precise dates were not important and that they should not value religious observation on one certain day more than on another.[130]

The people who celebrated Lent and Easter according to the older tradition possessed good arguments supporting their practice. Their timing of the fast was observed first, and it seemed to coincide better with Christ's experience. Besides, they were accustomed to the timing.[131] Chrysostom acknowledged that these claims were true, but argued that the Council at

---

[124] *Adv. Jud.* 2.1 (PG 48.857).   [125] *Adv. Jud.* 2.1 (PG 48.858).
[126] *Adv. Jud.* 4.1 (PG 48.873).   [127] *Adv. Jud.* 4.3 (PG 48.874).
[128] *Adv. Jud.* 3.1 and 3.5–6 (PG 48.861 and 868–72). Christians who celebrated Easter according to the Jewish calendar considered it a minor matter: *Hom. in Gen.* 12.1 (PG 53.98).
[129] Theodoret narrates a story about a monk living near Antioch who celebrated Easter on the wrong date, but dutifully changed his practices when the bishop informed him of the latest developments of orthodoxy, *HR* 3.17 (SC 234.278–80).
[130] On the constant nature of Christian worship: *Adv. Jud.* 3.5 (PG 48.868). Cf. the discussion of Chrysostom's objections to New Year's celebrations in chapter 6.
[131] Chrysostom acknowledged that Christ had celebrated Passover according to the Jewish calendar, *Adv. Jud.* 3.4 (PG 48.866). Christians used the argument that they had been fasting in this way for many years and did not want to change: ibid., 3.6 (PG 48.869).

Nicaea took precedence over any previous tradition.[132] In response to the concern for emulating their Savior's experience, the preacher pointed out that there were many aspects of this event that Christians should not act out precisely because they were rooted in Jewish practice. Moreover, the timing of Lent and Easter simply did not matter – they were arbitrary. In fact, the sacrifice of Jesus could be celebrated at any time, and would be just as holy on any day.[133]

After making this claim about the equality of all days, Chrysostom realized he had more explaining to do for a congregation that placed so much importance on the liturgical year. If each day was equally holy, then why did Christians fast for forty days before Easter? Chrysostom explained away the contradiction. These practices and their times were constructs: psychological or pedagogical tools that had been established to help ordinary people participate in Christian worship in the best way possible. In the past, laypeople had come to communion unprepared. Certain Church "Fathers" had sought to improve this situation by setting aside forty days for people to fast and to meet together for prayer.[134] As we have seen, Chrysostom never concealed his opinion that the observance of the fast was secondary to paying attention to his sermons. The preacher portrayed Lent as a method to inspire weak people to act like better Christians for at least a certain period of time, since most would not do it year-round. Therefore, preachers needed specific weeks to be set aside for the fast: "If I kept shouting and proclaiming a fast all year long, no one would pay attention to what I said."[135] Lent was a compromise that had been made with regard to normal human nature. The preacher observed that the majority of people missed the point: they did not always possess clean consciences, yet were careful to carry out the fast because it was traditional and to attend church services because of a feast day.[136]

---

[132] *Adv. Jud.* 3.3 (PG 48.864–6).

[133] *Adv. Jud.* 3.3–4 (PG 48.866–7). The Church did not consider the exact observance of dates to be important: *Adv. Jud.* 3.6 (PG 48.871–2). Some Christians wished to calculate more carefully the exact date of Jesus' crucifixion. Chrysostom responded that this calculation was too complicated to figure out, but more importantly, the exact time simply did not matter. Even the Jews, he pointed out, although they observed many precise rules in their worship, had no great concern about the exact time of their holidays, *Adv. Jud.* 3.5 (PG 48.868).

[134] *Adv. Jud.* 3.4 (PG 48.867). The Lenten fast may have been a recommendation not obligation at this time, see T. Finn, *The Liturgy of Baptism in the Baptismal Instructions of St. John Chrysostom* (Washington, DC, 1967) 48. The first references to a forty-day fast before Easter are after the Council of Nicaea, see Bradshaw, *The Search for the Origins of Christian Worship*, 183.

[135] *Adv. Jud.* 3.4 (PG 48.867).   [136] *Adv. Jud.* 3.5 (PG 48.868).

CONCLUSIONS

Many of the topics Chrysostom preached about were in response to certain Christian beliefs that members of his congregation already held. His complaints about their ignorance and his exhortations to improve their behavior can easily lead to an inaccurate impression of these people as reluctant or lukewarm Christians. Close attention to his comments, however, reveals that his listeners were serious about their religion. Much of the behavior that Chrysostom found objectionable stemmed more from a different interpretation of Christian piety than from actual ignorance or indifference. Many of the disagreements were due to the fact that a good deal of his teachings conflicted with previously held Christian traditions. The preacher and the congregation held different views about the importance of various aspects of Christian worship and about the relative significance of various sins and virtues: the two sides simply had different religious priorities. As we will see in the next chapter, there were also conflicting views about how far religious observance needed to extend outside the church into the daily life of ordinary people. The preacher's moral exhortations and the resistance to them, then, should not be seen in terms of correct Christianity and popular deviations, but as two perspectives that interacted with each other after having developed in different contexts.[137]

[137] On the process of Christianization as a dialogue preserved in sermons, at least in part, see E. Rebillard, "Interaction between the Preacher and his Audience: The Case-Study of Augustine's Preaching on Death," *Studia Patristica* 31 (1997) 86–96. Cf. P. Brown's discussion of the problems with viewing Late Antiquity in terms of a two-tiered model of "high" and "low" religion: *Cult of the Saints*, 1–22. In favor of the two-tiered model, see R. MacMullen, "Distrust of the Mind in the Fourth Century" in *Changes in the Roman Empire: Essays in the Ordinary* (Princeton, 1990), esp. 126–9.

CHAPTER 6

Habits and the Christianization of daily life

No sin was too small for Chrysostom to notice and then rebuke, but his ideal was not for all Christians to become ascetics. He insisted that people could live in the city, with jobs and families, and lead perfectly acceptable Christian lives. In order to do this, however, catechumens and baptized Christians required a great deal of instruction before they could sort out the non-Christian and/or sinful habits from their daily lives. Because of the difference between Chrysostom's view of the world and that of the majority of his congregation, there was no basis of common sense or inherited values that could assume the burden of coordinating the laity's reality with the clergy's expectations. Even though a gap between ideals and practice is present in any society, in the late fourth century innumerable behaviors reflected ancient traditions while ambitious church leaders aimed to change them as thoroughly as possible.

Chrysostom knew what he was up against when he took on what he called the "tyranny of ancient custom."[1] He knew that the unconscious repetition of actions and thoughts ingrained into daily activities was a powerful force to reckon with, especially when it involved religion: "When the custom is related to doctrines, it becomes even more established. For one would change anything more willingly than matters of religion."[2] Chrysostom was also aware that this had always been a difficult problem. In the time of the apostles, the old religion had custom on its side, while the novelty of Christianity could only have been an obstacle.[3] The power of custom had held sway over the Jews who had longed for Egypt after their escape because they had been accustomed to it. Likewise, Plato, although he did not believe in the gods, still took part in their rituals, while Socrates had lost his life because of new beliefs and practices.[4] Older practices clearly had a natural advantage.

[1] Chrysostom, *Hom. in I Cor.* 7.6 (PG 61.63).   [2] *Hom. in I Cor.* 7.7 (PG 61.64).   [3] Ibid.
[4] *Hom. in I Cor.* 7.7 (PG 61.63–4). Chrysostom also blamed man-made traditions for drawing the Jews away from the Law of God given to Moses toward what he considered to be human traditions, *Hom. in Mt.* 51.2 (PG 58.511).

Conversion to Christianity brought people from one set of customs, which could be observed without conscious effort, to a new, difficult set of rules, as well as threats of hell for those who did not follow these rules. Chrysostom observed that, because of the nature of human customs, there would have been no reason on earth for people to be attracted to a new, more demanding religion: thus such conversions were proof of the truth and power of Christian teachings.[5] He also made the point in this sermon that the Apostles, and presumably later preachers including himself, were engaged above all in changing the most stubborn customs among their people.[6] Nobody claimed that the moment of conversion automatically changed everything that needed to be changed. Initial, spiritual conversion was the easy part, but the actual fulfillment of the new religion's requirements called for constant concentration and willpower by each individual.

Breaking bad habits was even more important than attending church, while new habits were more essential than any other requirement expected of converts to Christianity. First of all, people needed to learn what activities and thoughts were sinful, so that they could pray for forgiveness and reform their behavior.[7] The significance of every action could not be underestimated – every small sin inevitably led to more serious ones: "One man laughed at the wrong time; another blamed him; a third took away his fear by saying that it was not important. 'For what is laughing? What could happen because of this?' From this come dirty jokes, from that foul language, and then filthy deeds."[8] This anecdote about ordinary men discussing the moral value of spontaneous laughter illustrates Chrysostom's wishes for a broad diffusion of the Christian ethos into everyday life, as well as its ambiguity when countered with the prevailing common sense. The preacher's judgment against laughter came down against what generally seemed to be reasonable.

The Antiochene preacher was not alone in his views. The generation of Church Fathers of the late fourth and early fifth centuries, including

---

[5] *Hom. in I Cor.* 7.7–8 (PG 61.64–5).
[6] Ibid. See S. Benin, *Footprints of God: Divine Accommodation in Jewish and Christian Thought* (Albany, NY, 1993) 59.
[7] *Hom. in Mt.* 14.4 (PG 57.221). See P. Brown, *The Body and Society: Men, Women and Sexual Renunciation in Early Christianity* (New York, 1988) 305–22 and *Authority and the Sacred: Aspects of the Christianisation of the Roman World* (Cambridge, 1995) 22–5, on Augustine's views of bad habits. In the second century, Clement of Alexandria had also highlighted the importance of habits as the foundation for faith, *Paedagogus* 1.1 (SC 70.108).
[8] *Hom. in Mt.* 86.3 (PG 58.767). For more against laughter and joking: *De Laz.* 1.11 (PG 48.978); *De stat.* 15.4 (PG 49.159).

Augustine, Ambrose, and Jerome, grappled with the problems of harmonizing orthodox doctrine with the way Christians led their lives.[9] Augustine, concerned with the strong grip that bad habits held upon his congregation, blamed the presence of these imperfections among Christians on a decline in behavior that occurred after mass conversions.[10] While these people were no longer worshiping pagan gods, many of their daily activities still bore the mark of the old religion, undetected by the practitioners themselves but unmistakable to the bishop. Chrysostom perceived the same problem in Antioch, spotting inconsistencies in worship unnoticed by the average Christian, particularly those related to the prominence of a large Jewish community in his city. In the end, though, the Church Fathers were not wrong to be preoccupied by these daily activities of ordinary people, for the Christianization of society that took place throughout the Roman world during Late Antiquity consisted of countless small changes. The conversion of everyday life by everyday people contributed greatly to the permanence of this larger transformation.[11]

HABITS AND *HABITUS*

Pagan authors had developed ideas about habits forming the backbone of society's morality and had written their own treatises on raising children, teaching students, and influencing rulers. As we have seen in the first chapter, some advocated the promotion of better habits and better morality among the masses instead of focusing solely on intellectuals and princes. From the fourth to sixth centuries, church leaders from Chrysostom to Caesarius of Arles made a concerted effort to reform, or sometimes form, Christian mores and behaviors. Much of their labor was spent meddling with the habits of ordinary people – their choice of entertainment, manner of doing business, the way they dressed or ate their food, and their celebrations. The scale of this interference in daily life and the church leaders' motivation for it marks a change in the history of the belief that habits are central to morality, and makes it worth looking at in the context of the Christianization of society in Late Antiquity.

[9] P. Brown, "Christianization and Religious Conflict" in *CAH*, vol. xiii (1998) 661–3; R. Markus, *The End of Ancient Christianity* (Cambridge, 1990) 107–23.

[10] P. Brown, *The Cult of the Saints: Its Rise and Function in Latin Christianity* (Chicago, 1981) 29.

[11] On local resistance to and adaptation of Christian precepts, see W. Klingshirn, *Caesarius of Arles: The Making of a Christian Community in Late Antique Gaul* (Cambridge, 1994), esp. 1–5; P. Brown, *The Rise of Western Christendom: Triumph and Diversity AD 200–1000*, 2nd edn. (Oxford, 2002) 72–92. Averil Cameron favors the changes in the "habits of the heart" over economic or institutional explanations of the rise of Christianity, in *Christianity and the Rhetoric of Empire: The Development of Christian Discourse* (Berkeley, 1991) 28.

The sociologist Pierre Bourdieu has focused scholarly attention on the importance of specific customs and everyday actions with his concept of *habitus*. His work emphasizes cultural communication formed by the particular tastes in consumption, associations, and habits that are critical aspects of what defines and reinforces one's social status. Although the details of Bourdieu's sociological research on French society of the 1960s and 1970s obviously cannot be matched in any pre-modern society, the weight that he gives to the activities of everyday life is useful to draw on in this context. In Chrysostom's sermons, we are given a glimpse of some of his contemporaries' customs, as well as the preacher's plan for a broad transformation of everyday life. Chrysostom also perceived the minutiae of everyday life as the key to defining a distinct category of people. He envisioned a "*homo Christianus,*" whose disposition (*habitus*) would be the result of a Christian environment of mutually reinforcing beliefs and practice. As we will see, he hoped that this would result in Christian choices in clothes, eating habits, entertainment, family life, etc. Chrysostom's goal was not social change (or control) as an end in itself, but to encourage a lifestyle conducive to collective salvation, which would include his own. With the knowledge of sins and virtues automatic, embedded in their *habitus*, people would reflexively withdraw from sin and temptation. In other words, the Christian ethos had to become common sense if it was going to work for ordinary people.

Bourdieu's *habitus* provides a middle way in sociological theory between "determinism and freedom, conditioning and creativity, consciousness and the unconscious, or the individual and society."[12] In Bourdieu's view, cultural tendencies and habits are not forced on people, yet they do not develop independently of their particular social environment. The *habitus* is the core of ideas that underlies the choices and attitudes of common-sense behaviors, which in turn reinforce social and economic status. In the model that Bourdieu used to analyze French society, the nexus of economic and cultural capital determines one's *habitus*. The combination of one's wealth and level of education would limit one's "choice" of hobbies, material possessions, entertainment, etc.[13] Applying this model to Late Antiquity, however, reveals the limitations of focusing exclusively on these two factors. In this context, religious identity would, perhaps, be an additional determinant. Or, at least, church authorities attempted to make it so. Chrysostom hoped to eclipse distinctions of class or culture, by making religious identity the primary marker of difference in society.[14]

---

[12] P. Bourdieu, *The Logic of Practice*, R. Nice, trans. (Stanford, CA, 1990) 55.

[13] P. Bourdieu, *Distinction: A Social Critique of the Judgment of Taste* (Cambridge, MA, 1984).

[14] He observed that upper-class people associated with non-Christians of their own social class rather than with lower-class Christians, and urged them to change this, *Hom. in Mt.* 59.5 (PG 58.581).

The prevailing *habitus* in fourth-century Antioch, however, was weighed down with the traditions of Hellenistic cities, the Roman Empire, and the old religion. And, as in Bourdieu's model, these dispositions were tenacious, even when the world that they developed in response to was fading.[15] Chrysostom reacted to the situation by demanding that people think consciously about things that they normally would not question – their patterns of thought, their food, their clothes, their speech, their laughter. Everyone would have a Christian response to any situation, he believed, if their religious disposition structured all of their thoughts and actions. In a few generations, with people raised with these tendencies from childhood, the Christian life could be effortless. In the end, though, it is clear that he and other Christian authorities of this time had limited success in reorienting the tastes and attitudes of the mass of Christians.

BAD HABITS

On the topic of habits and customs, Chrysostom spoke most often about the bad ones, explaining the sinful nature of practices that, to the laity, seemed desirable or even necessary to their daily routines. In many instances, Christians did not realize that certain actions could be considered sinful and were reluctant to believe their preacher when he explained why. It is not difficult to understand their doubt, since Chrysostom scrutinized every aspect of life through the lens of Christianity, from naming children to weeping at funerals. The preacher urged his listeners to identify and avoid not only sins, but also the thoughts and deeds which seemed insignificant but led to major sins.[16] Such dangers lurked everywhere: business transactions, birthday parties, the theater and other spectacles, dice-playing, jewelry, cosmetics, money lending, investments, conversations with friends, songs, hairstyles, clothing, and eating habits.[17] It is possible that the preacher depicted his listeners as ignorant of proper behavior in order to avoid admitting that they were actively disobeying him, but it is even more likely that many people were indeed confused or simply disagreed with their preacher's distinctions between correct and incorrect behavior. The fact that many of these customs were just then being denounced would have added to the

---

[15] Bourdieu, *The Logic of Practice*, 56 and 60–2.   [16] Chrysostom, *De stat.* 15.4 (PG 49.159).
[17] Various daily activities are condemned throughout Chrysostom's many sermons. A concentration of such admonitions can be found in his sermon *On the Kalends* (PG 48.953–62). Rabbinic literature also expresses concern about the temptations inherent in city life, especially those related to greed and luxury, see Z. Safrai, *The Economy of Roman Palestine* (London, 1994) 312–13.

laity's confusion and/or resistance because they had been acceptable for generations in the Christian community.

The problem of oath-swearing illustrates the dissonance between the preacher's moralizing and the audience's common sense. Chrysostom repeatedly informed his congregation that swearing oaths was a sin.[18] Not only did they often lead to perjury, oaths were disrespectful to God's name and the Scriptures. Nevertheless, since oaths were entrenched in the daily economic and social interaction among the people of the city, Chrysostom believed that most people would not suspect that this was a sin unless church authorities explained it to them. Apparently, all parts of society were susceptible to this problem: the preacher encouraged the men in his congregation to punish their wives and slaves who swore oaths by sending them to bed without their suppers.[19] Also, during a festival, when many country people were present who did not often attend church, Chrysostom took the opportunity to work in exhortations against oaths because he did not want the farmers to return home without this knowledge.[20] But this practice was so fundamental to the lives of the laity that even the people who frequently heard his sermons were unable or unwilling to quit.

People swore oaths in a range of situations: to make guarantees in business contracts, to promise a personal favor, or to force others to change their behavior. Swearing was a sin that workmen and artisans were in particular danger of falling into: according to the preacher, they could spoil the value of their honest labor by using oaths in the course of business.[21] Not only did Christians swear oaths in business transactions, some even used the communion table and the Gospels to make the bond stronger.[22] Even more disturbing for the preacher was the sight of a man forcing a woman into a synagogue to swear an oath regarding business matters. When questioned, the man explained that oaths sworn in synagogues were considered to be stronger. The preacher rescued the woman and took the opportunity to lecture the man on the sinfulness of both oaths and Judaizing.[23]

---

[18] Cf. the prohibitions of oaths in *Const. apost.* 5.11.1–12.5 (SC 329.242–6), 6.23.4 (SC 329.370), 7.3.4 (SC 336.32).

[19] *De stat.* 5.7 (PG 49.79).   [20] *De Anna* 1.1 (PG 54.631–2).   [21] *Hom. in Mt.* 61.2 (PG 58.591).

[22] *De stat.* 15.5 (PG 49.160). This passage also provides an interesting view into the average Christian's attitude toward and use of the church building. Chrysostom told his congregation that this sin was worse than the murder of Abel, worse than killing Christ.

[23] *Adv. Jud.* 1.3 (PG 48.847–8). Chrysostom told this anecdote in the context of trying to convince his listeners not to have such respect for Jewish holy places. Other evidence attests to healing in synagogues, but Chrysostom is the only source that attributes magical activities to them. See S. Fine, *This Holy Place: On the Sanctity of the Synagogue during the Greco-Roman Period* (South Bend, IN, 1997) 224–5.

In the case of oaths, Chrysostom's efforts had some success. After a number of consecutive sermons dealing with the issue, some members of the congregation reported that they had changed their ways and were attempting to enforce the preacher's rules on their brethren.[24] This triumph, however, was not complete. Later in the same series of sermons, he continued trying to convince his listeners that oath-swearing was a serious sin, telling them to envision the disembodied head of John the Baptist and the blood dripping from it and to keep the image with them all day, imagining that the gory head was crying out "hate my murderer, the oath!"[25]

Apparently, there was a range of opinions among the laity. On one occasion, the preacher worried that dwelling on this topic would bore the ones who understood the sinful nature of oath-swearing, while others conceded that it was a sin, but a small one.[26] Those who acknowledged that oaths could be sinful still argued that the custom was too entrenched in their lives to be stopped.[27] In a sermon on the Gospel of Matthew 5:33–4, Chrysostom read out the verse: "Again, you have heard that it was said to those of ancient times, 'you shall not swear falsely, but carry out the vows you have made to the Lord.' But I say to you, do not swear at all." Despite such unambiguous instructions, Christians agreed that perjury was a sin, but not all were convinced about oaths themselves.[28]

The context of these passages clearly indicates that the people had heard the preacher's view – for that matter, even Jesus' view – but still held onto their own interpretation: oaths simply did not seem sinful. The Antiochenes were not alone in their view of this matter: not all church leaders condemned the use of oaths. Theodoret narrates three separate saints' lives in which Syrian ascetics swear oaths without being corrected.[29] Augustine taught that oaths were not sinful in and of themselves, but that the casual use of them became a habit, which often led to the sin of perjury.[30]

---

[24] *De stat.* 9.1 (PG 49.103).
[25] *De stat.* 14.1 (PG 49.144). For a chart laying out the chronology of this series of sermons, see F. van de Paverd, *St. John Chrysostom, the Homilies on the Statues: An Introduction.* (Rome, 1991) 363; on the issue of oath-swearing: 249–50.
[26] *Cateches.* 2.2 (SC 366.172–4).   [27] *De stat.* 6.6 (PG 49.90).   [28] *Hom. in Mt.* 17.5 (PG 57.261).
[29] Theodoret, *HR* 3.18 (SC 234.282), 15.5 and 24.8 (SC 257.22–4 and 150). Chrysostom also refers to a situation in which a slave being punished would adjure his master by Christ to stop. Explaining how people should react to being adjured to do something by Christ's name, he tells a story of a slave-girl who adjured a woman by Christ to help her, and the woman helped her because of her fear of God. Similarly, when beggars adjure people by Christ, they should give money to them. Chrysostom treats this sort of oath differently than the others, perhaps because they bind people to perform good works they should have been doing anyway, *Hom. in I Thess.* 11.3 (PG 62.464–5).
[30] See K. Uhalde, "The Expectation of Justice, AD 400–700," Ph.D. dissertation, Princeton University (1999) 105–41.

Once an individual clearly understood that this practice was a sin, Chrysostom claimed that breaking the habit of oath-swearing was among the easiest transitions required for a Christian life. He suggested quitting oath-swearing as a good starting point for people hoping to improve their behavior.[31] The congregation countered that oaths were difficult to root out because they were habits deeply embedded in their daily activities outside church. Turning this argument to his own purposes, the preacher replied that, if the force of habit was so strong, then the laity should cultivate new, Christian habits, and their actions and beliefs would finally coincide. As an example of exactly how bad habits such as swearing could be changed, he referred to Demosthenes and his struggle against lisping and twitching, which he cured by giving speeches with his mouth filled with gravel.[32] Then, step by step, Chrysostom told his audience how to break their own habits: they should ask their slaves, wives, and friends to watch them and make sure they do not fall back into the old ways. If they kept at it for ten days, they would be able to break their bad habits. Chrysostom also insisted that the method would eventually work even if they fell back to old habits twenty times.[33] Elsewhere, he advised people to concentrate on stopping themselves from particular sins, and to sentence themselves to fasting when they failed.[34] In these discussions, it is clear that neither the preacher nor the congregation perceived habits such as oath-swearing as conscious actions or as matters of faith. The habits reflected only an ingrained routine and the correction required human repetition and practice, rather than spiritual inspiration. But for Chrysostom, this did not lessen the damage such sins could do to one's soul.

In addition to swearing oaths, numerous other aspects of daily life were problematic in Chrysostom's opinion. For example, local women put marks of mud on their children's foreheads, believing that the mark kept away the evil eye, witchcraft, and envy. He encouraged the women to stop using this technique because, first of all, their mud did not possess special powers. If mud could protect someone from evil, he argued, then the practice would not be confined to children or to foreheads: everyone would cover their entire bodies in it. Instead, they should put the sign of the cross on their children's foreheads: "From the beginning of their lives, protect them with spiritual armor and teach them to seal their foreheads with their hands. Also, before they are able to do this with their own hands, you should

---

[31] *Hom. in Mt.* 11.8 (PG 57.201).
[32] *Hom. in Mt.* 17.7 (PG 57.263) and *De stat.* 7.5 (PG 49.97). See Plutarch, *Demosthenes* 4, 6–7, and 11 for accounts of the orator's struggle to overcome his weaknesses.
[33] *Hom. in Mt.* 17.7 (PG 57.263–4).   [34] *Hom. in Mt.* 11.8 (PG 57.202).

imprint the cross upon them."[35] Aside from hinting at how new Christian customs would become second nature to future generations, Chrysostom's instruction is interesting because it acknowledges that people were correct in their fears of evil spirits, that they should still attempt to keep them away, and that a sign or a mark would work. The sign, however, should be overtly Christian.[36]

In the same sermon, the preacher also criticized the way in which people chose names for their children by lighting many lamps and naming each of them. They then chose the name of the longest-burning lamp for their child, as good luck for a long life. Again, Chrysostom had no sympathy for such a custom: he wanted the members of his congregation to name their children after saints.[37] The bells and amulets parents attached to their babies did not impress Chrysostom either. Here too, he prescribed the sign of the cross as the only protection a child would need.[38] Realizing that most people would not see this as crucial to their observance of Christianity, he responded, "If these things seem trivial to some, let them learn that they are the cause of great evils."[39] Eventually, some of the changes Chrysostom hoped for occurred. An eighth-century text of baptismal rites includes a prayer for infants to be said on the eighth day after birth. The child was then sealed on the forehead, chest, and mouth and given a name. In other cases, despite Christianization, earlier customs persisted with the pagan structures intact. In the Coptic Church, on the seventh day after the birth of a child, seven candles with seven names were used to determine the name of the child.[40]

It is unclear whether Chrysostom thought that these practices damaged the children's or the parents' souls. At any rate, he probably expected that if Christians were immersed in Christian customs from birth, future preachers would be able to concentrate upon theology and praise to God rather than

[35] *Hom. in I Cor.* 12.7 (PG 61.106).

[36] D. Kalleres emphasizes the prominence of beliefs in supernatural elements, particularly demons, in late antique orthodox Christianity, see "Exorcising the Devil to Silence Christ's Enemies: Ritualized Speech Practices in Late Antique Christianity," Ph.D. dissertation, Brown University (Providence, RI, 2002).

[37] For naming after the longest-burning light: *Hom. in I Cor.* 12.7 (PG 61.106); cf. *Hom. in Gen.* 21.3 (PG 53.179), where he advised parents to name their children for holy men, and not arbitrarily or for ancestors. Cf. *De Anna* 1.6 (PG 54.642) and *De inan.* 48.655–7 (SC 188.146).

[38] *Hom. in I Cor.* 12.7 (PG 61.106).   [39] Ibid.

[40] K. W. Stevenson discusses the baptismal rite found in Barberini Ms. 336, an eighth-century text that reflects even earlier practices, comparing it to Chrysostom's baptismal sermons and also later practices, "The Byzantine Liturgy of Baptism," *Studia Liturgica* 17 (1987) 176–90. On the Christian lamp-lighting, see G. Viaud, "Les rites du septième jour après la naissance dans la tradition copte," *Le Monde Copte* 2 (1977) 16–19. I thank Wendy Mayer for this last reference.

spending so much time on such simple and mundane matters. Ideally, he would be able to take basic knowledge of Christian behavior for granted and spend the time in church on more advanced teachings. Chrysostom lamented to his audience that their persistence in swearing prevented him from progressing in his explanations of the Scriptures:

> Look, this is the second year that I have been discussing this with you, dear ones, and I have not succeeded in explaining even one hundred lines of Scriptures to you . . . most of my exhortation is used up on ethical matters. But it did not have to be this way. Instead, you should have been taught diligence in behavior at home, among yourselves. But thoughts about and contemplation of the Scriptures, you should entrust to me.[41]

In this case, the congregation's ignorance of or resistance to the preacher's "diligence in behavior" affected the course of their instruction, and Chrysostom's own progress as an exegete. The laity's need for extensive explanation, repetition, and persuasion shaped Chrysostom's concerns and led him to slow down and focus upon behavior instead of theology.

Convincing the Christians of Antioch that even the smallest details of life were indeed matters of heaven or hell occupied a great deal of Chrysostom's attention. His important position in the community did not prevent him from concentrating on issues that many church authorities might have considered beneath them. In the forty-ninth sermon on the Gospel of Matthew, we find Chrysostom using all of his rhetorical power to fight the evils of decorated sandals. His passion about the importance of one's taste in shoes immediately calls to mind the modern concept of *habitus*, only in Chrysostom's view, one's choices in daily life are (or should be) the manifestations of religious identity rather than social status. There is no indication of a special event that would have provoked him to focus on shoes, although he also addressed this topic briefly in his sermon *On the Kalends*.[42] In this sermon, Chrysostom found his way to the subject at first with a metaphor about different types of artisans and how most crafts contributed something to society, with the exception of luxury trades, such as elaborate cooking and embroidery.[43]

Chrysostom promotes a very puritanical Christian aesthetic in this section, condemning paintings and decorations, and especially the gaudy shoes some of the sandal-makers were producing. Weaving was fine, but not

---

[41] *De stat.* 16.2 (PG 49.164).
[42] *On the Kalends* 5 (PG 48.960). See also *Const. apost.* 1.3.9 (SC 320.112), where luxurious sandals are forbidden as being unnecessary.
[43] *Hom. in Mt.* 49.4 (PG 58.500–1).

when it was too fancy, because shoes decorated so elaborately caused men to become irresponsible and effeminate.[44] The audience's reaction to this condemnation was evident in Chrysostom's defense of himself:

I know that to many I seem to be concerned with petty matters, meddling in other people's affairs. I shall not stop on account of this. For the cause of all evil is this: that these sins seem to be petty and because of this they are ignored. And you say, "What sin can be more worthless than this, of having a decorated and shining sandal fitted on one's foot, if it even seems right to call it a sin?"[45]

Either Chrysostom had heard his audience's opinions, or he merely expected that the average Christian considered fancy shoes to be a very negligible sin, or maybe not a sin at all. The preacher even expected the congregation to be angry at him for denouncing these shoes. He later explained that their refusal to acknowledge that wearing fancy shoes was immoral had forced him to expound upon the subject. The possession of such shoes was cruel, not only because unnecessary luxury was sinful, but also because they were wasting money that could have been given as alms to the poor.[46]

Meanwhile, apparently, the harangue did not go over very well. The preacher went on to condemn those who argued against him that wearing these shoes was not so wrong, and told the rest that they should be weeping, not laughing.[47] He closed by trying to persuade his listeners to understand the scope of sin, how, despite their views to the contrary, every little thing in life was relevant, and how even small habits could be great sins.[48] Although the small matters could lead to damnation, learning the details of the correct way to live could lead to greatness, Chrysostom explained, just as the rhetoricians and philosophers had to learn their letters carefully before they could use language for their great achievements.

CELEBRATING THE NEW YEAR

On the Kalends of January, Chrysostom faced a congregation at risk of being completely overwhelmed by the tyranny of ancient custom. In his sermon, *On the Kalends*, Chrysostom attempted to explain to his listeners why they should not participate in the New Year's celebrations. In Antioch, people decorated the marketplace, their workshops, and their own bodies, competing with each other for the best display. They lighted

---

[44] *Hom. in Mt.* 49.4–5 (PG 58.501–3). On proper Christian footwear, see also Clement of Alexandria, *Paedagogus* 2.11 (SC 108.220–2).

[45] *Hom. in Mt.* 49.5 (PG 58.501).   [46] *Hom. in Mt.* 49.5 (PG 58.502).

[47] *Hom. in Mt.* 49.6 (PG 58.503).   [48] *Hom. in Mt.* 49.6 (PG 58.503–4).

lamps outside and decorated the doors of their houses. At dawn, both men and women filled their libation bowls and wine cups in order to drink unmixed wine. The traditional festivities also included night choruses, gift exchanges, and the careful observation of omens to learn the luck of the New Year.[49]

While systematically condemning all of these practices, Chrysostom suggested substitutions. Christians should decorate their souls and minds rather than their workshops and the marketplace. They would still receive gifts – spiritual ones from God and honors from the angels. The preacher instructed his audience to replace strong drinks with prayer and wine with Scriptures: "Wine creates a storm, the *logos* calm."[50] If Christians were hoping to be in a good mood for the New Year, then they would achieve this state not with drinking parties, but through the words of Christian philosophy and by ignoring rather than embracing worldly matters of wealth, power, and honor.

Aside from the impious celebrations, the entire premise of the event was problematic to Chrysostom: a particular day simply should not be special for a non-Christian reason. As we have seen, even Christian reasons to favor one day over another were looked at with suspicion. Traditionally, the omens of this day would determine the luck for the entire year, but Chrysostom insisted that Christians should neither observe omens nor give such importance to any single day. Again, he provided an alternative for the custom: "Let the entire year be a good omen to you, not if you get drunk on the first of the month, but if on the first of the month and on each day you do the things that seem good to God."[51] Good or bad luck was not the result of a day's place in the calendar, but of one's actions on that day. Simply put, chance played no role: nothing led to evil but sin; nothing to goodness but virtue. Chrysostom told his potential augurers:

---

[49] *In Kalend.* (PG 48.953–62). For a detailed description of the festivities that took place during the Kalends of January in fourth-century Antioch, see M. W. Gleason, "Festive Satire: Julian's *Misopogon* and the New Year at Antioch," *JRS* 76 (1986) 106–19. See Libanius, *On the Kalends* (*Or.* 9) for a positive, pagan perspective on the holiday; text and translation by J. Martin in Libanius, *Discours*, vol. II: *Discours II–X*, J. Martin, ed. and trans. (Paris, 1988). The holiday also troubled Augustine, who gave a long sermon in the early 400s on the Kalends of January that kept his listeners away from the festivities, *Vingt-six sermons au peuple d'Afrique*, F. Dolbeau, ed. (Paris, 1996) 345–417. Caesarius of Arles condemned the singing, dancing, banquets, gift exchanges, and games in Sermons 192 and 193, see Klingshirn, *Caesarius of Arles*, 216–18. Asterius of Amaseia preached a sermon against the Kalends in 400 AD, in which he also describes the festival's customs in detail: *Hom.* 4 in Asterius of Amasea, *Homilies I–XIV. Text, Introduction and Notes*, C. Datema, ed. (Leiden, 1970). On the celebration of the Kalends in the Roman Empire, see M. Meslin, *La fête des Kalends de janvier dans l'empire romain: étude d'un rituel de Nouvel An* (Brussels, 1970).
[50] *In Kalend.* 2 (PG 48.955).   [51] Ibid.

If you philosophize on these [Christian] things and are thus disposed, you will have the entire year with good omens, by making prayers and giving alms each day. But if you neglect your own virtue, and you entrust the good cheer of your soul to the beginnings of months and the numbers of days, you will be deprived of all good things.[52]

Chrysostom was well aware, however, that he could not prevent people from marking the Kalends of January as special. For one thing, church authorities could not change the fact that it was the day when the newly elected political officials began their terms.[53] Since people were going to observe the Kalends regardless of their association with paganism, Chrysostom offered a compromise. Christians should celebrate the Kalends by giving thanks to God, by weighing their sins against their good works, and by meditating on the passage of time as it related to their Christian beliefs. Chrysostom expressed this advice quite eloquently:

When you see the year coming to completion, give thanks to the Lord that he brought you to this cycle of years. Put your heart to rest, count up the time of your life, say to yourself: "The days move quickly and pass by, the years come to an end, we have already traversed much of the road – but what noble thing have we done?" We will not go from here empty and lacking all righteousness. The judgment is at the doors. Life presses on and on toward our old age.[54]

Ideally, Christians would contemplate their deeds in this manner without any special occasion to prompt them. Chrysostom was sensible enough to realize that introspection once a year was better than nothing. From the traditions of a persistent pagan celebration, he singled out the impulse to become preoccupied with the passing of time. Instead of looking for omens, Christians were to concentrate on their mortality and on Judgment Day. In this manner, the different conceptions of time stemming from pagan and Christian beliefs could be reconciled to some degree and an old habit of thinking could help support the new one.[55]

Chrysostom's congregation was reluctant to believe that their traditional New Year's celebrations were incompatible with their Christian faith. In response, Chrysostom explained in detail that every action and every thought, no matter how inconsequential it seemed, should be done for the glory of God, that is, in a Christian way. This is the heart of his views of habit and the ideal Christian life, which must have seemed so simple to

[52] Ibid. Cf. Klingshirn, *Caesarius of Arles*, 215–35.
[53] See Meslin, *La fête des Kalends*, 23–35 for the civic celebrations.   [54] *In Kalend.* 3 (PG 48.956).
[55] For a discussion of pagan and Christian ways of perceiving time, see Meslin, *La fête des Kalends*, 7–18; Markus, *End of Ancient Christianity*, 85–135.

the ascetically trained preacher. He began with the question, how could it be possible to do everything for the glory of God? Regarding eating and drinking, the preacher recommended that they should summon the poor to their houses and offer communal meals. Staying at home all day could also be done for the glory of God, especially on the Kalends: "Whenever you hear a commotion, disorder, and diabolical parades, the marketplace filled with wretched people and excess, stay home and escape the tumult."[56] In their relationships with other people, it was possible for Christians both to praise others and to censure them for the glory of God. Chrysostom told his listeners to choose their friends, as well as their enemies, according to the glory of God, and even how to have conversations with these people:

If you are sitting next to someone, don't speak of any earthly business, about anything simple or at random, and not about anything unfit for us, but about our philosophy, about the King of heaven, but not about unnecessary or mindless things such as "who is going to be the new archon?" . . . "How did that man get so wealthy?"[57]

As another example of how seemingly insignificant actions could be adjusted for the glory of God, Chrysostom discussed personal grooming and posture. Christians should not examine their hair or decorate their faces, but remain in their natural state. By not taking part in forbidden activities and by not looking at members of the opposite sex, they would be acting piously. As we have already seen, both men and women could also demonstrate Christian precepts with their shoes, by not decorating them. If a man chose a wife based on her virtue, rather than the reputation or wealth of her family, he would be making a choice according to the glory of God. One should not speak, he added, even in one's working life, if the words did not glorify God. The preacher deflected potential job-related protests by referring to examples in the Scriptures: Paul's jailers and Phineas. If jailers and murderers could act in God's interests, then any occupation could be held with a view to God's glory.[58]

WEDDINGS AND FUNERALS

In addition to the Kalends of January, the Antiochenes refused to abandon their traditional celebrations of weddings and funerals. The line that divided customs which were compatible with a Christian life from the incompatible

---

[56] *In Kalend.* 3 (PG 48.957).   [57] *In Kalend.* 4 (PG 48.959).
[58] Ibid. For an earlier treatise on the religious relevance of daily activities, see Clement of Alexandria's *Paedagogus*, especially books 2 and 33 (SC 108 and 158).

ones was seldom clear. The fact that pagans celebrated certain events, such as weddings and funerals, did not necessarily require that the ceremony be condemned. But, on the other hand, many practices that had been observed for generations within Christian communities were condemned as pagan or simply immoral during this period.

In his preaching against traditional wedding ceremonies, Chrysostom faced the task of condemning many of the customs without speaking badly about the occasion itself. He tried to explain why many elements of marriage ceremonies should be discontinued: "Marriage is considered to be an honorable thing both by us and by outsiders: and it *is* honorable. But when marriages are solemnized, such absurd things happen . . ."[59] Chrysostom decided that his listeners needed a fresh look at these cherished traditions because most people, he assumed, were "bound and misled by custom" and were unable to see what was wrong.[60] Dancing, cymbal and flute music, traditional songs, drinking, and a bride made up with a painted face and colored eyebrows on the occasion of a wedding seemed perfectly acceptable to most Christians. Chrysostom understood this, but carried on, knowing that his condemnation of wedding ceremonies would seem ridiculous. He knew he had reached the limits of his authority over people's lives and tried to appear humble in his hope of change in these matters. He claimed only to expect that a few would join him to be laughed at by the rest.[61]

Chrysostom attacked the wedding ceremony for its inconsistency with all other rules of decorum: the benefit of a lifetime of feminine modesty and isolation could be undone in one day's festivities. The laity's logic of breaking everyday rules for a special occasion fell flat on Chrysostom's ears. He responded: "Do not speak to me of the custom, for if it is worthless, do not let it happen once. But if it is good, let it always happen."[62] Chrysostom described the ceremony from his perspective: to the sound of obscene songs, the garishly made-up bride paraded through the market place by torchlight, watched by many men.[63] A customary law required people to insult the bride, which became a competition. Chrysostom asked his listeners to stop and think rationally: why should they enjoy being abused in public? If they

---

[59] *Hom. in I Cor.* 12.5 (PG 61.103). Cf. *Hom. in Gen.* 48.6 (PG 54.443).
[60] *Hom. in I Cor.* 12.5 (PG 61.103). See A. Natali, "Les survivances païennes dans le rituel des mariages chrétiens à Antioche au IVe siècle d'après Jean Chrysostome: essai d'interprétation" in *Sociabilité, pouvoirs et société*, F. Thelamon, ed. (Rouen, 1987) 111–16.
[61] *Hom. in I Cor.* 12.5 (PG 61.103). [62] Ibid.
[63] On traditional Roman wedding ceremonies, see S. Treggiari, "Roman Marriage" in *Civilization of the Ancient Mediterranean*, vol. III, M. Grant and R. Kitzinger, eds. (New York, 1988) 1349–50 and *Roman Marriage: Iusti Coniuges from the Time of Cicero to the Time of Ulpian* (Oxford, 1991), esp. 161–70.

could only remove themselves from their attachment to tradition for its own sake, they would understand that these practices made no sense and that marriage required a solemn ceremony.[64]

Chrysostom also asked them to think of the effect of the festivities on the entire community; the light of the torches and loud music made the spectacle impossible to escape, and so everyone in the neighborhood was forced to observe and therefore be damaged by it. He was particularly concerned with the dancing: young women dancing in the street were a terrible sight, even if they were slaves. In another sermon, inspired by the story of Salome's dance, he condemned dancing in general, but particularly at weddings: the women for performing and the men for watching them. Dancing was a misuse of one's feet: "For where there is dancing, the devil is also there. For God did not give us feet for this purpose, but for us to walk with discipline: not for us to disgrace ourselves, not for us to leap like camels."[65] While Chrysostom could envision Christian versions of other traditional ways of celebrating, such as instrumental music and singing, wedding dances clearly were beyond the scope of tolerance or any sort of adaptation.

Funerals were another occasion for conflict.[66] Here, as with the Kalends celebration, Chrysostom condemned both the traditional practices and the premise for them. The funeral dinner was an acceptable practice because there was a "human law" that required it.[67] This attitude can also be seen in the discussion of funerary banquets in the *Apostolic Constitutions*, which were assembled during this period in Northern Syria. The compilers of this document treated the funeral dinner as an acceptable custom so long as the participants did not overeat or become drunk.[68] But any funerary observation beyond the dinner, according to Chrysostom, implied a non-Christian fear of death.

---

[64] By the ninth century in the Byzantine Empire, marriage required a priest's benediction. In the West, marriage never lost its fundamental connection with civil law. See P. L. Reynolds, *Marriage in the Western Church: The Christianization of Marriage during the Patristic and Early Medieval Periods* (Leiden, 1994).

[65] *Hom. in Mt.* 48.3 (PG 58.491).

[66] For an in-depth study of John Chrysostom's views on death, see F.-X. Druit, *Langage, images et visages de la mort chez Jean Chrysostome* (Namur, 1990). On Greek Church Fathers' condemnations of traditional funeral rituals, see M. Alexiou, *The Ritual Lament in Greek Tradition* (Cambridge, 1994) 24–35. See also F. Paxton, *Christianizing Death: The Creation of a Ritual Process in Early Medieval Europe* (Ithaca, NY, 1990) 19–46, and E. Rebillard, *In hora mortis: évolution de la pastorale chrétienne de la mort aux IVe et Ve siècles dans l'Occident latin* (Rome, 1994).

[67] *Hom. in I Cor.* 28.3 (PG 61.235). It is unclear what he means by "human law" since all customs could be considered such. See Brown, *Cult of the Saints*, 24, where he cites a sixth-century Egyptian epitaph referring to funerals as a "human law."

[68] *Const. apost.* 8.44.1–3 (SC 336.260–2).

The attack on funeral customs focused on excessive mourning. The preacher viewed an emotional display of grief as a pagan tendency and an implicit denial of the truth of the Resurrection. After the coming of Christianity, true believers had no reason to be upset by death. Instead, living sinners were to be mourned, because although worms were not yet eating their bodies, their passions were shredding their souls to pieces.[69] After the death of a loved one, men should not beat themselves or invite pagan women to sing dirges at funerals. The practice of inviting poor people and priests to pray in order to help the souls of the dead was, in Chrysostom's view, consistent with Christian teachings about death, so long as this was done with the proper acknowledgment that sin was the problem, not death.[70]

Chrysostom encouraged his congregation to try to impress their pagan neighbors by not mourning over death.[71] The stark difference between the behavior of Christians and pagans would emphasize Christianity's superiority, if only the flock would behave in ways consistent with their faith. Unfortunately, Christian women, according to Chrysostom, grieved even more than the unbelievers. They claimed that they were blinded by passion and wished to avoid offending non-Christians.[72] Such actions, especially their tears, were unavoidable: they could not imagine any other possible reaction, because they believed their mourning was natural. A confused layperson defended his grief with the simple point: "And what can I do? Such a thing is nature.'"[73] But to Chrysostom, grief was not due to human nature, but to old customs and the weakness of an individual's Christian faith. Like celebrating the Kalends, insisting upon grieving for the dead reflected non-Christian logic of how the world worked, and so people were told to leave behind these habits of thinking and feeling.[74] Again, Chrysostom tried to divert his congregation's tendencies into better practices. In this case, he encouraged his listeners to mourn for sinners rather than for the dead. Obvious and simple in the mind of the preacher, this substitution was

---

[69] Worms and beasts: *Hom. in Mt.* 27.3–4 (PG 57.347–50); *Hom. in Gen.* 45.2 (PG 54.416). After the riot of 387, Chrysostom comforted the Antiochenes about their fears of death by telling them that they should only fear sin: *De stat.* 5.2–6 (PG 49.70–8), 6.3 (PG 49.85), and 7.1 (PG 49.91).

[70] *Hom. in Mt.* 31.4 (PG 57.374–5).   [71] *Hom. in I Cor.* 3.5 (PG 61.28–9).

[72] *Hom. in I Cor.* 28.3 (PG 61.235–6). Here, Chrysostom acknowledged that many women grieved over lost children. On Chrysostom's descriptions of childbirth and early death of children, see B. Leyerle, "Appealing to Children," *JECS* 5.1 (1997) 243–70, esp. 246–9. See also D. O'Roark, "Parenthood in Late Antiquity: Evidence of John Chrysostom," *GRBS* 40 (1999) 53–81.

[73] *Hom. in Mt.* 31.4 (PG 57.375).

[74] Augustine's views on this matter softened over time. Eventually he conceded to his congregation that mourning was acceptable. See E. Rebillard, "Interaction between the Preacher and His Audience: The Case-Study of Augustine's Preaching on Death," *Studia Patristica* 31 (1997) 86–96.

most likely impossible, even laughable, for ordinary people. In Late Antiquity, Christian funerary epigraphy demonstrates active lay spirituality and concern for the dead.[75] Clearly, grief remained a part of Christian societies.

GOOD HABITS

Willpower and the force of habit were also involved in the adoption of specifically Christian customs. Again, Chrysostom viewed habit as a powerful force, though one that could be controlled by a considerable act of will. The application of the will was one of the keys to developing a Christian life: "For whenever you say, 'it is difficult for me to abstain from habit [swearing oaths],' for this same reason, you should make haste to abstain, confident that if you make another habit for yourself, one of not swearing, no future work will be necessary."[76] In other words, not swearing could become just as routine as swearing was. In response to people's claims of not having control over their habits, Chrysostom countered that they had already adopted a new custom: fasting at Lent. They fasted without hesitation because of the power of custom, which had, by that time, made the task easy. If someone tempted them with food forbidden during the fast, none of them would give in: "Through the habit in our conscience, we endure it all, suffering nobly."[77]

Chrysostom encouraged his flock to think about Christian self-restraint in general as a habit.[78] He told them to train themselves in this, with the help of their families, friends, and servants, just as he encouraged them to use such methods to get rid of bad habits, as discussed above. After telling his audience how to collect alms at home, Chrysostom described the role that habit formation played in the development of a Christian life:

If we establish ourselves in such a habit, afterwards we are pricked by our conscience if we ever abandon this law. Later, we will not even consider the matter to be oppressive, and little by little we will arrive at greater things, and by practicing contempt for wealth, and by pulling up the root of evils, we will live this life without fear and obtain the life to come.[79]

---

[75] On the importance of memorials for the dead, see Brown, "Christianization and Religious Conflict," 660–2. E. Rebillard demonstrates that there was little change in burial practices in the late Roman Empire, "Conversion and Burial in the Late Roman Empire," in *Conversion in Late Antiquity and the Early Middle Ages: Seeing and Believing*, K. Mills and A. Grafton, eds. (Rochester, NY, 2003) 61–83.

[76] *De stat.* 6.6 (PG 49.90).   [77] Ibid.   [78] *Hom. in Mt.* 11.8 (PG 57.202).

[79] *Hom. in I Cor.* 43.4 (PG 61.374). For the results of this attitude in the West, see P. Brown, "Pelagius and His Supporters: Aims and Environment," *JThS* 29 (1968) 93–114. The Pelagians believed that people could break their bad habits and become perfect on earth by following Christian rules of behavior.

Chrysostom argued that a virtuous life did not necessarily have to be a struggle. If people could make basic changes in their lives – if they were habitually virtuous – the ideal Christian life would be effortless.

In a surprisingly self-conscious passage, Chrysostom acknowledged that he tended to forbid all of the activities that people enjoyed. After condemning almost every detail of public spectacles and wedding parties, he admitted, "I know that I am a tiresome and annoying person – and hard to please – as though I were trimming some of the pleasure from life."[80] As a substitute for sinful entertainment, he encouraged his listeners to find pleasure in natural beauty, to go to the river and the gardens, to listen to grasshoppers, to go to the martyr shrines, and to enjoy their families. The preacher pointed out that they could learn a lot from the barbarians in this matter, since they were simple, family-oriented people without any customs of going to lewd spectacles.[81]

Chrysostom understood that associating new activities with already established daily routines would help embed them into people's lives. He instructed his congregation to include Christian practices at specific times outside the church services and festivals. For their mealtimes, he advised them to use a thanksgiving prayer of the monks in the nearby wilderness, and dictated it to his audience verse by verse.[82] Prayer was a good practice in itself, and could also help focus people's minds on avoiding habitual sins. In response to the laity's straightforward excuse for blasphemy – they claimed that they could not keep silent when suddenly distressed – he insisted that they could cry out in prayer instead. Although the bad words seemed to come out spontaneously, Chrysostom told his listeners to bite their tongues (literally) because they could choose whether they spoke evil or prayed.[83]

Singing (unlike dancing) could be beneficial and fully Christian, as long as the words came from the Scriptures. Traditional songs of farmers, wet-nurses, and women at their looms ranged from offensive to merely inconsequential. If, on the other hand, people accustomed themselves to singing psalms instead, they could infuse their working days with Christianity. Chrysostom also encouraged prayer while working, pointing out that repetitive motions did not prevent them from quietly worshiping in the meantime.[84]

---

[80] *Hom. in I Cor.* 12.6 (PG 61.104).

[81] *Hom. in Mt.* 37.7 (PG 57.427–8). Cf. P. Rousseau, *Basil of Caesarea* (Berkeley, 1994) 163. On the enjoyment of nature rather than spectacles or luxuries, see *Adv. oppug.* 2.5 (PG 47.338).

[82] *Hom. in Mt.* 55.5 (PG 58.545–7). For more on praying before and after eating: *De Anna* 2.5 (PG 54.650); *Ecloga de oratione* 2 (PG 63.584); *De Laz.* 1.9 (PG 48.974–5).

[83] *De Laz.* 3.7 (PG 48.1001).

[84] J. C. B. Petropoulos, "The Church Father as Social Informant: St John Chrysostom on Folk Songs," *Studia Patristica* 22 (1989) 159–64. Cf. Klingshirn, *Caesarius*, 184.

After attending church, the laity was advised not to hurry off to the agora, but to go home and contemplate the sermon they had just heard with their families, like children with their homework.[85] After work, they should write down their sins of the day. If they wrote down their sins, acknowledging them and asking for forgiveness, then God would erase them. Otherwise, God would inscribe the sins in His book and exact the penalty for them later on Judgment Day.[86] In addition to the regular contemplation of sins, singing psalms before and after eating was a good habit to adopt, even for people who did not understand the words.[87] In the evening, during the time between dinner and bedtime, instead of thinking about work, Christians should sit quietly alone and review their sins yet again, like judges sitting undisturbed behind a curtain.[88]

Trying to direct more attention to almsgiving, Chrysostom urged every-one to collect a small sum of money each day. He gave them precise instructions on how to do this: they should put a small chest near the place in their houses where they prayed. When they went to pray, they would deposit alms into the box first. In addition to helping the poor, the presence of this box of money would protect the house from demons and the sleepers from bad dreams. The preacher's advice – which proba-bly would have reminded people of a similar method of alms-collection among the Jews – took the fear of demons for granted, as well as prayer in homes, which was established enough to have space reserved for it.[89] Also, in this case, it is important to note that Chrysostom was attempt-ing to add a Christian habit of almsgiving to the already existing habit of praying.[90]

Another new and completely Christian activity was possible because of the proximity of the monastic communities. As we have seen, Chrysostom encouraged his people to visit the monks, in order to observe their pious way of life and receive prayers and instruction from them. The monks, he assured them, had moved to the mountains for the very reason of instruct-ing the townspeople on how to conduct their lives. The preacher even

[85] *Hom. in Mt.* 5.1 (PG 57.55).
[86] *Hom. in Mt.* 41.4 (PG 57.450). On the use of inscription imagery, see S. Elm, "Inscriptions and Conversions: Gregory of Nazianzus on Baptism (*Or.* 38–40)" in *Conversion in Late Antiquity and the Early Middle Ages: Seeing and Believing*, K. Mills and A. Grafton, eds. (Rochester, NY, 2003) 1–35.
[87] *Hom. in Psalmos* 41.1–2 (PG 55.156–8).
[88] *Hom. in Mt.* 42.4 (PG 57.455). Cf. Clement of Alexandria, *Stromateis* 7.7.49, where he recommends reading the Scriptures before meals and silent self-judging.
[89] *De eleem.* 3 (PG 51.265–6), and *Hom. in I Cor.* 43.4 (PG 61.372–3). In Jewish communities, alms were distributed to the poor from a money chest (*quppah*) kept in the synagogue, see G. Hamel, *Poverty and Charity in Roman Palestine, First Three Centuries CE* (Berkeley, 1989) 216–19.
[90] Another possible way to work almsgiving into one's routine was for Christians to invite the poor to their communal meals, *Hom. in Mt.* 48.7 (PG 58.495).

offered to guide a spiritual field trip out to where he had once lived as a monk.[91]

Some of these distinctively Christian activities were meant to substitute for sinful activities, while others were meant to reinforce lessons learned in church. Another function of Christian habits was to distinguish Christians from the rest of the population in Antioch. In these matters, it becomes clear that Chrysostom considered Christianity to be the most important aspect of a person's identity and that everyone should take care to reinforce and express this identity in every possible way.

NEW HABITS DEVELOPED BY LAY CHRISTIANS

While their preacher was telling them what to do and what not to do in order to be good Christians, the Antiochene laypeople did not lack initiative: they had their own Christian customs. Many of these customs were slightly misguided, from Chrysostom's point of view, since they reflected a different view of the hierarchy of sins and, in particular, a deep concern for physical purity. But the preacher did not condemn any of their practices *because* they came from the congregation. We know about these customs not from exhortations against them, but from Chrysostom's passing references to them or his suggestions of ways in which certain religious practices could be made more effective. In contrast to the preacher's frequent exclamations that his congregation was not actively "Christian" enough, these practices indicate that the laity was already quite Christianized.

Some of the Antiochenes displayed their respect for the Scriptures by incorporating them into their daily lives outside the church. When describing the phylacteries and borders on the clothing of the Jews in the Scriptures, Chrysostom compared the phylacteries to the Gospels that many of the women in the congregation were wearing around their necks.[92] Material evidence also testifies to this practice. Miniature parchment and papyrus codices survive, ranging in size from ten by fifteen centimeters down to five by six-and-a-half centimeters.[93] Smaller Christian papyri amulets also survive, inscribed mainly with psalm verses or the Lord's Prayer. This use of the Scriptures was popular but not universally approved of: the Council of

---

[91] *Hom. in Mt.* 72.4 (PG 58.672). For a description of Chrysostom's time as a monk, see Palladius, *Dial.* 5 (SC 341.108–10) and J. N. D. Kelly, *Golden Mouth: The Story of John Chrysostom – Ascetic, Preacher, Bishop* (Ithaca, NY, 1995) 24–35; A. Sterk, *Renouncing the World Yet Leading the Church: The Monk-Bishop in Late Antiquity* (Cambridge, MA, 2004) 141–62.

[92] *Hom. in Mt.* 72.2 (PG 58.669).

[93] The majority of these little codices are Christian apocryphal texts. See H. Y. Gamble, *Books and Readers in the Early Church: A History of Early Christian Texts* (New Haven, 1995) 235–6.

Laodicaea in 360 prohibited clergy from using such amulets.[94] Bits of the Scriptures were also hung above the beds of some Christians, in order to keep away evil spirits that brought bad dreams. Chrysostom told them that they would continue having nightmares unless they also kept an alms box in the room.[95] In such cases, believers observed Christian customs that were not specifically required or even encouraged. Chrysostom was not alone in his acceptance of these customs. Augustine believed that sleeping with the Gospel of John under one's pillow would help cure headaches. Likewise, Theodoret, bishop of Cyrrhus, kept oil blessed by martyrs hanging by his bed.[96]

The Christian communal dinner bringing rich and poor together had led to associated activities. In this case, new developments of a Christian custom were problematic. Some of the wealthier Antiochenes were indeed opening their houses to the poor, but mainly in order to become even wealthier at their expense. The rich used the occasion as a chance to offer loans to their poorer brethren. Chrysostom, of course, condemned this as a perversion of what the gathering should be, and also condemned the usurers' likely defense, that they give alms to the poor after they earn interest on the loans.[97]

As mentioned earlier, some of the congregation stayed home when they broke the fast. According to the preacher, the people who stayed home from church misjudged what was sinful: by not coming to church after breaking the fast, they compounded their problem.[98] For him, the believers' bodily purity was less important than their ability and willingness to pay attention to sermons. Although it is possible that the absent ones used their failed fast as an excuse to stay home from church, this attitude fits a broader pattern of thinking. From Chrysostom's sermons, it becomes clear that the believers were concerned about being physically pure before participating in Christian worship, even though this was not officially required or encouraged.

Besides their concern with observing Lent, Chrysostom believed that his congregation worried too much about cleanliness. Even though they were

---

[94] Canon 36. See Gamble, *Books and Readers*, 237–41 on the magical uses of Christian texts. Gamble does not see a specific influence from Jewish phylacteries inspiring the Christian use of amulets. Apotropaic formulae were used widely in antiquity and Christians developed their own expression of a broader cultural disposition. Cf. P. van der Horst, "Sortes: Sacred Books as Instant Oracles in Late Antiquity" in *The Use of Sacred Books in the Ancient World*, L. V. Rutgers, P. W. van der Horst, H. W. Havelaar, and L. Teugels, eds. (Leuven, 1998) 143–73.
[95] *Hom. in I Cor.* 43.4 (PG 61.372–3). Cf. *Hom. in John* 32.3 (PG 59.187), where Chrysostom states that the devil would not approach a house that contained a gospel. See Brown, *The Body and Society*, 313.
[96] Augustine, *Tractates on the Gospel of John* 7; Theodoret, *HR* 21.16 (SC 257.96).
[97] *Hom. in Mt.* 56.5 (PG 58.556–7).   [98] *De stat.* 9.1 (PG 49.104) and 10.1 (PG 49.111).

told that physical substances such as food and dirt did not pollute their bodies, lay Christians took care to wash their hands before prayer. Likewise, they believed that they should not pray after having sex with their spouses, even though this was permitted.[99] The *Apostolic Constitutions* also testify to these beliefs and condemn them. The compiler emphasized that legitimate sexual relations, nocturnal emissions, and menstruation did not pollute Christians or preclude them from religious activities. Similarly, Chrysostom attempted to convince the laity that a misdeed such as insulting another person created more pollution than dirt or marital sex.[100]

Chrysostom was worried that the concern with purity stemmed from a tendency toward Jewish customs. After discussing Jesus' rejection of Jewish dietary laws and bathing, he looked at his own audience and noticed Christians continuing suspiciously similar practices: "For even in the church we see such a custom holding sway among the many, how people take care to come in clean garments and to wash their hands. But how they might present a clean soul to God, they make no account."[101] Some Antiochenes had adopted attitudes and traditions that connected physical cleanliness and holiness, whether from observing the Jews, from adapting their own ancestors' Jewish traditions, or from their own spiritual logic which led them to believe that they must be clean when in church.[102] This type of behavior was difficult for Chrysostom to forbid, since, of course, people had to bathe and their desire to show respect to holy places was not objectionable. Despite his hostility to the adoption of seemingly Jewish practices by members of his congregation, he did not forbid them to wash themselves before religious activities, but only asked that they consider washing themselves in virtues as well.[103] All the preacher could do about the practice of ritual bathing was to set it in perspective. He asked people if they would dare to pray if they had dung on their hands. He assumed

[99] *Hom. in Mt.* 51.5 (PG 58.516). Cf. Caesarius of Arles, who instructed his congregation that abstinence *was* required before, Sermon 44.3 (SC 243.330–2).

[100] *Hom. in Mt.* 51.5 (PG 58.515–6); *Const. apost.* 6.27.1–3 (SC 329.378). On issues of purity, see D. Brakke, "The Problematization of Nocturnal Emissions in Early Christian Syria, Egypt and Gaul," *JECS* 3 (1995) 419–60.

[101] *Hom. in Mt.* 51.5 (PG 58.515–16).

[102] For interactions between Jews and Christians in Antioch and Chrysostom's attitude toward this, see R. Wilken, *John Chrysostom and the Jews: Rhetoric and Reality in the Late 4th Century* (Berkeley, 1983), and P. W. van der Horst, "Jews and Christians in Antioch at the End of the Fourth Century" in *Christian–Jewish Relations through the Centuries*, S. Porter and B. W. R. Pearson, eds. (Sheffield, 2000) 228–38; L. V. Rutgers' discussion of the Christianization of the Maccabean martyrs in "The Importance of Scripture in the Conflict between Jews and Christians: The Example of Antioch" in *The Use of Sacred Books in the Ancient World*, L. V. Rutgers, P. W. van der Horst, H. W. Havelaar, and L. Teugels, eds. (Leuven, 1998) 287–303.

[103] *Hom. in Mt.* 51.4 (PG 58.516).

that they would not, and asked them to think about the reasoning behind this. Why would anyone be reverential in ways that were inconsequential, such as bodily cleanliness, but negligent of sins?[104] These people, however, presumably believed that concern for purity expressed morality and was not a substitute for it.

Whether or not these practices stemmed from adherence to the habits of a different religion, it is significant that people adapted them to a Christian context – that is, actions such as hanging a passage of the Gospel above the bed or washing one's hands before prayer were not merely throwbacks to a non-Christian world, but an expression of belief in the power of the Christian religion and its symbols. Most importantly, these new customs indicate a community of laypeople thinking about their religion and incorporating it into their lives in ways that originated from their own experiences and logic, rather than solely from instructions from church authorities.

CONCLUSIONS

Chrysostom remarked that the adherents to different religions in Antioch were indistinguishable in the marketplace, on the streets, and in the theater. Christians were clearly separated from the rest only in church after the uninitiated were taken away so that the baptized could participate in the mysteries.[105] To the preacher's mind, this distinction ought to have been visible to everyone, always, in every aspect of the person: the clothing, the words, all of the daily activities. This vision of the Christian life required many practices to be reflexive, natural parts of each day. The new habits of thinking and acting that he tried to instill through his sermons would work together, Chrysostom hoped, eventually creating a truly Christian society.

In the cases of oath-swearers and the ones who stayed home from church because they broke their fast, some Christians did respond to their preacher's demands and change their behavior. But sermons also reveal instances when the laity rejected the preacher's program of Christianization. Most Christians apparently did not question the necessity of being baptized, receiving communion, or fasting during Lent, but they did argue back, require more explanation, or simply ignore proposed changes to some of their routine activities. In other words, people did not reject their preacher's demands because they were generally impious or unenthusiastic Christians. On the

---

[104] Ibid. Cf. *Hom. in Mt.* 37.6 (PG 57.426) where Chrysostom remarks that his listeners washed themselves after visiting a tomb, but not after attending the theater.
[105] *Hom. in Mt.* 4.7 (PG 57.48).

contrary, they even observed some aspects of their religion more carefully than Chrysostom advised. These values and customs rooted in the congregation reveal ordinary people who were engaged with their religion. Their tendency to reject certain teachings, which in turn inspired countless hours of preaching, can enhance our understanding of the religious mentality of lay Christians in Late Antiquity. The congregation sometimes accepted and sometimes rejected the demands of the preacher, and this determined how they would live their lives, how their preacher could progress with his teachings, and ultimately the manner of the Christianization of their society.

Conclusions

The chief difficulty of combining social with intellectual history is not the lack of ideas among regular people, but the lack of sources that survive to tell us about these ideas. Surely all communities have consisted of ordinary individuals with their own theories about cosmology and morality, but few have left written records of their thoughts. The ideal historical sources for social history almost never survive, at least not from pre-modern eras. We would like to have daily journals of late antique Christians who jotted down their responses to sermons, as well as statistical surveys allowing us to chart the demographics of the congregations and to poll their reactions. Given what we are left with, however, texts written by elites who came into contact with the general population are extremely valuable sources for learning about the world-views and experiences of ordinary people. The late fourth and fifth centuries – the Golden Age of Christian preaching – have left us with an abundance of such texts that provide insight into the changes of this period.

One of the most fascinating aspects of Late Antiquity is the prominence of theological debates. Public discussions and fights over such "intellectual" concerns point to the obvious fact that all people think about the nature of the world and the fate of their souls. In addition to theological controversies, quieter debates took place in Christian communities over the definition of orthodox behavior. We should not imagine this process as consisting entirely of preachers imposing their views upon uninformed congregations. In many instances, contact with lay Christians shaped the attitudes and expectations of Church Fathers. They responded to their congregations by attempting to reinforce what people knew and correct the ways in which they differed from official doctrines. In addition to affecting their leaders' agendas, laypeople also often simply rejected aspects of their teachings, as we have seen in the divergence between Chrysostom's high expectations and the real people he faced. The preacher's popularity gave him influence but not control over the laity's beliefs about their religious obligations. In the end, it is clear that both sides contributed to the emerging Christian common sense that would define what was acceptable and what was unacceptable in their communities.

When studying the transformation of social norms of this period, we need to avoid seeing everything from a Church Father's point of view, however much this perspective dominates our sources. In contrast to the standard narrative of Christianity's triumph in Late Antiquity, Christianization and "orthodoxification" were slow, uneven processes.[1] Regardless of the weight of later orthodox tradition on his side, it is necessary to remember that Chrysostom's views of Christianity were not necessarily dominant in his time and place. On the contrary, he had to use his powers of persuasion to try to gain supporters because he knew that various Christian world-views existed among the members of his own congregation. Church leaders attached the labels of heretical, pagan, or Judaizing to practices that diverged from official teachings. In order to establish their understanding of Christianity as the sole official doctrine, they attacked their rivals and critics. But we do not have to interpret divergent Christian views in the same negative light that the Church Fathers did. With this in mind, the study of sermons as dialogues between preachers and their audiences allows us to see ordinary Christians making an impact on the development of their religion, not just diluting it with their numbers, or degrading it with their negligence – the picture that is often the apparent conclusion to be drawn from a late antique Church Father's complaints.

In order to examine the Christianization and "orthodoxification" of ordinary people, this book has drawn on a range of topics related to the reception and impact of sermons, from the influence of the urban crowd on politics to the transformation of old philosophical traditions. When situated in the historical context of the late antique city, sermons illustrate the conflicts and compromises involved in the transmission of ideas. The interaction and the disagreements between Chrysostom and his listeners show how stark dichotomies between elites and masses, Christian and non-Christian, and orthodoxy and heresy are misleading. These groups were not as well defined or as isolated from each other as they sometimes appear; none of the categories worked as well in practice as

---

[1] See P. Brown, "Christianization and Religious Conflict" in *CAH*, vol. XIII (1998): 632–64, at 662–4; P. Garnsey and C. Humfress, *The Evolution of the Late Antique World* (Cambridge, 2001) 142–3 and 165; R. Lim, "Converting the Un-Christianizable: The Baptism of Stage Performers in Late Antiquity" in *Conversion in Late Antiquity and the Early Middle Ages: Seeing and Believing*, K. Mills and A. Grafton, eds. (Rochester, NY, 2003) 84–126, at 110.

in rhetorical pronouncements.² The interaction between preachers and their audiences allows us to look more closely at the problems with these categories, as recent work on social relations and Christianization shows.

ELITES, MASSES, AND THE DEMOCRATIZATION OF CULTURE

The nature of the relationship between the elites and masses is particularly important to the study of Late Antiquity because of the development of a common culture based on Christianity that, to some extent, transcended social class. As we have seen, the development of orthodox standards of behavior was in part the diffusion of older philosophical ideals, while the real innovation of Christian culture was the systematic attempt to spread these ideas to all levels of society. This transformation of culture can be interpreted in different ways. In a recent essay, Jean-Michel Carrié revives 'positive democratization' as an alternative to the "catastrophic democratization" proposed by Gibbon and others, for whom the contamination of elite culture by the uneducated masses explained many of the changes of the later Roman Empire.³ With "positive democratization," cultural change is seen as rooted in the increased communication between social groups spurred by Christianity, especially through sermons and hagiography. From this perspective, contact with and input from the lower classes is not a negative aspect of culture, but an expansion of the definition of "culture." Since church authorities addressed a range of social groups in a variety of ways, from complex theological arguments to simple parables, the continuum between "high" and "low" culture became more unified in Late Antiquity, with Christianity at its center.⁴ Linked to this idea of a continuum, the democratization of culture can also be viewed as both "descending" and "ascending," since upper-class ideas and values began to apply to the rest of society and vice versa. Preachers such as Chrysostom spoke about the poor as noble and elites as servile (in a spiritual sense). In this context, the

---

² For instance, see L. V. Rutgers' work emphasizing the interaction rather than isolation of Jewish communities in the Roman Empire, "Archaeological Evidence for the Interaction of Jews and Non-Jews in Late Antiquity," *AJA* 96.1 (1992) 101–18.

³ J.-M. Carrié, "Antiquité tardive et 'démocratisation de la culture': un paradigme à géométrie variable," *AntTard* 9 (2001) 27–46, at 30–3. This volume of articles reflects on Santo Mazzarino's work on "positive democratization" during the third century CE. Averil Cameron cautions against an overly simplistic conception of "democratization of culture." *Christianity and the Rhetoric of Empire: the Development of Christian Discourse* (Berkeley, 1991) 7–8.

⁴ Carrié, "Antiquité tardive," 45. On the new types of cultural production accessible to the masses, see also Cameron, *Christianity and the Rhetoric of Empire*, 187–8.

imagery and ideas emphasized by church leaders were not merely literary exercises, but were meant to transform the world-views and lives of the broader society.[5]

At the same time, many of the religious and intellectual developments in Late Antiquity were related to the democratization of theology. In contrast to the traditional cults, Christian communities expected everyone to share the same beliefs. One result of requiring ordinary people to grasp theological concepts and distinguish "correct" from "incorrect" beliefs was increased competition among religious groups for popular support.[6] When preachers promoted their views, people were not forced to agree, but chose to. A focus on elements of "positive," "ascending," and "descending" democratization can help identify the ways in which religious changes resulted from interaction between authorities and ordinary people. Studies of sermons as social communication fit into the broader project of understanding the Christianization of the Roman world as well as the relationship between the "elites and masses." An exchange of ideas between preachers and audiences is prominent in some of the sermon collections. But this type of information only becomes noticeable once a cultural chasm between the preachers and their audiences is no longer presupposed.[7]

CONVERSION AND CHRISTIANIZATION

The study of Christianization centers on the changes and continuity in the world-views and behavior of people during the late Roman Empire. Which beliefs and social norms were transformed, and which were merely adjusted or relabeled? This book has presented elements of both change and continuity, and focused on how the interactions between the elites and the masses affected the manner of Christianization. The study of this issue is complicated by the overlapping processes of conversion, Christianization, and "orthodoxification." The standard definition of "conversion," as an inner rejection of an old belief in favor of a new one, often does not

---

[5] J.-M. Salamito, "Christianisation et démocratisation de la culture: aspects aristocratiques et aspects populaires de l'être-chrétien aux IIIe et IVe siècles," *Ant Tard* 9 (2001) 165–78, at 174.

[6] Garnsey and Humfress, *Evolution of the Late Antique World*, 132–5, 151. On the reception by the masses of competing Christian doctrines, see M.-Y. Perrin, "A propos de la participation des fidèles aux controverses doctrinales dans l'Antiquité tardive: considérations introductives," *Ant Tard* 9 (2001) 179–99.

[7] Carrié, "Antiquité tardive," 46. On sermons as dialogues, see R. Van Dam, *Becoming Christian: The Conversion of Roman Cappadocia* (Philadelphia, 2003) 106–9. On the social and cultural connections that allow elite speakers to communicate with broader audiences, see S. Todd, "*Lady Chatterley's Lover* and the Attic Orators: The Social Composition of the Athenian Jury," *JHS* 110 (1990) 146–73.

fit what our sources describe. Many of the people who "converted" were nominal Christians already, while many of those who were accused of pagan, Jewish, or heretical practices probably considered themselves to be good Christians.[8] Even though this was the period of the emergence of orthodoxy, the power of the Church Fathers to impose their expectations on people was very limited: there was "no monolithic church able to dictate to its new members the exact terms of their faith."[9] When scholars distance themselves from the Church Fathers' point of view, the agenda of rigorous preachers is put into perspective as "hyper-Christianization," while the variations found in local Christian communities can be viewed more generously than before as "self-Christianization."[10]

In this context, the study of public spectacles has emerged as a particularly rewarding way to study the complex processes of Christianization from multiple perspectives.[11] Disagreement over the moral value of spectacles was not only a conflict between pagan and Christian culture, as preachers sometimes made it out to be, but it was also a conflict among Christians over the definition of acceptable behavior. Attitudes about public entertainment highlight the inadequacy of the bishops' power to implement their plans, illustrating how Christianization "involved the slow molding of attitudes and habits of life through pastoral care."[12] Studies of public entertainment also point to the ways in which the sermons and the rest of the liturgy competed with older forms of assembly and entertainment. Like the spectacles, the church became a place where different levels of society met. Gatherings in both the church and the theater display the same "intricate patterns forming of co-operation, interdependence and exploitation between the

---

[8] On conversion and baptism as ongoing, lifelong process: S. Elm, "Inscriptions and Conversions: Gregory of Nazianzus on Baptism (*Or.* 38–40)" in K. Mills and A. Grafton, *Conversion in Late Antiquity and the Early Middle Ages: Seeing and Believing* (Rochester, NY, 2003) 1–35. On efforts to convert nominal Christians, see Lim, "Converting the Un-Christianizable," 85.

[9] N. McLynn, "Seeing and Believing: Aspects of Conversion from Antoninus Pius to Louis the Pious" in K. Mills and A. Grafton, *Conversion in Late Antiquity and the Early Middle Ages: Seeing and Believing* (Rochester, NY, 2003) 224–70, at 224–5.

[10] On hyper-Christianization, see Brown, "Christianization and Religious Conflict," 655. For self-Christianization, see W. Klingshirn, *Caesarius of Arles: The Making of a Christian Community in Late Antique Gaul* (Cambridge, 1994) 2.

[11] Recent studies of religious and social implications of public spectacles include B. Leyerle, *Theatrical Shows and Ascetic Lives: John Chrysostom's Attack on Spiritual Marriage* (Berkeley, 2001); Lim, "Converting the Un-Christianizable"; J. Harries, "Favor Populi: Pagans, Christians and Public Entertainment in Late Antique Italy" in *Bread and Circuses: Euergetism and Municipal Patronage in Roman Italy*, K. Jones and T. Cornell, eds. (London, 2003) 125–41; A. Hartney, *John Chrysostom and the Transformation of the City* (London, 2004); D. Trout "Town, Countryside and Christianization at Paulinus' Nola" in *Shifting Frontiers in Late Antiquity*, R. Mathisen and H. Sivan, eds. (Aldershot, 1995) 175–86.

[12] Lim, "Converting the Un-Christianizable," 86.

rich and poor, the patron and the client."[13] This approach to the study of Christianization intersects with the study of elites and masses, especially when the focus is on the limitations of church leaders' authority.

In his sermons, Chrysostom expressed both his vision of an ideal Christian society and his frustrations when confronted with resistance from people with different conceptions of orthodoxy. His main purpose was not to convince anyone to accept Christianity – the people he spoke to were already inside his church. Instead, he was trying to convert Christians to his version of the faith. The concept of *habitus* helps us understand Chrysostom's notion of conversion: being a Christian did not only entail correct beliefs but a way of life based on a radical reorientation of common sense. But, as is clear in recent work cited above, the exact results of conversion could not be controlled by church authorities. The religious value of private, daily actions and feelings – the extent to which mealtimes became Christian, the extent to which Christian theology changed one's reaction to a loved one's death – these things would be determined by what was deemed acceptable by ordinary people.

Questions about the democratization of culture, conversion, and Christianization merge in the study of preachers and their audiences. Sermons allow us to learn about the world of non-elites and how they related to authorities by providing information about beliefs and behaviors that lay Christians considered to be acceptable as well as what they questioned. Various Christian leaders tried to prevent the appearance of social stratification within their churches, but elements of mundane relationships made their way into the church, not least in the popularity that a good speaker could gain. Chrysostom and many of his contemporaries used rhetorical skill in a traditional way, to reinforce their authority and prestige and to benefit from their followers' love of eloquence. But Chrysostom did not choose his topics and examples on the basis of rhetorical education alone, and the popularity won by eloquence was not an end in itself. His concerns were not disconnected from his congregation: his sermons addressed pressing issues of belief and behavior. He was trying to convince people to change their lives in countless ways. Furthermore, as is clear in the case of classical Greek oratory, when persuasion is necessary, the language and arguments are in part shaped by the listeners.[14] Even in contemporary politics, it would be difficult to say for certain whether a key issue originates among

---

[13] Harries, *"Favor Populi,"* 126–7.
[14] See J. Ober, *Mass and Elite in Democratic Athens: Rhetoric, Ideology and the Power of the People* (Princeton, 1989).

the people, or is something that political elites have chosen to be a popular concern. The diffusion of orthodox doctrine and behavior worked the same way through hagiography, liturgy, and sermons, and often the end result was not the same orthodoxy that its proponents had envisioned. Again, the democratization of theology and religious life was both ascending and descending.

Our sources and various strands of scholarship emphasize the importance of power and authority in the spread of Christianity, but much was out of the reach of authorities. Not all aspects of life would be Christianized. In Chrysostom's case, the fact that he had to concentrate so much on defending his ideas indicates that his world-view, although dominant in our sources, was not embraced wholeheartedly in its original context. The degree to which orthodox standards of behavior were embraced depended on their appeal to the masses and the ability of church authorities to persuade them to accept these standards. By looking closely at the church assembly as an encounter between an authoritative speaker and ordinary listeners, we can see that traditional urban culture helped both sides to communicate with each other and that the instructions promoting orthodoxy were contested. Ordinary people's inclinations affected the content and style of their preacher's sermons, and their refusal to accept all of his instructions often stemmed from different notions of what made a life a Christian life, rather than from a lack of enthusiasm or knowledge. Clearly, there is much more to be written on the sermons by Chrysostom and his contemporaries, especially as dialogues between preachers and their audiences.[15] Additional studies focused on the communication between preachers and their audiences in Late Antiquity will help to flesh out our understanding of the gray areas between elites and masses, pagan and Christian, orthodox and heretic, how these different groups saw each other, and, not least, instruct us about the impact of ordinary people on history.

---

[15] Future projects on Chrysostom will be facilitated by the online database, "A Social Lens: Late Antiquity in the Sermons of John Chrysostom," funded by the Australian Research Council and directed by Pauline Allen and Wolfram Kinzig. The database allows one to search sermons according to key words. It is accessible at: http://www.cecs.acu.edu.au/chrysostom/history.php.

Bibliography

PRIMARY SOURCES

Ammianus Marcellinus. *Histories*, 3 vols., ed. J. C. Rolfe. Cambridge, MA, 1935.
Römische Geschichte, 4 vols., ed. and trans. W. Seyfarth. Berlin, 1968.
Amphilochius of Iconium. *Amphilochii Iconiensis opera*, ed. C. Datema. CCSG 3. Turnhout, 1978.
Asterius of Amasea. *Homilies I–XIV. Text, Introduction and Notes*, ed. C. Datema. Leiden, 1970.
Augustine of Hippo. *De Doctrina Christiana*, ed. J. Marten and K.-D. Dauer. CCSL 32. Brepols, 1962.
Vingt-six sermons au peuple d'Afrique, ed. F. Dolbeau. Collections des Etudes Augustiniennes, Série Antiquité 147. Paris, 1996.
Basil. *Letters*, 4 vols., trans. R. J. Deferrari. Cambridge, MA, 1961–2.
Lettres, 3 vols., ed. and trans.Y. Courtonne. Paris, 1957–66.
Caesarius of Arles. *Sermons*, trans. M. M. Mueller. FOTC 31, 47, 66. Washington, DC, 1956–64.
Sermons au peuple, 3 vols., ed. and trans. M.-J. Delage. SC 175, 243, 330. Paris, 1971–86.
Choricius of Gaza. *Opera*, ed. R. Foerster. Stuttgart, 1972.
Constitutiones apostolorum (Les constitutions apostoliques), 3 vols., ed. and trans. M. Metzger. SC 320, 329, 336. Paris, 1985–7.
Clement of Alexandria. *Paedagogus (Le Pédagogue)*, 3 vols., ed. M. Harl, trans. and intro. H. I. Marrou. SC 70, 108, 158. Paris, 1960–70.
Dio Chrysostom. *Dionis Prusaensis quem vocant Chrysostomum quae exstant omnia*, 2 vols., ed. J. von Arnim. 2nd edn. Berlin, 1962.
Discourses, 5 vols., trans. J. W. Cohoon and H. Lamar Cosby. Cambridge, MA, 1932–51.
Eunapius. *Eunapii vitae sophistarum*, ed. J. Giangrande. Rome, 1956.
Eunapius and Philostratus: Lives of the Sophists, ed. W. C. Wright. Cambridge, MA, 1952.
Eusebius. *Werke: Über das Leben des Kaisers Konstantin*, ed. F. Winkelmann. Berlin, 1975.
Gregory of Nazianzus. *Discours 32–37*, ed. C. Moreschini, trans. P. Gallay. SC 318. Paris, 1985.

Epistles. PG 37.

"Gregory Nazianzen's Two Invectives against Julian the Emperor." In *Julian the Emperor*, trans. C. W. King, 1–121. London, 1888.

Lettres, 2 vols., ed. and trans. P. Gallay. Paris, 1964.

Gregory of Nyssa. *De deitate filii et spiritus oratio.* PG 46.

Lettres, ed. and trans. P. Maraval. SC 363. Paris, 1990.

Jerome. *De viris illustribus*, ed. A. Ceresa-Gastaldo. Florence, 1988.

On illustrious men, trans. T. P. Halton. FOTC 100. Washington, DC, 1999.

John Chrysostom. *Opera.* PG 47–64.

Works of St. Chrysostom. A Select Library of Nicene and Post-Nicene Fathers, ed. P. Schaff, ser. 1, vols. IX–XIV. Grand Rapids, MI, 1988.

Baptismal Instructions, trans. Paul W. Harkins. ACW 31. Westminster, MD, 1963.

Christianity and Pagan Culture in the Later Roman Empire. Together with an English Translation of John Chrysostom's Address on Vainglory and the Right Way for Parents to Bring Up their Children, trans. M. L. W. Laistner. Ithaca, NY, 1951.

Discourses against Judaizing Christians, trans. P. W. Harkins. FOTC 68. Washington, DC, 1979.

Homilies on Genesis, trans. R. C. Hill. FOTC 74, 82, 87. Washington, DC, 1986–92.

Homilies on the Incomprehensible Nature of God, trans. P. Harkins. FOTC 72. Washington, DC, 1984.

Huit catéchèses baptismales inédites, ed. and trans. A. Wenger. SC 50. 2nd edn. Paris, 1970.

On Repentance and Almsgiving, trans. G. G. Christo. FOTC 96. Washington, DC, 1998.

On Wealth and Poverty (translations of the nine sermons *On Lazarus*), trans. C. Roth. Crestwood, NY, 1984.

Sermons sur la Genèse, ed. and trans. L. Brottier. SC 433. Paris, 1998.

Sur la vaine gloire et l'éducation des enfants, ed. and trans. A.-M. Malingrey. SC 188. Paris, 1972.

Sur le sacerdoce: dialogue et homélie, ed. and trans. A.-M. Malingrey. SC 272. Paris, 1980.

Sur l'incompréhensibilité de Dieu, ed. A.-M. Malingrey, intro. J. Daniélou, trans. R. Flacelière. SC 28. 2nd edn. Paris, 1970.

Trois catéchèses baptismales, ed. and trans A. Piédagnel. SC 366. Paris, 1990.

Julian. *L'empereur Julien. Oeuvres complètes*, 2 vols., ed. J. Bidez, G. Rochefort, and C. Lacombrade. Paris, 1932–64.

The Works of the Emperor Julian, 3 vols., trans. W. C. Wright. Cambridge, MA, 1949–54.

Libanius. *Libanii Opera*, 12 vols., ed. R. Förster. Leipzig, 1903–27.

Antioch as a Centre of Hellenic Culture as Observed by Libanius (selected orations), trans. and intro. A. F. Norman. Translated Texts for Historians 34. Liverpool, 2000.

"Antiochikos (Oration II)," trans. G. Downey. *PAPS* 103 (1959): 652–86.

Discours, vol. I: *Autobiographie (Discours I)*, ed. J. Martin, trans. P. Petit. Paris, 1979.

Discours, vol. II: *Discours II–X*, ed. and trans. J. Martin. Paris, 1988.

Libanios: Briefe, ed. and trans. G. Fatouros and T. Krischer. Munich, 1980.

Libanius: Imaginary Speeches: A Selection of Declamations, trans. and intro. D. A. Russell. London, 1996.

Selected Works, 2 vols., ed. A. F. Norman. Cambridge, MA, 1969–77.

Lucian. *Luciani opera*, 4 vols., ed. M. D. Macleod. Oxford, 1972–87.

Works, 8 vols., trans. A. M. Harmon. Cambridge, MA, 1947.

Maximus of Tyre. *Dissertationes*, ed. M. B. Trapp. Stuttgart, 1994.

Maximus of Tyre: The Philosophical Orations, trans. M. B. Trapp. Oxford, 1997.

Menander Rhetor. *Menander Rhetor*, ed., trans., and intro. D. A. Russell and N. G. Wilson. Oxford, 1981.

Origen. *Contre Celse*, ed. and trans. M. Borret. SC 132, 136, 147, 150, 227. Paris, 1967–76.

Contra Celsum, trans. into English and intro. H. Chadwick. Cambridge, 1953.

Palladius. *Dialogus de vita S. Joannis Chrysostomi*, ed. P. R. Coleman-Norton. Cambridge, 1928.

Dialogue sur la vie de Jean Chrysostome, ed., trans., and intro. A.-M. Malingrey and P. Leclercq. SC 341 and 342. Paris, 1988.

Philostratus, Flavius. *Flavii Philostrati opera*, 2 vols., ed. C. L. Kayser. Leipzig, 1870–1, repr. Hildesheim, 1985.

Eunapius and Philostratus: Lives of the Sophists, ed. W. C. Wright. Cambridge, MA, 1952.

Plutarch. *De liberis educandis*, ed. and trans. J. Sirinelli, intro. R. Flacelière and J. Irigoin. Paris, 1987.

De recta ratione audiendi in *Oeuvres morales*, vol. VII. 2., *Traités 37–41*, ed. and trans. R. Klaerr, A. Philippon, and J. Sirinelli. Paris, 1989.

Moralia, 14 vols. Cambridge, MA, 1927–69.

Porphyry. *Vita Plotini* in *Opera*, vol. I, ed. P. Henry and H.-R. Schwyzer. Leiden, 1951.

Socrates Scholiasticus. *Ecclesiastica historia*, 2 vols., ed. R. Hussey. Oxford, 1853, repr. Hildesheim, 1992.

Ecclesiastical History, ed. A. C. Zenos. A Select Library of Nicene and Post-Nicene Fathers, ed. P. Schaff, ser. 2, vol. II. Grand Rapids, MI, 1979.

Sozomen. *Ecclesiastical History*, ed. C. Hartranft. A Select Library of Nicene and Post-Nicene Fathers, ed. P. Schaff, ser. 2, vol. II. Grand Rapids, MI, 1979.

Kirchengeschichte, ed. J. Bidez and G. C. Hansen. Berlin, 1960.

Synesius. *Dion*. In *Synesii Cyrenensis opuscula*, ed. N. Terzaghi. Rome, 1944.

Themistius. *Orationes*, 3 vols., ed. G. Downey and A. F. Norman. Leipzig, 1965–74.

Politics, Philosophy and the Empire in the Fourth Century: Select Orations of Themistius, trans. and intro. P. Heather and D. Moncur. Translated Texts for Historians 36. Liverpool, 2001.

The Private Orations of Themistius, trans. and intro. R. Penella. Berkeley, 2000.

Theodoret of Cyrrhus. *Histoire des moines de Syrie*, 2 vols., ed. and trans. P. Canivet and A. Leroy-Molinghen. SC 234 and 257. Paris, 1977–9.
A History of the Monks of Syria, trans. R. M. Price. Cistercian Studies 88. Kalamazoo, MI, 1985.
The Theodosian Code and Novels, and the Sirmondian Constitutions, trans. C. Pharr. Corpus of Roman Law 1. Princeton, 1952.
Zosimus. *Histoire nouvelle*, 3 vols., ed. and trans. F. Paschoud. Paris, 1971–89.
New History, trans. R. T. Ridley. Byzantina Australiensia 2. Canberra, 1982.

SECONDARY SOURCES

Adkin, N. "A Problem in the Early Church: Noise during Sermon and Lesson." *Mnemosyne* 4.38 (1985): 161–3.
Alcock, S. *Graecia Capta: The Landscapes of Roman Greece*. Cambridge, 1993.
Alexiou, M. *The Ritual Lament in Greek Tradition*. Cambridge, 1994.
Allen, P. "The Homilist and the Congregation: A Case Study of John Chrysostom's Homilies on Hebrews." *Augustinianum* 36 (1996): 397–421.
"John Chrysostom's Homilies on I and II Thessalonians: The Preacher and His Audience." *Studia Patristica* 31 (1997): 3–21.
Allen, P., R. Canning, and L. Cross, eds. *Prayer and Spirituality in the Early Church*, vol. 1. Brisbane, 1998.
Allen, P. and M. B. Cunningham, eds. *Preacher and Audience: Studies in Early Christian and Byzantine Homiletics*. Leiden, 1998.
Allen, P. and W. Mayer. "Traditions of Constantinopolitan Preaching: Towards a New Assessment of Where John Chrysostom Preached What." *Byzantinische Forschung* 24 (1997): 93–114.
John Chrysostom. London, 2000.
Ameringer, T. E. *The Stylistic Influence of the Second Sophistic on the Panegyrical Sermons of St. John Chrysostom*. Washington, DC, 1921.
Anderson, G. *Philostratus: Biography and Belles Lettres in the Third Century* AD. London, 1986.
The Second Sophistic: A Cultural Phenomenon in the Roman Empire. London, 1993.
Ashbrook-Harvey, S. "Antioch and Christianity." In *Antioch: The Lost Ancient City*, ed. C. Kondoleon, 39–49. Princeton, 2000.
Athanassiadi, P. *Julian: An Intellectual Biography*. London, 1992.
Auerbach, E. *Literary Language and Its Public in Late Latin Antiquity and in the Middle Ages*, trans. R. Manheim. New York, 1965.
Auksi, P. *Christian Plain Style: The Evolution of a Spiritual Ideal*. Montreal, 1995.
Bagnall, R. *Egypt in Late Antiquity*. Princeton, 1993.
Baldovin, J. F. *The Urban Character of Christian Worship: The Origins, Development and Meaning of Stational Liturgy*. Orientalia Christiana Analecta 228. Rome, 1987.
Barkhuizen, J. H. "Proclus of Constantinople: A Popular Preacher of Fifth-Century Constantinople." In *Preacher and Audience: Studies in Early Christian and*

Byzantine Homiletics, ed. P. Allen and M. B. Cunningham, 179–200. Leiden, 1998.

Barnes, T. D. "Christians and the Theater." In *Roman Theater and Society*, ed. W. J. Slater, 161–80. Ann Arbor, MI, 1996.

Barry, W. "Aristocrats, Orators and the 'Mob': Dio Chrysostom and the World of the Alexandrians." *Historia* 42.1 (1993): 82–103.

Baur, C. *John Chrysostom and His Time*, trans. M. Gonzaga. London, 1959.

Beacham, R. C. *The Roman Theatre and Its Audience*. London, 1991.

Beard, M., ed. *Literacy in the Roman World* (*JRA* Supplement 3) Ann Arbor, MI, 1991.

Becker, A. H. and A. Yoshiko Reed, eds. *The Ways That Never Parted: Jews and Christians in Late Antiquity and the Early Middle Ages*. Tübingen, 2003.

Benin, S. *Footprints of God: Divine Accommodation in Jewish and Christian Thought*. Albany, NY, 1993.

Berger, K. "Antike Rhetorik und christliche Homiletik." In *Spätantike und Christentum: Beiträge zur Religions und Geistesgeschichte der griechisch-römischen Kultur und Zivilisation der Kaiserzeit*, ed. C. Colpe, L. Honnefelder, and M. Lutz-Bachmann, 173–87. Berlin, 1992.

Bergmann, B. and C. Kondoleon, eds. *The Art of Ancient Spectacle*. New Haven, 1999.

Bériou, N. and D. D'Avray, eds. *Modern Questions about Medieval Sermons: Essays on Marriage, Death, History and Sanctity*. Spoleto, 1994.

Blänsdorf, J., ed. *Theater und Gesellschaft im Imperium Romanum*. Tübingen, 1990.

Bonz, M. P. "The Jewish Donor Inscriptions from Aphrodisias: Are They Both Third-Century, and Who Are the Theosebeis?" *HSCPh* 96 (1994): 281–99.

Bourdieu, P. *Distinction: A Social Critique of the Judgment of Taste*. Cambridge, MA, 1984.

The Logic of Practice, trans. R. Nice. Stanford, CA, 1990.

Bowersock, G. W. *Greek Sophists in the Roman Empire*. Oxford, 1969.

Julian the Apostate. Cambridge, MA, 1978, repr. 1997.

Hellenism in Late Antiquity. Ann Arbor, MI, 1996.

Bowersock, G. W., P. Brown, and O. Grabar, eds. *Late Antiquity: A Guide to the Postclassical World*. Cambridge, MA, 1999.

Bowman, A. K. "Literacy in the Roman Empire: Mass and Mode." In *Literacy in the Roman World* (*JRA* Supplement 3), ed. M. Beard, 119–31. Ann Arbor, MI, 1991.

Life and Letters on the Roman Frontier: Vindolanda and Its People. London, 1998.

Bowman, A. K. and G. Woolf, eds. *Literacy and Power in the Ancient World*. Cambridge, 1996.

Bradshaw, P. *The Search for the Origins of Christian Worship: Sources and Methods for the Study of Early Liturgy*. 2nd edn. Oxford, 2002.

Brakke, D. "The Problematization of Nocturnal Emissions in Early Christian Syria, Egypt and Gaul." *JECS* 3 (1995): 419–60.

Brancacci, A. *Rhetorike philosophousa: Dione Crisostomo nella cultura antica e bizantina*. Naples, 1985.

"Cinismo e predicazione popolare." In *Lo spazio letterario della Grecia antica*, vol. I.3, ed. G. Cambiano, L. Canfora, and D. Lanza, 433–55. Rome, 1994.

Branham, R. B. *Unruly Eloquence: Lucian and the Comedy of Traditions*. Cambridge, MA, 1989.

Branham, R. B. and M.-O. Goulet-Cazé, eds. *The Cynics: The Cynic Movement in Antiquity and Its Legacy*. Berkeley, 1996.

Braniste, E. "The Liturgical Assembly and Its Functions in the Apostolic Constitutions." In *Roles in the Liturgical Assembly: The 23rd Liturgical Conference*, trans. M. J. O'Connell, 73–99. New York, 1981.

Brauch, T. "Themistius and the Emperor Julian." *Byzantion* 63 (1993): 79–115.

Bregman, J. *Synesius of Cyrene: Philosopher-Bishop*. Berkeley, 1982.

Brink, F. "Dio on the Simple and Self-Sufficient Life." In *Dio Chrysostom: Politics, Letters and Philosophy*, ed. S. Swain, 261–78. Oxford, 2000.

Brock, S. "Greek and Syriac in Late Antique Syria." In *Literacy and Power in the Ancient World*, ed. A. K. Bowman and G. Woolf, 149–60. Cambridge, 1996.

Brown, P. "Pelagius and His Supporters: Aims and Environment." *JThS* 29 (1968): 93–114.

"The Rise and Function of the Holy Man in Late Antiquity." *JRS* 61 (1971): 80–101.

The Philosopher and Society in Late Antiquity. Berkeley, 1978.

The Cult of the Saints: Its Rise and Function in Latin Christianity. Chicago, 1981.

The Body and Society: Men, Women and Sexual Renunciation in Early Christianity. New York, 1988.

Power and Persuasion in Late Antiquity: Towards a Christian Empire. Madison, WI, 1992.

Authority and the Sacred: Aspects of the Christianisation of the Roman World. Cambridge, 1995.

"Augustine and a Practice of the *Imperiti*: *Qui Adorant Columnas in Ecclesia*." In *Augustin prédicateur*, ed. G. Madec, 367–75. Paris, 1998.

"Asceticism: Pagan and Christian." In *CAH*, vol. XIII (1998): 601–31.

"Christianization and Religious Conflict." In *CAH*, vol. XIII (1998): 632–64.

Poverty and Leadership in the Late Roman Empire. Hannover, NH, 2002.

The Rise of Western Christendom: Triumph and Diversity AD 200–1000, 2nd edn. Oxford, 2002.

Browning, R. "Literacy in the Byzantine World." *BMGS* 4 (1978): 39–54.

Medieval and Modern Greek. Cambridge, 1983.

Brunt, P. A. "Aspects of Social Thought of Dio Chrysostom and of the Stoics." *PCPhS* 199 (1973): 9–34.

"Did Imperial Rome Disarm Her Subjects?" *Phoenix* 29 (1975): 260–70.

Burns, T. S. and J. W. Eadie, eds. *Urban Centers and Rural Contexts in Late Antiquity*. East Lansing, MI, 2001.

Cambiano, G., L. Canfora, and D. Lanza, eds. *Lo spazio letterario della Grecia antica*, vol. I.3. Rome, 1994.

Cameron, Alan. *Circus Factions: Blues and Greens at Rome and Byzantium*. Oxford, 1976.

Cameron, Averil. *Christianity and the Rhetoric of Empire: The Development of Christian Discourse*. Berkeley, 1991.

Campbell, J. *The Influence of the Second Sophistic on the Style of the Sermons of St. Basil the Great*. Cleveland, OH, 1983.

Carrié, J.-M. "Antiquité tardive et 'démocratisation de la culture': un paradigme à géométrie variable." *AntTard* 9 (2001): 27–46.

Carruthers, M. *The Craft of Thought: Meditation, Rhetoric, and the Making of Images, 400–1200*. Cambridge, 1998.

Caseau, B. "Sacred Landscapes." In *Late Antiquity: A Guide to the Postclassical World*, ed. G. Bowersock, P. Brown, and O. Grabar, 21–59. Cambridge, MA, 1999.

Clark, E. *Jerome, Chrysostom and Friends: Essays and Translations*. New York, 1979.

Reading Renunciation: Asceticism and Scripture in Early Christianity. Princeton, 1999.

Clark, G. "Philosophic Lives and the Philosophic Life." In *Greek Biography and Panegyric in Late Antiquity*, ed. T. Hägg and P. Rousseau, 29–51. Berkeley, 2000.

Christianity and Roman Society. Cambridge, 2004.

Clarke, M. L. *Rhetoric at Rome: A Historical Survey*. New York, 1996.

Coleman-Norton, P. R. "St. Chrysostom and the Greek Philosophers." *CPh* 25 (1930): 305–17.

Colin, J. *Les villes libres de l'Orient greco-romain et l'envoi au supplice par acclamations populaires*. Collection Latomus 82. Brussels, 1965.

Colpe, C., L. Honnefelder, and M. Lutz-Bachmann, eds. *Spätantike und Christentum: Beiträge zur Religions und Geistesgeschichte der griechischrömischen Kultur und Zivilisation der Kaiserzeit*. Berlin, 1992.

Corbier, M. "L'écriture en quête de lecteurs." In *Literacy in the Roman World (JRA Supplement 3)*, ed. M. Beard, 99–118. Ann Arbor, MI, 1991.

Cribiore, R. *Writing, Teachers, and Students in Graeco-Roman Egypt*. Atlanta, 1996.

Crook, J. A. *Legal Advocacy in the Roman World*. London, 1995.

Cunningham, M. B. "Preaching and Community." In *Church and People in Byzantium*, ed. R. Morris, 29–46. Birmingham, 1986.

"Andreas of Crete's Homilies on Lazarus and Palm Sunday: The Preacher and His Audience." *Studia Patristica* 31 (1997): 22–41.

Daly, L. J. "Themistius' Concept of *Philanthropia*." *Byzantion* 45 (1975): 22–40.

Danassis, A. *Johannes Chrysostomos: pädagogisch-psychologische Ideen in seinem Werk*. Bonn, 1971.

Daniélou, J. "La catéchèse dans la tradition patristique." In *Conversion, Catechumenate, and Baptism in the Early Church*, ed. E. Ferguson, 279–92. New York, 1993.

Datema, C. "Amphiloque d'Iconium et Pseudo-Chrysostom." *JÖB* 23 (1974): 29–32.

Deferrari, R. J. "St. Augustine's Method of Composing and Delivering Sermons." *AJPh* 43 (1922): 97–123.

Dekkers, E. "Limites sociales et linguistiques de la pastorale liturgique de S. Jean Chrysostome." *Augustinianum* 20 (1980): 119–29.

Dentzer, J.-M. and W. Orthomann, eds. *Archéologie et histoire de la Syrie*, vol. II: *La Syrie de l'époque achéménide à l'avènement de l'Islam*. Saarbrücken, 1989.

Dominik, W. J., ed. *Roman Eloquence: Rhetoric in Society and Literature*. London, 1997.

Dorival, G. "L'image des Cyniques chez les Pères grecs." In *Le Cynisme ancien et ses prolongements: actes du colloque international du CNRS*, ed. M.-O. Goulet-Cazé and R. Goulet, 419–43. Paris, 1993.

Downing, F. G. *Cynics and Christian Origins*. Edinburgh, 1992.

Druit, F.-X. *Langage, images et visages de la mort chez Jean Chrysostome*. Namur, 1990.

Dudley, D. R. *A History of Cynicism*. London, 1937.

Dujarier, M. *A History of the Catechumenate*, trans. E. Haasl. New York, 1979.

Dumortier, J. "Une assemblée chrétienne au IVe siècle." *Mélanges de Science Religieuse* 29 (1972): 15–22.

Elm, S. "Orthodoxy and the True Philosophical Life: Julian and Gregory of Nazianzus." *Studia Patristica* 38 (2001): 69–85.

"Inscriptions and Conversions: Gregory of Nazianzus on Baptism (*Or.* 38–40)." In *Conversion in Late Antiquity and the Early Middle Ages: Seeing and Believing*, ed. K. Mills and A. Grafton, 1–35. Rochester, NY, 2003.

Escolan, P. *Monachisme et église. Le monachisme syrien du IVe au VIIe siècle: un monachisme charismatique*. Paris, 1999.

Fantham, E. "The Contexts and Occasions of Roman Public Rhetoric." In *Roman Eloquence: Rhetoric in Society and Literature*, ed. W. J. Dominik, 111–28. London, 1997.

Fatouros, G. and T. Krischer, eds. *Libanios*. Darmstadt, 1983.

Ferguson, E. "Inscriptions and the Origin of Infant Baptism." *JThS* 30.1 (1979): 37–46.

ed. *Conversion, Catechumenate, and Baptism in the Early Church*. New York, 1993.

Festugière, A. J. *Antioche païenne et chrétienne: Libanius, Chrysostome et les moines de Syrie*. Paris, 1959.

Fine, S. *This Holy Place: On the Sanctity of the Synagogue during the Greco-Roman Period*. South Bend, IN, 1997.

Finn, T. *The Liturgy of Baptism in the Baptismal Instructions of St. John Chrysostom*. Washington, DC, 1967.

"Quodvultdeus: Preacher and the Audience. The Homilies on the Creed." *Studia Patristica* 31 (1997): 42–58.

Foss, C. "The Near Eastern Countryside in Late Antiquity: A Review Article." In *The Roman and Byzantine Near East: Some Recent Archaeological Research*, ed. J. H. Humphrey, 214–34. Ann Arbor, MI, 1995.

Fowden, G. "The Pagan Holy Man in Late Antique Society." *JHS* 102 (1982): 33–59.

Fox, R. L. "Literacy and Power in Early Christianity." In *Literacy and Power in the Ancient World*, ed. A. K. Bowman and G. Woolf, 126–48. Cambridge, 1996.

Francis, J. A. *Subversive Virtue: Asceticism and Authority in the Second-Century Pagan World*. University Park, PA, 1995.

Franklin, J. L. Jr. "Literacy and the Parietal Inscriptions of Pompeii." In *Literacy in the Roman World (JRA* Supplement 3), ed. M. Beard, 77–98. Ann Arbor, MI, 1991.

Frézouls, E. "Recherches sur les théâtres de l'Orient syrien." *Syria* 38 (1961): 54–86.

Gamble, H. Y. *Books and Readers in the Early Church: A History of Early Christian Texts*. New Haven, 1995.

Garnsey, P. and C. Humfress. *The Evolution of the Late Antique World*. Cambridge, 2001.

Gleason, M. W. "Festive Satire: Julian's *Misopogon* and the New Year at Antioch." *JRS* 76 (1986): 106–19.

Making Men: Sophists and Self-Presentation in Ancient Rome. Princeton, 1995.

Goulet-Cazé, M.-O. and R. Goulet, eds. *Le Cynisme ancien et ses prolongements: actes du colloque international du CNRS*. Paris, 1993.

Graumann, T. "St. Ambrose on the Art of Preaching." In *Vescovi e pastori in epoca teodosiana: XXV incontro di studiosi dell'antichità cristiana*. Rome, 1997.

Greatrex, G. and J. Watt. "One, Two, or Three Feasts? The Brytae, the Maiuma and the May Festival at Edessa." *Oriens Christianus* 83 (1999): 1–21.

Gregory, T. E. *Vox Populi: Popular Opinion and Violence in the Religious Controversies of the Fifth Century AD*. Columbus, OH, 1979.

Grimm, V. *From Feasting to Fasting, the Evolution of a Sin: Attitudes to Food in Late Antiquity*. New York, 1996.

Hägg, T. and P. Rousseau, eds. *Greek Biography and Panegyric in Late Antiquity*. Berkeley, 2000.

Hahn, J. *Der Philosoph und die Gesellschaft: Selbstverständnis, öffentliches Auftreten und populäre Erwartungen in der hohen Kaiserzeit*. Stuttgart, 1989.

Hamel, G. *Poverty and Charity in Roman Palestine, First Three Centuries CE*. Berkeley, 1989.

Harmless, W. "'Salt for the Impure, Light for the Pure': Reflections on the Pedagogy of Evagrius Ponticus." *Studia Patristica* 37 (2001): 514–25.

Harries, J. *Law and Empire in Late Antiquity*. Cambridge, 1999.

"Favor Populi: Pagans, Christians and Public Entertainment in Late Antique Italy." In *Bread and Circuses: Euergetism and Municipal Patronage in Roman Italy*, ed. K. Jones and T. Cornell, 125–41. London, 2003.

Harris, W. *Ancient Literacy*. Cambridge, MA, 1989.

Hartney, A. *John Chrysostom and the Transformation of the City*. London, 2004.

Haubold, J. and R. Miles. "Communality and Theatre in Libanius' Oration LXIV." In *Culture and Society in Later Roman Antioch*, ed. I. Sandwell and J. Huskinson, 24–34. Oxford, 2004.

Heather, P. and D. Moncur. *Politics, Philosophy, and Empire in the Fourth Century: Select Orations of Themistius*. Liverpool, 2001.

Herrin, J. *The Formation of Christendom*. Princeton, 1987.

Hock, R. "Cynics and Rhetoric." In *Handbook of Classical Rhetoric in the Hellenistic Period, 330 BC–AD 400*, ed. S. E. Porter, 755–73. Leiden, 1997.

Holl, K. *Amphilochios von Ikonium in seinem Verhältnis zu den grossen Kappadoziern.* Tübingen, 1904.

Holum, K. *Theodosian Empresses: Women and Imperial Dominion in Late Antiquity.* Berkeley, 1982.

Hopkins, K. "Conquest by Book." In *Literacy in the Roman World* (*JRA* Supplement 3), ed. M. Beard, 133–58. Ann Arbor, MI, 1991.

Horsfall, N. "Statistics or States of Mind?" In *Literacy in the Roman World* (*JRA* Supplement 3), ed. M. Beard, 59–76. Ann Arbor, MI, 1991.

The Culture of the Roman Plebs. London, 2003.

Horst, P. van der. "Sortes: Sacred Books as Instant Oracles in Late Antiquity." In *The Use of Sacred Books in the Ancient World*, ed. L. V. Rutgers, P. W. van der Horst, H. W. Havelaar, and L. Teugels, 143–73. Leuven, 1998.

"Jews and Christians in Antioch at the End of the Fourth Century." In *Christian–Jewish Relations through the Centuries*, ed. S. E. Porter and B. W. R. Pearson, 228–38. Sheffield, 2000.

Hubbell, H. "Chrysostom and Rhetoric." *CPh* 19.3 (1924): 261–76.

Humphrey, J. H., ed. *The Roman and Byzantine Near East: Some Recent Archaeological Research.* Ann Arbor, MI, 1995.

Jaeger, W. *Early Christianity and Greek Paideia.* Cambridge, MA, 1961.

Jansen, K. *The Making of the Magdalen: Preaching and Popular Devotion in the Later Middle Ages.* Princeton, 2000.

Jones, A. H. M. *The Later Roman Empire, 284–602: A Social, Economic and Administrative Survey.* Baltimore, MD, 1964, repr. 1986.

Jones, C., G. Wainwright, and E. Yarnold, eds. *The Study of Liturgy.* Revised edn. Oxford, 1992.

Jones, C. P. *Culture and Society in Lucian.* Cambridge, MA, 1986.

Jones, K. and T. Cornell, eds. *Bread and Circuses: Euergetism and Municipal Patronage in Roman Italy.* London, 2003.

Judge, E. A. "The Rhetoric of Inscriptions." In *Handbook of Classical Rhetoric in the Hellenistic Period, 330 BC–AD 400*, ed. S. E. Porter, 807–28. Leiden, 1997.

Kalleres, D. "Exorcising the Devil to Silence Christ's Enemies: Ritualized Speech Practices in Late Antique Christianity." Ph.D. dissertation, Brown University. Providence, RI, 2002.

Kaster, R. *Guardians of Language: The Grammarian and Society in Late Antiquity.* Berkeley, 1988.

"Controlling Reason: Declamation in Rhetorical Education at Rome." In *Education in Greek and Roman Antiquity*, ed. Y. L. Too, 317–37. Leiden, 2001.

Kelly, J. N. D. *Jerome: His Life, Writings, and Controversies.* New York, 1975.

Golden Mouth: The Story of John Chrysostom – Ascetic, Preacher, Bishop. Ithaca, NY, 1995.

Kennedy, G. *Greek Rhetoric under Christian Emperors.* Princeton, 1983.

Kennedy, H. "From *Polis* to *Madina*, Urban Change in Late Antique and Early Islamic Syria." *Past & Present* 106 (1985): 3–27.

Kinzig, W. "The Greek Christian Writers." In *Handbook of Classical Rhetoric in the Hellenistic Period, 330 BC–AD 400*, ed. S. E. Porter, 633–70. Leiden, 1997.

Klingshirn, W. *Caesarius of Arles: The Making of a Christian Community in Late Antique Gaul*. Cambridge, 1994.

Klingshirn, W. and M. Vessey, eds. *The Limits of Ancient Christianity: Essays on Late Antique Thought and Culture in Honor of R. A. Markus*. Ann Arbor, MI, 1999.

Kohn, H. *Versorgungskrisen und Hungerrevolten im spätantiken Rom*. Bonn, 1961.

Kolbet, P. "The Cure of Souls: St. Augustine's Reception and Transformation of Classical Psychagogy." Ph.D. dissertation, University of Notre Dame. South Bend, IN, 2002.

Kondoleon, C., ed. *Antioch: The Lost Ancient City*. Princeton, 2000.

Kontoulis, G. *Zum Problem der Sklaverei (ΔΟΥΛΕΙΑ) bei den kappadokischen Kirchenvätern und Johannes Chrysostomus*. Bonn, 1993.

Krueger, D. *Symeon the Holy Fool: Leontius's Life and the Late Antique City*. Berkeley, 1996.

"The Bawdy and Society: The Shamelessness of Diogenes in the Roman Imperial Culture." In *The Cynics: The Cynic Movement in Antiquity and Its Legacy*, ed. R. B. Branham and M.-O. Goulet-Cazé, 222–39. Berkeley, 1996.

Lassus, J. *Sanctuaires chrétiens de Syrie: essai sur la genèse, la forme et l'usage liturgique des édifices du culte chrétien, en Syrie, du IIIe siècle à la conquête musulmane*. Paris, 1947.

Levi, D. *Antioch Mosaic Pavements*, 2 vols. Princeton, 1947.

Leyerle, B. "John Chrysostom on Almsgiving and the Use of Money." *HTR* 87.1 (1994): 29–47.

"Appealing to Children." *JECS* 5.2 (1997): 243–70.

Theatrical Shows and Ascetic Lives: John Chrysostom's Attack on Spiritual Marriage. Berkeley, 2001.

Lieberman, S. "Roman Legal Institutions in Early Rabbinics and in the *Acta Martyrum*." *Jewish Quarterly Review* 35.1 (1944): 1–57.

Liebeschuetz, J. H. W. G. *Antioch: City and Imperial Administration in the Later Roman Empire*. Oxford, 1972.

Barbarians and Bishops: Army, Church and State in the Age of Arcadius and Chrysostom. Oxford, 1990.

Lieu, S. N. C., ed. *The Emperor Julian: Panegyric and Polemic*. Liverpool, 1989.

Lim, R. *Public Disputation, Power and Social Order in Late Antiquity*. Berkeley, 1995.

"In the 'Temple of Laughter': Visual and Literary Representations of Spectators at Roman Games." In *The Art of Ancient Spectacle*, ed. B. Bergmann and C. Kondoleon, 343–65. New Haven, 1999.

"Converting the Un-Christianizable: The Baptism of Stage Performers in Late Antiquity." In *Conversion in Late Antiquity and the Early Middle Ages: Seeing and Believing*, ed. K. Mills and A. Grafton, 84–126. Rochester, NY, 2003.

Ma, J. "Public Speech and Community in the *Euboicus*." In *Dio Chrysostom: Politics, Letters and Philosophy*, ed. S. Swain, 108–24. Oxford, 2000.

MacCormack, S. *Art and Ceremony in Late Antiquity*. Berkeley, 1981.

MacMullen, R. "Two Types of Conversion to Early Christianity." *VChr* 37 (1983): 174–92.

Christianizing the Roman Empire, AD 100–400. New Haven, 1984.

"What Difference did Christianity Make?" *Historia* 35 (1986): 322–43.

"The Preacher's Audience (AD 350–400)." *JThS* 40 (1989): 503–11.

"Distrust of the Mind in the Fourth Century." In *Changes in the Roman Empire: Essays in the Ordinary*. Princeton, 1990.

Christianity and Paganism in the Fourth to Eighth Centuries. New Haven, 1997.

Madec, G., ed. *Augustin prédicateur*. Paris, 1998.

Markus, R. A. *The End of Ancient Christianity*. Cambridge, 1990.

"How on Earth could Places become Holy? Origins of the Christian Idea of Holy Places." *JECS* 2.3 (1994): 257–71.

Marrou, H. I. *A History of Education in Antiquity*, trans. G. Lamb. London, 1956.

Mathisen, R. and H. Sivan, eds. *Shifting Frontiers in Late Antiquity*. Aldershot, 1995.

Mayer, W. "The Provenance of the Homilies of St. John Chrysostom: towards a New Assessment of Where He Preached What." Ph.D. dissertation, University of Queensland. Brisbane, 1996.

"John Chrysostom and His Audiences: Distinguishing Different Congregations at Antioch and Constantinople." *Studia Patristica* 31 (1997): 70–5.

"The Dynamics of Liturgical Space: Aspects of the Interaction between John Chrysostom and His Audience." *Ephemerides Liturgicae* 111 (1997): 104–15.

"Monasticism at Antioch and Constantinople in the Late Fourth Century: A Case of Exclusivity or Diversity?" In *Prayer and Spirituality in the Early Church*, ed. P. Allen, R. Canning, and L. Cross, vol. 1, 275–88. Brisbane, 1998.

"John Chrysostom: Extraordinary Preacher, Ordinary Audience." In *Preacher and Audience: Studies in Early Christian and Byzantine Homiletics*, ed. P. Allen and M. B. Cunningham, 105–37. Leiden, 1998.

"Constantinopolitan Women in Chrysostom's Circle." *VChr* 52 (1998): 1–24.

"Female Participation and the Late Fourth-Century Preacher's Audience." *Augustinianum* 39 (1999): 139–47.

"Who Came to Hear John Chrysostom Preach? Recovering a Late Fourth-Century Preacher's Audience." *Ephemerides Theologicae* 76 (2000): 73–87.

"At Constantinople, How Often Did John Chrysostom Preach? Addressing Assumptions about the Workload of a Bishop." *Sacris Erudiri* 40 (2001): 83–105.

Mazzarino, S. *Aspetti sociali del quarto secolo: ricerche di storia tardo-romana*. Rome, 1951.

McLaughlin, E. "The Word Eclipsed? Preaching in the Early Middle Ages." *Traditio* 46 (1991): 77–122.

McLynn, N. "Seeing and Believing: Aspects of Conversion from Antoninus Pius to Louis the Pious." In *Conversion in Late Antiquity and the Early Middle Ages:*

Seeing and Believing, ed. K. Mills and A. Grafton, 224–70. Rochester, NY, 2003.

Méridier, L. *Le philosophe Thémistios: devant l'opinion de ses contemporains.* Paris, 1906.

Merkt, A. "Mündlichkeit: ein Problem der Hermeneutik patristischer Predigten." *Studia Patristica* 31 (1997): 76–85.

Meslin, M. *La fête des Kalends de janvier dans l'empire romain: étude d'un rituel de Nouvel An.* Brussels, 1970.

Mills, K. and A. Grafton, eds. *Conversion in Late Antiquity and the Early Middle Ages: Seeing and Believing.* Rochester, NY, 2003.

Mitchell, S. *Anatolia: Land, Men and Gods in Asia Minor*, vol II: *The Rise of the Church.* Oxford, 1993.

Moles, J. L. "The Career and Conversion of Dio Chrysostom." *JHS* 98 (1978): 79–100.

"'Honestius quam ambitiosius?' An Exploration of the Cynic's Attitude to Moral Corruption in His Fellow Men." *JHS* 103 (1983): 103–23.

"Cynic Cosmopolitanism." In *The Cynics: The Cynic Movement in Antiquity and Its Legacy*, ed. R. B. Branham and M.-O. Goulet-Cazé, 114–20. Berkeley, 1996.

Momigliano, A. "Popular Religious Beliefs and the Late Roman Historians." In *Popular Belief and Practice*, ed. G. J. Cuming and D. Baker, 1–18. Cambridge, 1972.

Mormando, F. *The Preacher's Demons: Bernardino of Siena and the Social Underworld of Early Renaissance Italy.* Chicago, 1999.

Morris, R., ed. *Church and People in Byzantium.* Birmingham, 1986.

Muessig, C., ed. *Medieval Monastic Preaching.* Leiden, 1998.

Mühlenberg, E. and J. van Oort, eds. *Predigt in der Alten Kirche.* Kampen, 1994.

Munitiz, J. A. "Catechetical Teaching-Aids in Byzantium." In *ΚΑΘΗΓΗΤΡΙΑ: Essays Presented to Joan Hussey for Her 80th Birthday*, ed. J. Chrysostomides, 69–83. Camberley, Surrey, 1988.

Natali, A. "Eglise et évergétisme à Antioche à la fin du IVe siècle d'après Jean Chrysostome." *Studia Patristica* 17 (1982): 1176–84.

"Tradition ludique et sociabilité dans la pratique religieuse à Antioche d'après Jean Chrysostome." *Studia Patristica* 16 (1985): 463–70.

"Les survivances païennes dans le rituel des mariages chrétiens à Antioche au IVe siècle d'après Jean Chrysostome: essai d'interprétation." In *Sociabilité, pouvoirs et société*, ed. F. Thelamon, 111–16. Rouen, 1987.

Norman, A. F. "The Book Trade in Fourth-Century Antioch." *JHS* 80 (1960): 122– 6.

"Libanius: The Teacher in an Age of Violence." In *Libanios*, ed. G. Fatouros and T. Krischer, 150–69. Darmstadt, 1983.

Ober, J. *Mass and Elite in Democratic Athens: Rhetoric, Ideology and the Power of the People.* Princeton, 1989.

Oberg, E. "Das Lehrgedicht des Amphilochios von Ikonium." *JbAC* 16 (1973): 67–97.

O'Connell, M. J., trans. *Roles in the Liturgical Assembly: the 23rd Liturgical Confer-ence*. New York, 1981.

Olivar, A. *La predicación cristiana antigua*. Barcelona, 1991.

Ong, W. *Orality and Literacy: The Technologizing of the Word*. London, 1982.

O'Roark, D. "Parenthood in Late Antiquity: Evidence of John Chrysostom." *GRBS* 40 (1999): 53–81.

Parkin, A. "Poverty in the Early Roman Empire: Ancient and Modern Conceptions and Constructs." Ph.D. dissertation, Cambridge University, 2001.

Pasquato, O. *Gli spettacoli in S. Giovanni Crisostomo: paganesimo e cristianesimo ad Antiochia e Constantinopoli nel IV secolo*. Rome, 1976.

I laici in Giovanni Crisostomo: tra chiesa, famiglia e città. Rome, 1998.

Patlagean E. *Pauvreté économique et pauvreté sociale à Byzance 4e–7e siècles*. Paris, 1977.

Paverd, F. van der. *Zur Geschichte der Messliturgie in Antiocheia und Konstantinopel gegen Ende des vierten Jahrhunderts: Analyse der Quellen bei Johannes Chrysos-tomos*. Rome, 1970.

St. John Chrysostom, the Homilies on the Statues: An Introduction. Rome, 1991.

Paxton, F. *Christianizing Death: The Creation of a Ritual Process in Early Medieval Europe*. Ithaca, NY, 1990.

Penella, R. *Greek Philosophers and Sophists in the 4th c. AD: Studies in Eunapius of Sardis*. Leeds, 1990.

"The Rhetoric of Praise in the Private Orations of Themistius." In *Greek Biog-raphy and Panegyric in Late Antiquity*, ed. T. Hägg and P. Rousseau, 194–208. Berkeley, 2000.

ed., trans., and intro. *The Private Orations of Themistius*. Berkeley, 2000.

Pernot, L. *La rhétorique de l'éloge dans le monde gréco-romain*. Paris, 1993.

Perrin, M.-Y. "A propos de la participation des fidèles aux controverses doctrinales dans l'Antiquité tardive: considérations introductives." *AntTard* 9 (2001): 179–99.

Petit, P. *Libanius et la vie municipale à Antioche au IVe siècle après J.-C*. Paris, 1955.

"Recherches sur la publication et la diffusion des discours de Libanius." *Historia* 5 (1956): 479–509.

Les étudiants de Libanius. Paris, 1957.

Petropoulos, J. C. B. "The Church Father as Social Informant: St John Chrysostom on Folk Songs." *Studia Patristica* 22 (1989): 159–64.

Polecritti, C. *Preaching Peace in Renaissance Italy: Bernardino of Siena and his Audience*. Washington, DC, 2000.

Porter, S. E., ed. *Handbook of Classical Rhetoric in the Hellenistic Period, 330 BC–AD 400*. Leiden, 1997.

Porter, S. E. and B. W. R. Pearson, eds. *Christian–Jewish Relations through the Centuries*. Sheffield, 2000.

Potter, D. "Martyrdom as Spectacle." In *Theater and Society in the Classical World*, ed. R. Scodel, 53–88. Ann Arbor, MI, 1993.

"Performance, Power and Justice in the High Empire." In *Roman Theater and Society*, ed. W. J. Slater, 129–59. Ann Arbor, MI, 1996.

Pouchet, R. *Basil le Grand et son univers d'amis d'après sa correspondance: une stratégie de communion*. Rome, 1992.

Quaeston, J. *Patrology*, vol. III. Utrecht, 1963.

Rappe, S. "The New Math: How to Add and to Subtract Pagan Elements in Christian Education." In *Education in Greek and Roman Antiquity*, ed. Y. L. Too, 405–32. Leiden, 2001.

Rebillard, E. *In hora mortis: évolution de la pastorale chrétienne de la mort aux IVe and Ve siècles dans l'Occident latin*. Rome, 1994.

"Interaction between the Preacher and His Audience: The Case-Study of Augustine's Preaching on Death." *Studia Patristica* 31 (1997): 86–96.

Religion et sépulture: l'église, les vivants et les morts dans l'antiquité tardive. Paris, 2003.

"Conversion and Burial in the Late Roman Empire." In *Conversion in Late Antiquity and the Early Middle Ages: Seeing and Believing*, ed. K. Mills and A. Grafton, 61–83. Rochester, NY, 2003.

Rey-Coquais, P. (1997) "La culture en Syrie à l'époque romaine." In *Donum Amicitiae: Studies in Ancient History*, ed. E. Dabrowa, 139–60. Krakow, 1997.

Reynolds, P. L. *Marriage in the Western Church: The Christianization of Marriage during the Patristic and Early Medieval Periods*. Leiden, 1994.

Rich, J., ed. *The City in Late Antiquity*. London, 1992.

Robert, L. *Les gladiateurs dans l'Orient grec*. Paris, 1940.

Roueché, C. "Acclamations in the Later Roman Empire: New Evidence from Aphrodisias." *JRS* 74 (1984): 181–99.

Performers and Partisans at Aphrodisias in the Roman and Late Roman Periods. London, 1993.

Rousseau, P. *Basil of Caesarea*. Berkeley, 1994.

"'The Preacher's Audience': A More Optimistic View." In *Ancient History in a Modern University*, vol. II: *Early Christianity, Late Antiquity and Beyond*, ed. T. W. Hillard and E. A. Judge, 391–400. Grand Rapids, MI, 1998.

"Antony as Teacher in the Greek *Life*." In *Greek Biography and Panegyric in Late Antiquity*, ed. T. Hägg and P. Rousseau, 89–109. Berkeley, 2000.

The Early Christian Centuries. New York, 2002.

Rubenson, S. "Philosophy and Simplicity: The Problem of Classical Education in Early Christian Biography." In *Greek Biography and Panegyric in Late Antiquity*, ed. T. Hägg and P. Rousseau, 110–39. Berkeley, 2000.

Ruether, R. R. *Gregory of Nazianzus, Rhetor and Philosopher*. Oxford, 1969.

Russell, D. A. "Rhetors at the Wedding." *PCPhS* 205 (1979): 104–17.

Greek Declamation. Cambridge, 1983.

ed. and trans. *Libanius: Imaginary Speeches: A Selection of Declamations*. London, 1996.

"The Panegyrists and Their Teachers." In *The Propaganda of Power: The Role of Panegyric in Late Antiquity*, ed. Mary Whitby, 17–50. Leiden, 1998.

Rutgers, L. V. "Archaeological Evidence for the Interaction of Jews and Non-Jews in Late Antiquity." *AJA* 96.1 (1992): 101–18.

"The Importance of Scripture in the Conflict between Jews and Christians: The Example of Antioch." In *The Use of Sacred Books in the Ancient World*, ed. L. V. Rutgers, P. W. van der Horst, H. W. Havelaar, and L.Teugels, 287–303. Leuven, 1998.

Rutgers, L. V., P. W. van der Horst, H. W. Havelaar, and L. Teugels, eds. *The Use of Sacred Books in the Ancient World*. Leuven, 1998.

Rylaarsdam, D. "The Adaptability of Divine Pedagogy: Sunkatabasis in the Theology and Rhetoric of John Chrysostom." Ph.D. dissertation, University of Notre Dame. South Bend, IN, 2000.

Saddington, D. B. "The Function of Education according to Christian Writers of the Latter Part of the Fourth Century." *Acta Classica* 8 (1965): 86–101.

Safrai, Z. *The Economy of Roman Palestine*. London, 1994.

Salamito, J.-M. "Christianisation et démocratisation de la culture: aspects aristocratiques et aspects populaires de l'être-chrétien aux IIIe et IVe siècles." *AntTard* 9 (2001): 165–78.

Sallmann, K. "Christen vor dem Theater." In *Theater und Gesellschaft im Imperium Romanum*, ed. J. Blänsdorf, 243–59. Tübingen, 1990.

Sandwell, I. and J. Huskinson, eds. *Culture and Society in Later Roman Antioch*. Oxford, 2004.

"Christian Self-Definition in the Fourth Century AD: John Chrysostom on Christianity, Imperial Rule and the City." In *Culture and Society in Later Roman Antioch*, ed. I. Sandwell and J. Huskinson, 35–58. Oxford, 2004.

Schäublin, C. "Zum paganen Umfeld der christlichen Predigt." In *Predigt in der Alten Kirche*, ed. E. Mühlenberg and J. van Oort, 25–49. Kampen, 1994.

Scodel, R., ed. *Theater and Society in the Classical World*. Ann Arbor, MI, 1993.

Siegert, F. "Homily and Panegyrical Sermon." In *Handbook of Classical Rhetoric in the Hellenistic Period, 330 BC–AD 400*, ed. S. E. Porter, 421–43. Leiden, 1997.

Simon, M. *Verus Israel: A Study of the Relations between Christians and Jews in the Roman Empire AD 135–425*, trans. H. McKeating. London, 1996.

Sironen, E. *The Late Roman and Early Byzantine Inscriptions of Athens and Attica*. Helsinki, 1997.

Slater, W. J., ed. *Roman Theater and Society*. Ann Arbor, MI, 1996.

Soury, G. *Aperçus de philosophie religieuse chez Maxime de Tyr, platonicien éclectique*. Paris, 1942.

Spira, A. "Volkstümlichkeit und Kunst in der Griechischen Vaterpredigt des 4. Jahrhunderts." *JÖB* 35 (1985): 55–73.

Stander, H. "The Clapping of Hands in the Early Church." *Studia Patristica* 26 (1993): 75–80.

Stanton, G. R. "Sophists and Philosophers: Problems of Classification." *AJPh* 94 (1973): 350–64.

Sterk, A. *Renouncing the World Yet Leading the Church: The Monk-Bishop in Late Antiquity*. Cambridge, MA, 2004.

Stevenson, K. W. "The Byzantine Liturgy of Baptism." *Studia Liturgica* 17 (1987): 176–90.

Swain, S., ed. *Dio Chrysostom: Politics, Letters and Philosophy*. Oxford, 2000.

"Reception and Interpretation." In *Dio Chrysostom: Politics, Letters and Philosophy*, ed. S. Swain, 13–51. Oxford, 2000.

Taft, R. "Women at Church in Byzantium: Where, When – and Why?" *DOP* 52 (1999): 27–87.

Tate, G. *Les campagnes de la Syrie du Nord du IIe au VIIe siècle*. Paris, 1992.

"Expansion d'une société riche et égalitaire: les paysans de Syrie du Nord du IIe au VIIe siècle." *Comptes Rendus de l'Académie des Inscriptions et Belles-Lettres*, 913–41. Paris, 1997.

Thelamon, F., ed. *Sociabilité, pouvoirs et société*. Rouen, 1987.

Tiersch, C. *Johannes Chrysostomus in Konstantinopel (398–404)*. Tübingen, 2002.

Tod, M. "Sidelights on Greek Philosophers." *JHS* 77 (1957): 132–41.

Todd, S. "*Lady Chatterley's Lover* and the Attic Orators: The Social Composition of the Athenian Jury." *JHS* 110 (1990): 146–73.

Too, Y. L., ed. *Education in Greek and Roman Antiquity*. Leiden, 2001.

Trapp, M. B. "Philosophical Sermons: The 'Dialexis' of Maximus of Tyre." In *ANRW* II.34.3 (1997): 1945–76.

Treggiari, S. "Roman Marriage." In *Civilization of the Ancient Mediterranean*, vol. III, ed. M. Grant and R. Kitzinger, 1349–50. New York, 1988.

Roman Marriage: Iusti Coniuges from the Time of Cicero to the Time of Ulpian. Oxford, 1991.

Trout, D. "Town, Countryside and Christianization at Paulinus' Nola." In *Shifting Frontiers in Late Antiquity*, ed. R. Mathisen and H. Sivan, 175–86. Aldershot, 1995.

Uhalde, K. "*The Expectation of Justice, AD 400–700*." Ph.D. dissertation, Princeton University, 1999.

Urbainczyk, T. *Socrates of Constantinople: Historian of Church and State*. Ann Arbor, MI, 1997.

"Vice and Advice in Socrates and Sozomen." In *The Propaganda of Power: The Role of Panegyric in Late Antiquity*, ed. Mary Whitby, 299–310. Leiden, 1998.

Theodoret of Cyrrhus: The Bishop and the Holy Man. Ann Arbor, MI, 2002.

Uthemann, K.-H. "Forms of Communication in the Homilies of Severian of Gabala: A Contribution to the Reception of the Diatribe as a Method of Exposition." In *Preacher and Audience: Studies in Early Christian and Byzantine Homiletics*, ed. P. Allen and M. B. Cunningham, 139–77. Leiden, 1998.

Van Dam, R. "Emperors, Bishops and Friends in Late Antique Cappadocia." *JThS* 37 (1986): 53–76.

Becoming Christian: The Conversion of Roman Cappadocia. Philadelphia, 2003.

Families and Friends in Late Roman Cappadocia. Philadelphia, 2003.

Vanderspoel, J. *Themistius and the Imperial Court: Oratory, Civic Duty and Paideia from Constantius to Theodosius*. Ann Arbor, MI, 1995.

Viaud, G. "Les rites du septième jour après la naissance dans la tradition copte." *Le Monde Copte* 2 (1977): 16–19.

Warren, J. "Diogenes Epikourios: Keep Taking the Tablets." *JHS* 120 (2000): 144–8.

Whitby, Mary, ed. *The Propaganda of Power: The Role of Panegyric in Late Antiquity.* Leiden, 1998.

Whitmarsh, T. *Greek Literature and the Roman Empire: The Politics of Imitation.* Oxford, 2001.

Wiemer, H.-U. "Der Sophist Libanios und die Bäcker von Antiocheia." *Athenaeum* 84 (1996): 527–48.

Wilken, R. *John Chrysostom and the Jews: Rhetoric and Reality in the Late 4th Century.* Berkeley, 1983.

The Christians as the Romans Saw Them. New Haven, 1984.

Zanker, P. *The Mask of Socrates: The Image of the Intellectual in Antiquity,* trans. A. Shapiro. Berkeley, 1995.

Index

acclamations 56–7, 58–9
  in churches 61–3
  see also applause
almsgiving 70–2, 112, 126, 137, 154, 161, 163
Ambrose 36, 67
Ammianus Marcellinus 58, 59, 60
Amphilochius of Iconium 36–9
  style of sermons 38–9
amulets
  Christian use of 152, 164–5
Antioch 3–4, 45, 52, 54–6, 69
  competing religious communities in 4
  monastic communities nearby 34, 107–8, 115–16
  see also John Chrysostom, Judaism, laypeople, Libanius, riots
Apostolic Constitutions 75–6, 79–80, 85, 99, 115, 159, 166
applause
  in church 52, 54–6, 61–2, 63, 133–4
  for public speakers 19, 28, 45, 46, 52, 54–6
  for public spectacles 54, 133–4
  see also acclamations, rhetoric, sermons
Aristotle, contact with public 28
artisans, *see* workers
ascetics, *see* monks
Augustine of Hippo 61, 67, 146, 150

baptism 121
  see also catechism
Basil of Caesarea
  attitude toward laypeople 34–5
  correspondence with Amphilochius of Iconium 37, 38
  correspondence with Libanius 31
  on social class of congregation 75
beggars 125, 127–8
  in Antioch 71–2
  see also poverty
Bourdieu, Pierre 147–8
Brown, Peter 69

Carrié, Jean-Michel 171
catechism 85, 90–1, 120–1
children 84–5, 91, 113, 122, 151–2
  amulets for 152
  naming ritual for 152
  see also family life
congregation, *see* laypeople
Constantine, emperor 58
contemplative life 13–16, 33–4
conversion to Christianity 7, 145, 172–3
Crook, John 49
cross, sign of as protection 151–2
Cunningham, Mary 93
customs, *see* habits
Cynics 12, 18, 20, 22–4, 25, 27
  Christian views of 30–1, 32–3
  rejection of wealth 29
  see also Dio Chrysostom, Lucian, philosophers

daily life
  Christianization of 145, 146, 147–8, 156–7, 161, 164, 174
  see also habits, meals, shoes, songs
dancing, sinfulness of 159
death
  fear of 159–60
  see also funerals
debates, theological, *see* theology
declamations 44–5
  see also rhetoric, Libanius, Second Sophistic
democratization
  of culture 171–2, 174–5
  of theology 172
demon-possession 85
Demosthenes 151
Dio Chrysostom 15, 17–19, 20, 22–4, 25, 26–7
  Euboicus 17–18
  see also Cynics, philosophers, rhetoric, Second Sophistic, sophists
Diogenes Laertius 23, 25, 30

194

Easter, controversy over the dating of 140–2
education
  broad definition 88–9
  Christian and pagan 61, 116–17
  church attendance as a form of 88–9, 116, 119,
    121–4
  see also psychagogy
elites, *see* rich, the; social classes
entertainment, public, *see* spectacles, theater
equality, of all Christians 68
Eunapius 21, 58
  on Christian monks 130
Eusebius 52–3, 61
evil eye, belief in 151–2

family life and religious practices 98–9, 149, 151,
    162–3
farmers 78–9, 149
  see also Syriac speakers
fasting 126, 136–7, 140, 161, 165
  Jewish 140–1
  laypeople's concerns about 138–9
  see also Lent
Frézouls, Edmond 55
funerals, sinful aspects 159–61

Galen 30
greed, *see* luxury
Gregory of Nazianzus
  admiration for Themistius and Libanius 31
  correspondence with Amphilochius of
    Iconium 37
  on public and private life 34
  on rhetorical style 35–6
  on theater 52
Gregory of Nyssa 68
  correspondence with Libanius 31–2

habits
  bad 148–54
  breaking of 151
  and Christianization 144–8
  good 161–3, 164
  see also daily life
habitus 147–8, 174
Hahn, Johannes 25
heretics 120–1, 122–3, 170
  in the congregation 85–6
  conversion of 114–15
  see also Judaizing
holy days
  disagreements about 135, 142, 155–6
  see also Easter, Kalends of January
holy places 118
homilies, *see* sermons

Jerome 33, 67
John Chrysostom
  attitude toward laypeople 108–12, 121–3, 124,
    143, 153
  on children 91, 113, 122, 151–2
  on education of Christians 88–9, 90–2,
    102–3
  on eloquence of preachers 62, 95
  on keeping the congregation's attention 94–5,
    96–8, 104–5
  and Libanius 2, 39, 60
  limits of power 173–5
  and monastic life 34, 131–3
  as patriarch of Constantinople 62–3
  pedagogical methods 105–6, 107–9, 110, 113,
    150
  on riots in Antioch 59
  on sexuality 124–6
  on shoes 153
  on slavery 76–8
  on wealth and poverty 69–72
  on women 80–3
  see also laypeople
Judaism
  in Antioch 4, 83–4
  and fasting 140–1
  influence on Christian practice 40
Judaizing Christians 83–4, 123, 134, 140–2, 149,
    166, 170
Julian, emperor 14–15, 27, 29
  decree against Christian teachers 60–1
  promotion of pagan worship 48–9
  on public speaking 47–8
  response to acclamations 58–9
  on similarity between monks and Cynics 30–1

Kalends of January 47, 154–7
Kaster, Robert 100

lalia 24–5
  see also rhetoric, Second Sophistic, Menander
    Rhetor
laughter
  at John Chrysostom 154, 158
  as leading to sins 145
  at philosophers 13–14
  by philosophers 26–7
lawyers 49–51
  rhetorical skill of 49–50
  see also rhetoric
laypeople
  attention to sermons 94–5, 104–5, 109–16,
    138, 143
  Christianization of 7–8, 119, 170–1, 172–5
  church attendance 73, 109, 133–6

laypeople (*cont.*)
concern for purity 118–19, 165–7
demon-possessed 85
depictions of 108–10
disagreements with John Chrysostom 124–9,
144–8, 149–50, 154, 158–61, 166–8
education of 68, 90–2, 103–4, 119, 121–4
equality of 68
fear of demons 163
heretical 85–6
knowledge of Christian doctrine 111–12,
113–16, 121, 123–4, 125, 172
literacy of 96, 98–100, 102–3
and monks 131–3, 163–4
and public spectacles 133–4
reaction to sermons 94, 96–8, 150
relationship with church leaders 1–2, 4, 95,
116–17, 118–20, 143, 169–70
relationship with non-Christians 115–16
see also children, farmers, fasting, Judaizing
Christians, slaves, social classes, women
Lazarus 70, 97
Lent 5, 136–40, 141–2, 161
celebrations related to 139–40
Leyerle, Blake 54
Libanius 3, 6, 31
on acclamations 57
and Amphilochius of Iconium 36–8, 39
and Christian students 60
correspondence with Basil of Caesarea 31
declamations by 44
in defense of Julian 47
and John Chrysostom 2, 39, 60
on lawyers 50
on monks 129–30
panegyrics by 45
on public speaking in Antioch 55–6
on public spectacles 43, 88
relationship with people of Antioch 46
on riots 56, 59
Lim, Richard 115
literacy 48, 96
archaeological evidence for 100–1
associated with monks 99, 101
extent in Late Antiquity 98–102, 104
of laypeople 96, 98–100, 102–3
and publicly posted documents 102
Lucian 17, 20, 25, 26, 30
Demonax 25, 26
see also Cynics, philosophers, rhetoric, Second
Sophistic, sophists
luxury, sinfulness of 70–1, 125–6, 138, 153–4

MacMullen, Ramsey 66
martyrs 51, 57–8, 126–7

Maximus of Tyre 13–14, 17, 19
see also Cynics, philosophers, rhetoric, Second
Sophistic, sophists
Mayer, Wendy 66
meals, Christianization of 162, 163
memory
aids for 106
as alternative to literacy 104–7
Menander Rhetor 46
see also *lalia*
miracles 114–15, 127
monks 73–4, 128–33
and literacy 99, 107–8
as models for laypeople 130–3, 162
as philosophers 32–3
relationship with laypeople 73–4, 107–8,
128–33
social status 132
as viewed by non-Christians 129–30

New Year's Eve, *see* Kalends of January

oath-swearing, sinfulness of 78–9, 112–13, 149–51
oratory, *see* rhetoric, sermons
Origen of Alexandria 30
orthodoxy 118–20, 122–3, 170–1, 172–3, 175

pagans
friendships with Christian intellectuals 31–2,
37–8, 39
and lay Christians 115–16
see also education, philosophers, Julian,
Libanius, Themistius
paideia, see education, rhetoric, philosophers
Palladius 34
panegyric 45–6
see also Libanius, rhetoric, Second Sophistic
Paul, Apostle
rhetorical skill 115–16
as tent-maker 73, 95
views on women 80–1
peasants, *see* farmers
philosophers
compared to Christians 29–31, 32–4
contact with public 13–19, 22–8, 29
debates with Christians 116
Epicurean 26–7
"false" 25, 30
lifestyle 13–16
physical appearance 26, 30–1, 32
popularity 40
as sarcophagus motif 27
and sophists 15–16, 18–19
see also Cynics, Dio Chrysostom, Lucian,
Plutarch, sophists, Themistius

Plato, contact with public 28
Plotinus 15, 21
  see also philosophers
Plutarch 18–19, 20, 46
  see also Cynics, philosophers, rhetoric, Second
    Sophistic, sophists, Themistius
Porphyry 21
  see also philosophers
Potter, David 51, 58
poverty 69–72
  see also almsgiving, beggars
preaching, *see* sermons
Proclus 15
  see also philosophers
psychagogy 89
purity, Christian concern for 118–19, 165–7

Quintilian 25

rhetoric
  accessibility 19–22, 25–6, 42–3, 46, 65–7, 93–4
  Christian approach to 35, 36, 40–1, 62, 65–7,
    91–4, 174–5
  contests 43–6, 47
  and education 43, 45–6, 60
  of lawyers 49–50
  and philosophers 17
  popularity 1–2, 11, 15, 42–7, 62
  taught to laypeople 115–16
  and urban culture 63–4
  see also declamations, *lalia*, Libanius,
    panegyrics, Second Sophistic, sophists,
    Themistius
rich, the
  and almsgiving 70–1
  equality with other Christians 68
  sins of 127–8, 165
  see also almsgiving, luxury, social classes
riots 59, 60
  church-related 3, 62–3
  Riot of the Statues 56, 59, 78, 136
Roueché, Charlotte 57
Rousseau, Philip 66–7

Second Sophistic 12, 16–19, 88
  influence on Christians 40–1
  rhetorical style of 19–21
  see also Dio Chrysostom, Lucian, Maximus of
    Tyre, philosophers, Plutarch, rhetoric,
    sophists, Themistius
sermo humilis 35, 94
  see also sermons, rhetoric
sermons
  accessibility/popularity 65–7, 93–4, 95, 174–5
  as education for laity 119, 121–4, 134

  as historical sources 4–7, 169, 172
  and the layout of churches 5
  methods of recording 6
  reactions to 94, 114–15
  rhetorical style of 6–7, 11, 35, 62, 93–4,
    95
  scholarship on 65–7
  see also laypeople, rhetoric
shoes, luxurious 153–4
sins
  differing views of 124–9
  seemingly insignificant 145, 148–9, 152, 153–4,
    157
  sexual 124–6, 127–8
  and social class 127–9
  see also habits, bad; luxury
slaves 76–8, 149, 151
  see also family life, laypeople
social classes
  archaeological evidence of 79
  Christian attitudes toward 34–5, 95, 138
  equality of all groups 68
  interaction among 169, 171–2, 174–5
  of laypeople 33–4, 65–8, 69–76, 79, 99–102
  of "middling classes" 67–9, 74–5
  and sins 127–9
  see also farmers, laypeople, slaves, workers
Socrates, church historian 6, 67
soldiers 73–4, 99
songs, Christianization of 162, 163
sophists
  associated with heretics 35
  as distinct from philosophers 15–16, 18–19
  see also Dio Chrysostom, Lucian, Maximus of
    Tyre, philosophers, rhetoric, Second
    Sophistic, Themistius
Sozomen 2, 114
spectacles
  public 43, 51–2, 133–4
  buildings for 55–6
  Christian critique of 52–4, 133–4, 173
  scholarship on 173
  see also rhetoric, theater
Syriac speakers, near Antioch 32, 78–9

Tertullian 30
  on spectacles 53
theater 53, 114
  buildings for 54–5
  popularity 42, 51–2, 54, 88, 133–4
  see also spectacles, public
Themistius 14–16, 21–2, 31–2, 37, 47, 86
  see also philosophers, rhetoric, Second
    Sophistic, sophists
Theodoret of Cyrrhus 108, 150

theology, debates about 115, 116, 169–70
thieves, in church 75

urban life
    influence on Christianity 42–3, 175
    and public speaking 55–6, 63–4
    see also acclamations; Antioch; spectacles,
        public; theater

virginity 126
virtues
    differing views of 124–9
    see also almsgiving; fasting; habits, good;
        virginity

wealth, *see* luxury; rich, the
weddings, sinful aspects 158–9
women
    biblical models for 82–3
    as members of the congregation
        79–83
    typical sins 81–2, 151–2, 160
    see also family life, laypeople
workers 25, 68, 72–6, 99–102, 149
    as Christian philosophers 33–4
    see also laypeople, social classes

Zanker, Paul 27
Zosimus 3